The Spirit Renews

the Face of the Earth

The Spirit Renews

the Face of the Earth

Pentecostal Forays in Science and
Theology of Creation

EDITED BY

Amos Yong

☙PICKWICK *Publications* • Eugene, Oregon

THE SPIRIT RENEWS THE FACE OF THE EARTH
Pentecostal Forays in Science and Theology of Creation

Pickwick Publications
A Division of Wipf and Stock Publishers
199 W. 8th Ave., Suite 3
Eugene, OR 97401

www.wipfandstock.com

ISBN 13: 978-1-4982-5244-7

Cataloging-in-Publication data:

The spirit renews the face of the earth : pentecostal forays in science and
theology of creation / edited by Amos Yong.

xxiv + 246 p. ; 23 cm. Includes indexes.

ISBN 13: 978-1-4982-5244-7

1. Pentecostalism. 2. Theology. 3. Christianity and Science. I. Yong, Amos.
II. Title.

BL241 .S68 2009

Manufactured in the U.S.A.

To Dennis W. Cheek

Contents

PART THREE: Theological Explications

PART FOUR: Contextual and Disciplinary Applications

Preface

Each of the essays in this book, with one exception, was originally presented at the thirty-eighth annual meeting of the Society for Pentecostal Studies, jointly held with the Wesleyan Theological Society, at Duke University Divinity School on March 13–15, 2008. I was privileged to co-chair that meeting with the Wesleyan Theological Society vice-president elect, Thomas J. Oord. Thanks, Tom, for doing more than your fair share of the work in planning the conference.

Thanks also the John Templeton Foundation for the grant which underwrote part of the conference expenses as well as subsidized the editorial cost for this volume.

Each of the contributors to this book has been conscientious in meeting the deadlines I have set for them. I am grateful for this as well as for the efforts they have put into their essays in this pioneering book on the interface between Pentecostal studies, theology of creation, and science.

I have also been supported in various ways by my deans here at Regent University School of Divinity. Thanks to Dean Michael Palmer, Associate Dean of Academics Donald Tucker, and Assistant Dean of Administration Joy Brathwaite for their consideration. Thanks also to Pidge Bannin for all she does at the School of Divinity office to make my work more manageable.

My graduate assistant Timothy Lim Teck Ngern helped with proofreading the manuscript (especially my introductory chapter), getting it ready for publication, and preparing the index. He did all of this joyfully, skillfully, and efficiently while transitioning with his family into a new living situation and adjusting to his first two semesters of doctoral studies.

Thanks to Charlie Collier and the editorial team at Pickwick Publications for their guidance. Diane Farley at Pickwick has been very helpful in working through the details of the publication process. Last but not least, I am indebted to Halden Doerge and Kristen Bareman at Wipf and Stock for their patience with me through the proofreading, copy-editing, and typesetting process.

In 1996, I moved with my wife and three young children from Vancouver, Washington, to the Boston, Massachusetts, area to begin doctoral studies in theology at Boston University. We settled into the North Attleboro suburb of Boston, and on the day of our move into our apartment, were helped by Rev. Dr. Dennis W. Cheek, then pastor of New Beginnings Christian Fellowship in Mansfield, Massachusetts (a town next door), an adjunct faculty member in the Education Department at the University of Rhode Island, and director of the Office of Research, High School Reform and Adult Education and State Superintendent for Area Career and Technical Centers, both with the Rhode Island Department of Education. Dennis had completed his PhD in science and technology education a few years before at the University of Pennsylvania, but remained firmly committed to the life of the church. He invited me to join him as associate pastor at New Beginnings, and even paid me a part-time salary—quite remarkable, since he himself served as pastor of the church on a voluntary basis—to help us get through financially. I have since been grateful that the Lord guided me to work with one of the few fellow Pentecostal pastors who understood the value of doctoral education, having been through the process himself, to the point of being willing to go the extra mile on my/our behalf. He read and gave me feedback on my earliest doctoral seminar papers, and over the years has found ways to support my scholarship and research from a distance. A few years ago, Dennis completed his second PhD, this time in theology at the University of Durham, writing a dissertation on theology and technology, all the while being active as a scholar-academic, working full time in the public sector, and serving graciously in pastoral roles wherever he has gone. Thanks for your collegiality and friendship, Dennis! I am dedicating this book to you as but a small token of my appreciation for all you have done to encourage Pentecostal scholarship to engage the sciences.

Introduction

Poured Out on All Creation!? Searching for the Spirit in the Pentecostal Encounter with Science

Amos Yong

While there has been a long history of the Pentecostal encounter with science stretching to the beginning of Pentecostalism early in the twentieth century, there has not been much scholarly study or analysis of this phenomenon.[1] This book is an attempt to fill the gap in the scholarly literature. In this introductory chapter, I will identify some of the salient factors in the background that might help explain why we have not seen more scholarship on the Pentecostalism-and-science interface, present a typology of the various modes of engagement especially with an eye toward possible developments of the encounter, and provide an overview of the scope of this volume in light of the past and in anticipation of the future. My overarching goal is to set the stage for the chapters to follow, both in terms of providing a historical context that can help readers appreciate the timeliness of this volume and in terms of sketching the conceptual terrain that will also set in bold relief the achievements of the authors and contributors in the pages to come.

---

1. One of the few attempts is Ronald L. Numbers, "Creation, Evolution, and Holy Ghost Religion: Holiness and Pentecostal Responses to Darwinism," *Religion and American Culture* 2:2 (1992) 127–58.

Pentecostalism and Science: A "History" of a Missed Encounter?

Ironically, Pentecostalism as a modern religious movement was birthed during the period when science contributed to the parting of ways between what we now call the fundamentalists and the modernists.[2] Not surprisingly, then, almost from the beginning we can detect a "love-hate" relationship between Pentecostalism and science.[3] On the one hand, Pentecostals were suspicious of any scientific advances that threatened to undermine belief in the reality, power, and personality of God and the Holy Spirit. As Bernie Van De Walle's chapter in this book documents, this was especially the case with scientific technologies like medicine. Even for later generations that adapted to accept the use of medicine, there has always been the concern that over-reliance on medicine will undermine authentic faith in God.

Yet on the other hand, Pentecostals were pragmatists urgently focused on carrying out the Great Commission in anticipation of the soon return of Christ.[4] For this task, they have always availed themselves of the applied sciences, especially the mass media, beginning with the use of radio as an evangelistic tool.[5] As scientific advances have been made

2. See George M. Marsden, *Fundamentalism and American Culture: The Shaping of Twentieth Century Evangelicalism, 1870–1925* (New York: Oxford University Press, 1980) esp. 93–96 and 194–95, and Robert Mapes Anderson, *Vision of the Disinherited: The Making of American Pentecostalism* (New York: Oxford University Press, 1979).

3. See Amos Yong and Paul Elbert, "Christianity, Pentecostalism: Issues in Science and Religion," in J. Wentzel van Huysteen, gen. ed., *Encyclopedia of Science and Religion*, 2 vols. (New York: Macmillan Reference Library, 2003) I:132–35.

4. On Pentecostal pragmatism, see Grant Wacker, "Searching for Eden with a Satellite Dish: Primitivism, Pragmatism, and the Pentecostal Character," in Richard T. Hughes, ed., *The Primitive Church in the Modern World* (Urbana, IL: University of Illinois Press, 1995) 139–66, and *Heaven Below: Early Pentecostals and American Culture* (Cambridge, MA: Harvard University Press, 2001) 267–68 and passim. On Pentecostalism's eschatologically-informed missionary vision, see James R. Goff Jr., *Fields White unto Harvest: Charles F. Parham and the Missionary Origins of Pentecostalism* (Fayetteville, AK: University of Arkansas Press, 1988); D. William Faupel, *The Everlasting Gospel: The Significance of Eschatology in the Development of Pentecostal Thought* (Sheffield: Sheffield Academic, 1996); and Allan Anderson, *Spreading Fires: The Missionary Nature of Early Pentecostalism* (London: SCM, and Maryknoll, NY: Orbis, 2007).

5. On the use of radio in Pentecostalism, see W. E. Warner, "Radio," in Stanley M. Burgess and Eduard M. Van Der Maas, eds., *The New International Dictionary of Pentecostal and Charismatic Movements*, rev. and expanded ed. (Grand Rapids, MI: Zondervan, 2002) 1015–16; Matthew Sutton, *Aimee Semple McPherson and the*

in the various communication technologies, Pentecostals have been quick to adopt television, the big screen of film, and the internet.[6] Given the prevalence of the use of media technologies in Pentecostal mission and evangelism, it is not surprising to note the emergence of scholarship on the subject, especially on developments in the global south.[7] However, most of these studies have been and are being done by outsiders to the movement, even as the absence of substantive theological reflection on these matters by Pentecostal scholars or insiders has itself been somewhat remarkable.

Why then have Pentecostals themselves not deliberated more intentionally about medicine, the mass media, and other related scientific and technological matters? One reason is certainly related to the fact that Pentecostal scholarship is still a fairly new phenomenon. The Society for Pentecostal Studies (SPS), the thirty-seventh annual meeting of which was the occasion for the essays published in this volume, was not established until the eighth decade of the modern Pentecostal movement. Since its charter in the early 1970s, the SPS has steadily expanded its scholarly horizons, beginning first with history (reflecting the doctoral training of the majority of the SPS "founding fathers" who were seeking to preserve the oral history of the movement before the last eyewitnesses of the first generation passed from the scene), moving on the biblical studies in the 1980s (a natural progression given Pentecostalism's biblicistic orientation), and then to theological stud-

---

Resurrection of Christian America (Cambridge, MA: Harvard University Press, 2007) ch. 3 (on McPherson's media savviness); and Benjamin A. Wagner, "'Full Gospel' Radio: Revivaltime and Pentecostal Uses of Mass Media, 1950–1979," *Fides et Historia* 35 (2003) 107–22.

6. D. J. Hedges, "Television," in Stanley M. Burgess and Eduard M. Van Der Maas, eds., *The New International Dictionary of Pentecostal and Charismatic Movements*, rev. and expanded ed. (Grand Rapids, MI: Zondervan, 2002) 1118–20, and David Edwin Harrell, "Pentecost at Prime Time: Early Religious TV Presented Huge Challenges, which Pentecostals Met Better than Most," *Christian History* 49 (1996) 52–54.

7. E.g., Birgit Meyer, "Pentecostalism, Prosperity, and Popular Cinema in Ghana," in S. Brent Plate, ed., *Representing Religion in World Cinema: Filmmaking, Mythmaking, Culture Making* (New York: Palgrave, 2003) 121–45; J. Kwabena Asamoah-Gyadu, "Anointing through the Screen: Neo-Pentecostalism and Televised Christianity in Ghana," *Studies in World Christianity* 11:1 (2005) 9–28; and Pradip Thomas, *Strong Religion, Zealous Media: Christian Fundamentalism and Communication in India* (Thousand Oaks, CA: SAGE, 2008) esp. part III.

ies broadly conceived in the 1990s.[8] As a scholarly enterprise that is arguably still in its gestational stage, Pentecostals in the academy have worked primarily in the arena of humanities in general, and in theological studies more specifically. In these contexts, the scholarly work of engaging with the sciences or with issues in the religion- or theology-and-science encounter have been either off the radar altogether or have been deemed less pressing.

Historically, however, there are also other reasons that, when combined with the Pentecostal ambivalence to things scientific noted earlier, have contributed to the delay of serious Pentecostal interactions with science. Here I am referring to the general anti-intellectualism which permeated the Pentecostal movement especially during the 1920s and 1930s when it aligned itself with the fundamentalist stream of American Christianity. Jerry King's chapter in this volume demonstrates that leading up to and then following from the Scopes Trial of 1925, Pentecostals increasingly came to understand themselves on the same side as the fundamentalists in defending the veracity of the scriptural account of God and creation against the modernist and liberal attacks. Such an alignment led, inevitably, to a suspicion about higher education in general, as well as about the scientific research in particular. This explains, at least in part, the resistance toward the (very gradual) transformation of Pentecostal "Bible institutes" to "Bible schools" to "Bible colleges" to "liberal arts colleges" and, finally, to "universities."[9] The legacy of this anti-intellectualism has been the reluctance, even in the Pentecostal academy, to seriously engage modern science until now.[10] Yet the emergence of Pentecostal universities offering a full range of science majors

8. I provide an overview of these developments in my "Pentecostalism and the Theological Academy," *Theology Today* 64:2 (2007) 244–50.

9. For an overview of these categories of Pentecostal institutions of higher education, see Jeff Hittenberger, "The Future of Pentecostal Higher Education: The Ring, the Shire, or the Redemption of Middle Earth?" in Eric Patterson and Edmund J. Rybarczyk, eds., *The Future of Pentecostalism in the United States* (Lanham, MD: Lexington, 2007) esp. 84–86.

10. The stereotype of Pentecostalism as being anti-intellectual continues to persist—e.g., Roger E. Olson, "Pentecostalism's Dark Side," *Christian Century* 123:5 (7 March 2006) 27–30. Pentecostals have recently begun to address the issue, however—e.g., Rick M. Nañez, *Full Gospel, Fractured Minds? A Call to Use God's Gift of the Intellect* (Grand Rapids, MI: Zondervan, 2005).

means that Pentecostal scholars will no longer be able to put off thinking theologically about science.[11]

Yet there may be other reasons internal to the logic of Pentecostal spirituality and piety that have so far hindered a Pentecostal engagement with science. In an essay presented also at the same conference that produced this volume's collection of papers, Telford Work, an ecumenical theologian in the Foursquare Church has suggested that Pentecostal intuitions and sensibilities will lead its practitioners to take up issues more relevant to certain aspects of the human sciences.[12] More specifically, like those in the Wesleyan tradition in which are found the roots of the modern Pentecostalism, Pentecostal scholars seem less interested in pursuing vocations in the natural sciences (or at least this is what the anecdotal "evidence" suggests) and more predisposed to engage the humanities (especially history) and the social and behavioral sciences (e.g., psychology, sociology, and cultural anthropology). Perhaps the centrality of the experience of the Spirit in the Pentecostal mode of being-in-the-world has something to do with nurturing certain interests and provoking some questions rather than others, with the result being that initial Pentecostal interfaces with the sciences on Pentecostal terms—i.e., in which Pentecostals have engaged the issues as Pentecostals rather than as evangelicals or as Christians in general—have been more noticeable in these "softer" rather than "harder" scientific disciplines.

11. One of the first published calls for a more integrative (rather than apologetic) approach to science within a Pentecostal educational context was Robert O'Bannon, Lois Beach, and J. Patrick Daugherty, eds., *Science and Christianity: Friends or Foes? Proceedings of the 1977 Bible-Science Symposium Sponsored by Lee College and the Liaisons* (Cleveland, TN: Pathway, 1977). Yet not only are the dominant categories oppositional—e.g., as in the "Friends or Foes" subtitle—but the Lee faculty published in this volume all wrote from out of a "conservative evangelical" rather than explicitly Pentecostal frame of reference. (Thanks to my student, Adam Tripp, for making a copy of this rare book available to me.)

12. See Telford Work, "The Science Division: Pneumatological Relations and Christian Disunity in Theology-Science Dialogue," *Zygon: The Journal of Religion and Science* 43:4 (2008) 897–908.

The "Rules" of Religion-Science Engagement: Existing Models, Pentecostal Re-appropriations

Whither therefore the Pentecostal encounter with science? As latecomers to the theology-and-science arena, of course, Pentecostals have the advantage of learning from the history of the conversation. Whereas the conflict model has been widely published as characterizing a large part of the history of interactions between religion and science—such that disagreements or contradictions between theology and science means that either that the former trumps the latter (for religionists) or vice versa (for anti-religious scientists)[13]—the last generation has seen the emergence of other approaches including dialogue, convergence, mutuality, complementarity, as well as the view that each concerns separate domains of reality and human endeavor.[14] Within Pentecostal circles one might be able to find advocates all along the broad spectrum of positions.

For example, many working scientists who are Pentecostals (i.e., are active member of or attend Pentecostal churches) have so far neither asked specifically Pentecostal questions about their science vocation nor asked specifically scientific questions about their religious practices or theological beliefs. In a sense, they live and work in two separate worlds, at the science workbench or in the lab on weekdays and tarrying at the altar or lifting up holy hands on weekends. Their science training does

---

13. For the dispute in the nineteenth century and earlier, see John William Draper, *History of the Conflict between Religion and Science* (New York: Appleton, 1892) and Andrew Dickson White, *A History of the Warfare of Science with Theology in Christendom*, 2 vols. (New York: Appleton, 1897). More recently, we have anti-religious naturalists like Richard Dawkins and Daniel Dennett on the one side and those who wish to subordinate at least the social sciences to theology like folk in the Radical Orthodoxy movement on the other.

14. E.g., Alister E. McGrath, *The Foundations of Dialogue in Science and Religion* (Malden, MA: Blackwell, 1998); Ted Peters and Martinez Hewlett, *Evolution from Creation to New Creation: Conflict, Conversation, and Convergence* (Nashville: Abingdon, 2003); Alan G. Padgett, *Science and the Study of God: A Mutuality Model for Theology and Science* (Grand Rapids and Cambridge, UK: Eerdmans, 2003); Niels Henrik Gregersen and J. Wentzel Van Huyssteen, eds., *Rethinking Theology and Science: Six Models for the Current Dialogue* (Grand Rapids: Eerdmans, 1998); Richard F. Carlson, ed., *Science and Christianity: Four Views* (Downers Grove: InterVarsity, 2000); and Stephen Jay Gould, "Nonoverlapping Magisteria: Science and Religion are Not in Conflict, for Their Teachings Occupy Distinctly Different Domains," *Natural History* 106:2 (1997) 16–22 and 60–62.

not help or encourage them to integrate their faith and their occupation (usually implicitly communicating that faith is an impediment to rigorous scientific work), and their Pentecostal churches and traditions are ill-equipped to handle such tasks. This kind of two-worlds approach is not unique only to Pentecostals, of course, and in many cases, enables successful scientific careers and spiritual commitments simultaneously (albeit separately).

Yet given the long alliance between evangelicalism and Pentecostalism, however, there are also an emerging number of Pentecostals who have taken up the task left over from previous generations of apologetic scholarship. The difference now, however, is at least twofold. First, that, for the most part, the natural theology approaches of the past have given way to the "humble approaches" of the present,[15] and, second, that Pentecostal apologists are to be found not only on the traditional side of defending more-or-less accepted theistic commitments but also on the other (more progressive?) side of advocating for a more scientifically informed theology. Representative of the former is Paul Elbert, a physicist and New Testament scholar in the Church of God (Cleveland), whose publications on theology and science reflect an evangelical orientation toward identifying new theistic evidences especially in light of recent experimental findings in the cosmological sciences.[16] Representative of the latter is the Pentecostal-charismatic biologist Denis Lamoureux, whose recent work has been devoted to defending a version of theistic evolution he calls evolutionary creationism over and against young-earth creationism and even intelligent design creationism.[17] Both Elbert and

15. John Marks Templeton, *The Humble Approach: Scientists Discover God*, rev. ed. (New York: Continuum, 1995).

16. See Paul Elbert, review of *God of the Astronomers* by Robert Jastrow in *The Evangelical Quarterly* 52 (1980) 242–44; "Biblical Creation and Science: A Review Article," *Journal of the Evangelical Theological Society* 39:2 (1996) 285–89; review of *Being a Christian in Science* by Walter Hearn in *Ashland Theological Journal* 34 (2002) 177–80; and, most explicitly bringing his Pentecostal sensibilities to bear on theology and science issues, "Genesis 1 and the Spirit: A Narrative-Rhetorical Ancient Near Eastern Reading in Light of Modern Science," *Journal of Pentecostal Theology* 15:1 (2006) 23–72.

17. See Denis O. Lamoureux, *Evolutionary Creation: A Christian Approach to Evolution* (Eugene, OR: Wipf & Stock, 2008) and Phillip E. Johnson, Denis O. Lamoureux, et al., *Darwinism Defeated? The Johnson-Lamoureux Debate on Biological Origins* (Vancouver, BC: Regent College, 1999); cf. my discussion of the latter volume, in "God and the Evangelical Laboratory: Recent Conservative Protestant Thinking about Theology and Science," *Theology & Science* 5:2 (2007) 203–21, esp. 209–11.

Lamoureux are insistent that God continues to be present and active personally in the human domain via the power of the Holy Spirit. They disagree, however, about how the Spirit worked in the pre-human evolutionary history of the world, with Elbert open to seeing certain events—such as the Big Bang, the origins of life, and the origins of modern *homo sapiens*, etc.—as signs of the Spirit's interventionist activity, while Lamoureux is more inclined to talk about evolutionary continuities even at these "junctures" so that the Spirit is understood to have worked immanently through the natural processes of the world instead of intermittently as in the traditional model.

More recently, however, Pentecostal scholars have been more actively taking up the questions arising specifically at the intersection of Pentecostalism and science. Along with James K. A. Smith, I have been spearheading "Science and the Spirit: Pentecostal Perspectives on the Science/Religion Dialogue" since 2006, a Templeton-funded research project involving ten other scientists and scholars. Within this group we have had a biologist exploring the interface of evolutionary theory, altruism, and the charismatic gifts; an anthropologist comparing anthropological and scientific method in the context of Afropentecostal praxis; and a theologian rethinking Newtonian and Einsteinian cosmologies using pneumatological categories; among other projects.[18] My co-director, James K. A. Smith (a philosopher by training), has attempted to ensure that the encounter between Pentecostalism and science is genuinely dialogical (a real two-way interaction) rather than monological (in which one partner dominates the discussion). More specifically, he has sought to explore how Pentecostalism might even "push back" on science, its assumptions and methods.[19] In fact, science

18. See, respectively, the preliminary work of Jeffrey P. Schloss, "Introduction: Evolutionary Ethics and Christian Morality: Surveying the Issues," in Philip Clayton and Jeffrey Schloss, eds., *Evolution and Ethics: Human Morality in Biological and Religious Perspective* (Grand Rapids: Eerdmans, 2004) 1–26; Craig Scandrett-Leathermann, "Anthropology, Polanyi, and Afropentecostal Ritual: Toward a Scientific and Theological Epistemology of Participation," *Zygon: Journal of Religion and Science* 43:4 (2008) 909–24; and Wolfgang Vondey, "The Holy Spirit and Time in Catholic and Protestant Theology," *Scottish Journal of Theology* 58:4 (2005) 393–409, and "The Holy Spirit and the Physical Universe: The Impact of Scientific Paradigm Shifts on Contemporary Pneumatology," *Theological Studies* 70:1 (2009) 1–34.

19. James K. A. Smith, "Is the Universe Open for Surprise? Pentecostal Ontology and the Spirit of Naturalism," *Zygon: Journal of Religion and Science*, 43:4 (2008) 879–96.

itself should be understood as being defined by a set of cultural practices and constructions, so that it is not only Pentecostalism that is a
cultural phenomenon which must kow-tow to the claims of "objective"
science.

In my own work, I have sought to contribute to the emerging
discussion of theology of nature from a Pentecostal and especially
pneumatological perspective.[20] Whereas the natural theology projects
of preceding generations attempted to formulate theological notions in
light of the deliverances of science, contemporary theology of nature
proposals recognize the validity of theological approaches as at least
equally viable if not superior to scientific methods since science cannot
claim any privileged or objective perspective informed by unproven
presuppositions.[21] What I have called a pneumatological theology of
nature—or pneumatological theology of creation—starts with the Spirit
(experientially and theologically) and from that vantage point seeks to
engage, interact with, and perhaps even include scientific perspectives
in attempting to comprehend the natural world.[22]

My work exemplifies the blurred lines between theology of nature
and theology of creation.[23] The concept of nature itself is theologically
ambiguous since historically, it has been defined in relationship or opposition to grace, and, since the Enlightenment, nature itself has been
opposed to super-nature. On the other hand, the notion of *creation* is
explicitly theological, assuming a creator—which for Christians and
Pentecostals is the God of Jesus Christ and of the Holy Spirit—thereby
securing the theological and even trinitarian credentials of any such

20. See my forthcoming *The Spirit, Creation, and New Creation: Modern Science
and the God-World Relation in the Pentecostal-Charismatic Imagination* (Minneapolis:
Fortress, 2010).

21. For articulation of the distinction, see Ian G. Barbour, *Nature, Human Nature,
and God* (Minneapolis: Fortress, 2002) 2.

22. See Yong, *The Spirit Poured Out on All Flesh: Pentecostalism and the Possibility
of Global Theology* (Grand Rapids: Baker Academic, 2005) ch. 7.

23. I wrestle with the distinction in my *Spirit Poured Out on All Flesh*, 267–68. Thus
also note that R. J. Berry's *God's Book of Works: The Nature and Theology of Nature*
(London and New York: T. & T. Clark, 2003) is actually a theology of the environment—i.e., a theology of creation—as is the case with Pentecostal theologian, Andrew
K. Gabriel, "Pneumatological Perspectives for a Theology of Nature: The Holy Spirit
in Relation to Ecology and Technology," *Journal of Pentecostal Theology* 15:2 (2007)
195–212.

undertaking.[24] The differences thus might be that a theology of creation is clearly theological discourse, whereas theology of nature is thought to represent the (impossible, for some) effort to find a middle way between that and the naturalistic discourse of natural theology.[25]

It is probably fair to say that given the theological and pneumatological commitments of Pentecostal scholars, few will be attracted to the project of natural theology. Further, given Pentecostal commitments to scriptural language and categories, most Pentecostal scholars who interface with the sciences will in all probability tend to think of the world in terms of creation rather than that of nature. We may now be in a better situation to appreciate the work that constitutes this volume.

Overview of the Book and the Essays

The twelve essays in this book are equally divided in four sections: biblical, historical, theological, and contextual/applicational. The three essays in section one are clearly contributions toward a Pentecostal theology of creation. Scott Ellington plies his skills as a scholar of the Hebrew Bible to uncover another "face" of the "Creator Spirit," that revealed in the face (*panim*) of yhwh, while Jerome Boone spans the biblical canon—from the creation narratives in Genesis through the Lukan narratives in the New Testament—in quest for a pneumatological theology of shalom for the created world. This is followed by Robert Waddell's theology of *new* creation, focused on John's Revelation, especially with regard to how such an eschatological vision has implications for present beliefs and practices regarding the environment. In each case, Pentecostal perspectives are engaged with the goal of formulating

24. E.g., David A. S. Fergusson, *The Cosmos and the Creator: An Introduction to the Theology of Creation* (London: SPCK, 1998).

25. John F. Haught, *Christianity and Science: Toward a Theology of Nature* (Maryknoll, NY: Orbis, 2007) attempts to walk a fine line between allowing theology to be informed by science and allowing theology to be governed by science—which raises the catch-22 question about whether science is an "equal" dialogue partner with theology; if yes, then is not the theological meta-discourse already compromised from the beginning, and if not, is dialogue even possible or desirable? For further discussion of the continuities and discontinuities between the older project of natural theology and the newer forms of theology of nature, see Gert Hummel, ed., *Natural Theology versus Theology of Nature? Tillich's Thinking as Impetus for a Discourse among Theology, Philosophy and Natural Sciences*, Theologische Bibliothek Töpelmann 60 (Berlin and New York: de Gruyter, 1994).

a biblical theology of creation even as Pentecostal stereotypes regarding the creation are challenged.

The historical discussions in section two are more loosely categorized as essays in the history of science drawn from the earlier history of Pentecostalism during the first part of the twentieth century. More specifically, Bernie Van De Walle's is in the history of applied science, David Norris' in the history of the epistemology of science, and Jerry King's in the history of religion-and-science. As already mentioned, Van De Walle recounts holiness (late nineteenth century) and Pentecostal (early twentieth century) attitudes toward medicine, medical practice, and medical science, while King tells about the Pentecostal alignment with fundamentalist views against modernist science. In the middle is the only essay on Oneness Pentecostal views regarding science in this volume, wherein Norris elaborates on how Garfield Haywood's theology of revelation provided a hermeneutic that helped interpret the "days" of the creation narrative. If these historical essays basically tell the story of the classical Pentecostal apologetic stance vis-à-vis science, they also clearly illuminate the early Pentecostal resistance to naturalism, naturalistic theologies, and even natural theology, without ever using these specific terms.

The theology section provides three contributions to theology of creation. The first two, by Shane Clifton and Matt Tallman, are more specifically Pentecostal theologies of the environment. Interestingly, both approach their topic creatively using the Pentecostal four-fold gospel of Jesus as savior, healer, baptizer (with the Spirit), and coming king, although Clifton's deployment of the four-fold gospel motif is intertwined with other analytical methods while Tallman works much more intentionally and persistently within the four-fold framework. Peter Althouse's essay, however, dovetails with that of Waddell in seeking an eschatological theology of creation. The difference is that Waddell works from the biblical text (Revelation) to new creation and then back to explore implications for us today, while Althouse works theologically and pneumatologically—through a dialogue with the work of Moltmann, especially his notion of the kenosis of the Spirit into creation—toward a soteriology or redemption of the present creation as a means of anticipating the new creation. In any case, when combined, Clifton, Tallman, and Althouse (as well as Waddell and Boone from section one) together invite Pentecostals to think about the theological implications of the environmental or ecological sciences, thus opening up to the scientific applications of the final section of the book.

We begin the final part of this volume with Kwabena Asamoah-Gyadu's African Pentecostal theology of creation. Although Asamoah-Gyadu was unable to attend and present his paper at the SPS conference (after his proposal was accepted), I nevertheless am glad that I invited him to write his essay for inclusion in the book. The African perspective reveals the complexity of the Pentecostal position on science: on the one hand, scientific knowledge is always subordinated to theological revelation; on the other hand, the sciences are methods which reveal the power, wisdom, and majesty of God the creator. Ed Decker's essay then focuses on showing how the behavioral and psychological sciences can illuminate Pentecostal experience. Finally Steve Badger and Mike Tenneson show how Pentecostal pedagogy can be helpful in teaching about origins. Together, these last two pieces reflect the promise of the Pentecostal dialogue with science: on the one hand learning from the sciences, on the other hand illuminating and informing a responsible Pentecostal approach to science.

In sum, as one of the first books on Pentecostalism and science, the essays in this volume represent nascent efforts of Pentecostal scholars to come to grips with science, and much of this is grappled with at the level of theology of creation rather than at the level of science specifically. Noticeably absent in this volume is the presence of Pentecostals who are working scientists; while this may reflect the nature of the SPS (its being comprised primarily of scholars in the humanities), it also probably also signals both that scientists are more focused on science research and willing to leave theology to theologians, and that it is in the nature of the theological task in general (with Pentecostal theologians and scholars being no exception to the rule) to ask questions which spill over into other disciplines (science included). So on the one hand, this is a book by Pentecostal scholars for other Pentecostals and other Christians seeking a more integrated theological world- and life-view that includes the sciences; on the other hand, perhaps this collection of essays will also inform the religion and science conversation in general.

In the end, however, *The Spirit Renews the Face of the Earth* reflects no more than an initial foray of Pentecostal engagement with the sciences in general and theology of creation more particularly. Much more work needs to be done, and we hope that the following essays will motivate others to go on from here. More precisely, however, in the spirit of the Pentecostal tradition, we hope that these essays may be a means through which we bear witness to the wondrous works of God in the Pentecostal encounter with science. In that case, there is a performative dimension to this book whereby what emerges is a theology which empowers a praxis through which the Holy Spirit renews and transforms not only the scientific practice, but also our own lives as well as the world as a whole, so we might hope.

PART ONE

Biblical Interpretations

1

The Face of God as His Creating Spirit

The Interplay of Yahweh's panim *and* ruach *in Psalm 104:29–30*

Scott A. Ellington

Introduction

This essay is occasioned by the unusual relationship found in Psalm 104 between two words used to describe somewhat different aspects of the presence and activity of God. *Ruach* indicates, among other things, the activity of God's spirit. The spirit is mentioned already in the second verse of Genesis with the *ruach elohim* hovering over the waters. *Panim*, translated most often as "face" or "presence," in reference to God implies both his proximity and his active presence to deliver and protect. After Israel's sin with the Golden Calf in Exodus 32, Moses is unwilling to continue the journey toward the new land if attended only by Yahweh's messenger (*malak*) but instead insists on and is granted Yahweh's *panim*, his accompanying presence, for the journey (Exod

33:12–16): "And he said to him, 'If your presence will not go, do not carry us up from here.'"

In Ps 104:27–30 these two terms are woven together to describe Yahweh's ongoing creative activity:

> These all look to you to give them their food in due season;
> when you give to them, they gather it up;
> when you open your hand, they are filled with good things.
> When you hide your *face*, they are dismayed;
> when you take away their *breath*, they die and return to dust.
> When you send forth your *spirit*, they are created [*bara*];
> and you renew the *face* of the ground.[1]

There is in this passage a three-part movement from filling, to emptiness and death, to fresh creation and new life that is reminiscent of the cycles and seasons of creation. The psalmist affirms that creation, far from being an event confined to the past, is ongoing. Von Rad's description of this active creation is representative of the views of many biblical scholars.

> The intention of Ps. CIV, which is in many respects paradig-
> matic, is indeed to show how the whole world is open to God—
> in every moment of its existence it requires to be sustained by
> God, everything "waits" on him (vs. 27); and it also receives
> this sustenance all the time. Were Jahweh to turn away from the
> world even for just one moment, then its splendour would im-
> mediately collapse (vs. 29).[2]

I will argue that the interweaving of *panim* and *ruach* in this passage suggests that both are seen by the psalmist as active agents in God's *creatio continua*. Also, the joining of these descriptors, with the rich and varied sets of meaning that each brings to this affirmation of God's creative activity, adds to our understanding of each. As von Rad suggests, this declaration truly is paradigmatic, being greater than the sum of its parts.

1. Italics added. Unless otherwise indicated I will utilize the New Revised Standard Version.

2. Gerhard von Rad, *Old Testament Theology*, vol. 1, trans. D. M. G. Stalker (San Francisco: Harper, 1962) 361.Though a general scholarly consensus accepts the notion of continuing creation, that acceptance is certainly not universal. Kraus sees in this psalm an emphasis rather on complete dependence, concluding that "The attempt to find in the psalm a clue for the dogmatic statement of *creatio continua* would be inappropriate"; Hans-Joachim Kraus, *Psalms* 60-150, trans. Hilton C. Oswald (Minneapolis, MN: Fortress , 1993) 303.

My interest here is in the unusual pairing of *ruach* and *panim* in the context of God's ongoing creation. I will develop the thesis that the *ruach Yahweh*, which normally represents a passive creative force, takes on a greater sense of being an active agent when paired with *panim*. Also that the *panim Yahweh*, which is most often associated with his blessing, deliverance, and protection, takes on a significantly different role in Psalm 104, where it is seen as a creative, life-giving force.

The Varied Faces of God's *Ruach*

God's spirit is present quite literally in the beginning of the biblical account. The creative role of the *ruach elohim* in the second verse of Genesis, though, has been widely debated and is by no means clear. Both von Rad and Westermann reject the notion that this is in any sense a reference to the person of God or a personal agent of God, translating *ruach elohim* as the "storm of God" or "God's wind," understanding it to be part of the three-clause description of chaos in verse 2: ". . . the earth was a formless void and darkness covered the face of the deep, while a wind from God swept over the face of the waters."[3]

Hildebrandt, on the other hand, argues that the *ruach elohim* in verse 2 should be understood in an adversative relationship with the formless void and the darkness.[4] He offers a compelling argument for understanding *ruach* as God's spirit, rather than as a wind from him or his breath, pointing to the uniform translation of *ruach elohim* as the "spirit of God" in each of its other occurrences in the biblical text.[5] Having rejected the translation "breath," though, Hildebrandt then adopts Stek and Tengstrom's connection between the "breath of God"

3. Gerhard von Rad, *Genesis: A Commentary*, rev. ed., trans. John H. Marks (Philadelphia, PA: Westminster, 1972) 49; Claus Westermann, *Genesis: A Practical Commentary*, trans. David Green (Grand Rapids, MI: Eerdmans, 1987) 8. This view is also adopted in Tanakh and the NRSV.

4. Fabry also argues for an adversative sense, but on very different grounds. Drawing on the adversarial relationship between wind and water in many Near Eastern cosmologies, he asserts that the wind of God would be understood as raging against the primordial sea in a "fundamental preexisting polarity"; H.-J. Fabry, "Ruach," in Johannes Botterweck, et al., eds., *Theological Dictionary of the Old Testament*, vol. 13 (Grand Rapids, MI: Eerdmans, 2004) 384–85. See also Lloyd Neve, *The Spirit of God in the Old Testament* (Tokyo: Seibunsha, 1972) 66.

5. Also Fabry, "Ruach," 382; Neve, *Spirit of God*, 67–68; and Robert Davidson, *Genesis 1–11* (Cambridge: Cambridge University Press, 1973) 16.

in 1:2 and the creative word spoken by God in 1:3. Hildebrandt's insistence on the translation "spirit of God," though probably correct, serves to weaken the argument that he then builds upon it. "It is evident," he states, "that the *ruach elohim* is not only superintending the work of creation but in fact brings creation about through the word. The passage is emphasizing the actual, powerful presence of God, who brings the spoken word into reality by the Spirit."[6] Hildebrandt collapses the distinction between God's spirit and the breath expelled in the act of speech as a means of maintaining the spirit's involvement in creation as an active agent, a conclusion which seems unwarranted and that is somewhat in tension with his insistence on translating *ruach elohim* as the spirit rather than the breath of God.

Certainly it would go beyond to text to see in Gen 1:2 a reference to the spirit as a divine person, distinguishable from the action of God. The *ruach elohim* is not a personal agent here and does not appear to be directly and explicitly involved in the process of creation that follows. The spirit is at best an evocative presence and a creative potential. John Walton suggests that we should understand the spirit's presence brooding above the chaotic waters as an intentional allusion to the motif of creation, being that which confronts chaos.

> Here the *ruah* may be seen as disrupting the power of chaos by bringing chaos into the realm of chaos. No citizen of the ancient Near East would miss the reference to the chaos motif, and no Israelite would fail to understand the potential for action inherent in the divine spirit.[7]

But the role of the *ruach elohim* is more symbolic than active. The presence of the spirit here at best bespeaks creative potential. But when Walton says "no Israelite would fail to understand the potential for action inherent in the divine spirit," he stops short of expressly identifying the nature and extent of that action. A clear connection between the *ruach elohim* and creation is both tenuous here and rare elsewhere in the biblical text. As we shall see, it appears most clearly stated in the third and final section of the Old Testament canon.

6. Wilf Hildebrandt, *An Old Testament Theology of the Spirit of God* (Peabody, MA: Hendrickson, 1995) 35.

7. John H. Walton, "Creation," in T. Desmond Alexander and David W. Baker, eds., *Dictionary of the Old Testament: Pentateuch* (Downers Grove, IL: InterVarsity, 2003) 157–58.

The phrase *ruach elohim* is primarily associated not with God's creation, but with his empowerment. The giving of God's *ruach* is described as the imparting of a *prophetic spirit* (Num 24:2; 1 Sam 10:10; 19:20, 23; 1 Chr 12:18; 2 Chr 15:1; 24:20; cf. Gen 41:38; Num 11:17, 25–26, 31; 1 Sam 10:6; 19:20, 23; 1 Kgs 22:24; Isa 48:16; 59:21; 61:1; Ezek 11:5; Joel 2:28–29; Mic 3:8; Neh 9:30; 2 Chr 18:23; 20:14), a *spirit of boldness* (1 Sam 11:6), or a *spirit of wisdom* (Exod 31:3; 35:31; cf. Gen 41:38; Exod 28:3; Deut 34:9; Isa 11:2–4; Dan 4:8–9; 5:11–12, 14; Neh 9:20) on chosen individuals.[8] Among the judges the *ruach Yahweh* is particularly associated with imparting the ability to lead and judge the people (Judg 3:10; 6:34; 11:29; 13:25; 14:6, 19; 15:14). The notion of the spirit as a *physically active agent* that can enter people or physically carry them from place to place is infrequent in the Old Testament, but is a particularly prominent image for the prophet Ezekiel (Ezek 2:2; 3:12, 14, 24; 8:3; 37:1; cf. 1 Kgs 18:12; 2 Kgs 2:16).[9] Creation, then, is not the dominant image associated with the presence and activity of God's spirit in the Old Testament.

Creation language outside of the opening chapters of Genesis is far from plentiful in the Old Testament, and even less common are references to the spirit as a creative, life-giving force. The Psalmist makes reference to God's creative word in Genesis 1, "By the word of the LORD the heavens were made, and all their host by the breath of his mouth" (Ps 33:6), but without closing the gap that we have already observed between the brooding spirit in 1:2 and the spoken word in 1:3. Ezekiel and Job come closest to affirming the activity of the spirit in the ongoing work of sustaining life. Ezekiel, in his prophecy at the Valley of Bones, refers to the life-giving power of Yahweh's spirit: "I will put my spirit within you, and you shall live" (37:14). Job speaks of the *ruach elohim* not as a creative agent, but as the breath of life that sustains him: "as long as my breath is in me and the spirit of God is in my nostrils" (27:3). He goes on, though, to make a more explicit connection between creation, life, and spirit: "The spirit of God (*ruach el*) has made me, and the breath of the Almighty gives me life" (Job 33:4). Here we have the clearest reference thus far to the spirit as creative agent and the suggestion, made explicit in Psalm 104, that the spirit's creative activity is ongoing.

8. In the Deutero-canonical writings, wisdom is personified and is expressly identified with the "breath" that emanates from God; Wis 7:25 and Sir 24:3.

9. Fabry, "Ruach," 382, elects a translation of "wind" rather than "spirit" in such instances.

Pointing to the priestly origins of Gen 1:2, Neve argues that the spirit as creator is primarily an exilic concept.

> For whatever reason, creation emerges as a major emphasis in literature that has been dated to the exile, Job, Deutero-Isaiah, Gen 1 (P) and some of the Psalms. In these writings the spirit of God is associated for the first time with the creation tradition, not only as the agent of cosmic creation, but also identified as the creator of man and the source of life in the regeneration of both man and the cosmos.[10]

The experience of exile, along with the confrontation both with Babylonian gods and the Babylonian creation mythology provided the impetus, Neve speculates, for Israel to articulate a more robust creation theology.

In summary, references to the *ruach elohim* or the *ruach Yahweh* as a creative agent are surprisingly uncommon in the Old Testament tradition and, though alluded to in prophetic writings, are associated most clearly with the *kethuvim* or writings, that part of the Old Testament which was canonized last. Such images as the spirit of wisdom, the spirit of leadership, and the prophetic spirit are far more representative of the Old Testament understanding of the action and function of the divine spirit.

The Spirit of God's *Panim*

The *panim* of God suggests a greater sense of the person of God than does his *ruach*. *Panim* refers to more than simply God's presence, but also implies a degree of relatedness, of ongoing interaction. In his study of the use of the noun with God as the subject, Simian-Yofre describes *panim* principally in terms of relatedness: "Insofar as *panim* bespeaks presence, its purpose is to underline the positive aspect of the interpersonal relationship. The negative aspect of the relationship is expressed by the separation from *panim*."[11] This connection is suggested already in Moses' demand for the accompanying *panim* in Exod 33:16. Presumably the angel of Yahweh would have been sufficient to provide guidance, protection, and empowerment for conquest. The *panim Yahweh* implied something more, a sense of identity and belonging: "For

10. Neve, *Spirit of God*, 63–64.

11. F. Simian-Yofre, "Panim," in. G. Johannes Botterweck, et al., eds., *Theological Dictionary of the Old Testament*, vol. 11 (Grand Rapids, MI: Eerdmans, 2001) 607.

how shall it be known that I have found favor in your sight, I and your people, unless you go with us? In this way, we shall be distinct, I and your people, from every people on the face of the earth" (Exod 33:16). Whereas God's *ruach*, at least in the Old Testament, suggests the notion of the activity and empowerment of God, God's *panim* comes closer to the idea of God as personal agent.

That which Moses sought, the accompanying *panim* of God, most frequently implies his blessing and protection. For Cain to be hidden from God's *panim* is to be made outlaw in the literal sense of that term, that is, to be outside the protection afforded by the law so that "anyone who meets me may kill me" (Gen 4:14). With the promise to Moses of God's accompanying *panim* comes the resulting assurance from Yahweh, "I will give you rest" (Exod 33:14).

The *panim* of God can be a source of both judgment and blessing. For Yahweh to "set his face against" a people is to judge and destroy them: "For I have set my face against this city for evil and not for good, says the LORD: it shall be given into the hands of the king of Babylon, and he shall burn it with fire" (Jer 21:10; cf. Lev 20:3, 5–6; 26:17; Jer 44:11; Ezek 7:22; 15:7; Ps 34:16; 80:16). For the psalm writers, though, the *panim* of God can be seen positively as a source of blessing and deliverance. The light of Yahweh's face shines and gives deliverance: "Let your face shine upon your servant; save me in your steadfast love" (Ps 31:16; cf. Pss 4:6; 16:11; 17:2, 15; 44:3; 67:1; 80:3, 7, 19; 89:15; 119: 135; Dan 9:17–18).[12] Craigie[13] is representative of those commentators who find a connection between the liturgical use of this expression in the Psalter and the priestly blessing formula in Num 6:24–26:

> The LORD bless you and keep you;
> the LORD make his face to shine upon you,
> and be gracious to you;
> the LORD lift up his countenance upon you,
> and give you peace.

Reference to the light of God's *panim* as a source of blessing and salvation is a favored expression of the psalm writers, appearing only rarely

---

12. Though speaking of the face of a human king, rather than God, Prov 16:15a offers insight into the metaphor of a shining face as a source of blessing and life: "In the light of a king's face there is life."

13. Peter C. Craigie, *Psalms 1–50* (Waco, TX: Word, 1983) 81.

outside of the Psalms. This, I will argue, accords well with the understanding of *panim* as a life-giving force in Psalm 104.

References to the hiding of God's face (*satar panim*) frequently identify the face of God with protection and deliverance by equating the hiding of his face with the removal of that protection and with handing over to judgment. In his landmark study of the hiding of God's face, Samuel Balentine draws attention to a distinction between the way this expression is used in the prophets and its appropriation in the Psalter. "Whereas the prophets stress the 'specific sense' of God's hiddenness in reaction to a guilty people, the psalmists complain of a hiddenness which to them seems inexplicable."[14] In the Psalter, the hiding of God's face appears most frequently in the context of lament, and is often not seen to be the result of sin. Of particular interest to this present study is Balentine's observation that in the psalms of lament the hiddenness of God's face is often associated with "the threat of death and confinement to Sheol" (Pss 22:16; 30:4; 88:5; 102:4; 143:7).[15] So, for example, Ps 143:7 reads: "Answer me quickly, O LORD; my spirit fails. Do not hide your face from me, or I shall be like those who go down to the Pit." Just as the shining forth of his face brings blessing, so too the hiding of the divine face leads to a diminishing of life. The hiding of God's face in the Psalms is also tied to his lack of deliverance, so that he forgets, does not hear, and does not answer (Pss 10:11; 13:1; 44:24; 69:17; 143:7).

In the Pentateuch and particularly in the prophetic writings, the hiding of Yahweh's *panim* results in the withdrawal of protection and the withholding of deliverance for the nation of Israel.

> My anger will be kindled against them on that day. I will forsake them and hide my face from them; they will become easy prey, and many terrible troubles will come upon them. On that day they will say, "Have not these troubles come upon us because our God is not in our midst?" On that day I will surely hide my face on account of all the evil they have done by turning to other gods (Deut 31:17–18).

Israel also experiences that hiddenness of the divine *panim* as judgment in a more active sense. "There is no one who calls on your name, or at-

---

14. Samuel E. Balentine, *The Hidden God: The Hiding of the Face of God in the Old Testament* (Oxford: Oxford University Press, 1983) 166.

15. Balentine, *Hidden God*, 60.

tempts to take hold of you; for you have hidden your face from us, and have delivered us into the hand of our iniquity" (Isa 64:7; cf. Gen 4:14; Deut 32:20; Isa 8:17; 54:8; 59:2; Jer 18:17; 33:5; Ezek 7:22; 39:21–29; Mic 3:4).

In summary, then, the *panim* of God describes his relational presence. He can punish his people either by setting his face against them or by hiding his face, thus withdrawing his protection and provision. In the Psalter the hiding of the divine face is often not tied to sin or a specific act of judgment and the psalm writer experiences the concealment of *panim* as a diminishing of life, a movement toward Sheol. The shining forth of God's face, by contrast, is a particular idiom of the psalm writers and expresses God's blessing and deliverance.

The Pairing of *Panim* and *Ruach*

Panim and *ruach* appear together only occasionally in descriptions of God's activities. The prophet Ezekiel understands the hiding of God's face in the sense typical of prophetic writers, that is, as a withdrawal of divine protection and/or as an active expression of judgment by Yahweh against the nation. In the thirty-ninth chapter of his prophecy, Ezekiel pairs the redirecting of Yahweh's face toward Judah with both their restoration from captivity and with the pouring out of his spirit. Ezekiel 39:23–29 reads:

> And the nations shall know that the house of Israel went into captivity for their iniquity, because they dealt treacherously with me. So I *hid my face* from them and gave them into the hand of their adversaries, and they all fell by the sword. I dealt with them according to their uncleanness and their transgressions, and *hid my face* from them. Therefore, thus says the Lord GOD: Now I will restore the fortunes of Jacob, and have mercy on the whole house of Israel; and I will be jealous for my holy name. They shall forget their shame, and all the treachery they have practiced against me, when they live securely in their land with no one to make them afraid, . . . and I will never again *hide my face* from them, when I *pour out my spirit* upon the house of Israel, says the Lord GOD [italics added].

The pouring out of God's spirit does not appear to imply a creative or re-creative act, though, such as is the case with the reanimation of the dry bones in chapter thirty-seven. Nor do we find the use of creation language associated with the restoration of Israel in Ezekiel, as we do in Deutero-Isaiah.[16]

Psalm 139:7 also pairs the *ruach* and *panim* of Yahweh: "Where can I go from your spirit? Or where can I flee from your presence?" This usage is interesting in that it shifts noticeably the understanding of spirit. The *ruach Yahweh* is not now an empowerment for prophecy and wisdom or an anointing for leadership, but a personal presence, an active agent.

In Ps 51:9–12, the psalmist pairs *panim* and *ruach* in calling on God for personal restoration, specifically selecting language of new creation.

> Hide your *face* from my sins,
> and blot out all my iniquities.
> Create [*bara*] in me a clean heart, O God,
> and put a new and right *spirit* within me.
> Do not cast me away from your *presence*,
> and do not take your holy *spirit* from me.
> Restore to me the joy of your salvation,
> and sustain in me a willing *spirit*.

The synonymous parallelism in verse 9 between "hide your face from my sins" and "blot out all my iniquities" is suggestive. For God to hide his face from sin is to withhold that which sustains it. Metaphorically sin will "die" if God will but hide his face from it. Restoration in verse 10 requires a fresh act of creation. Neither the heart nor the spirit marred by sin can be rehabilitated. They must be created anew. The relationship between God's *panim* and his *ruach* in verse 11 is also evocative. To be cast away from the face of God is to lose his sustaining spirit. Presumably, then, both the face and the spirit of Yahweh are involved in restoring salvation and sustaining a willing spirit. Here we come closest to the interplay between *panim*, *ruach*, and *bara* found more expressly stated in Ps 104:29–30. The face of God sustains life, poetically speaking, even the "life" of the psalmist's sins. The spirit of God stands together with his face and, in so doing, is credited with being more than simply the activity or empowerment of God. Also the creative activity of both *panim* and *ruach* are not conceived of as a one-time, past event, but are ongoing. Each act of restoration requires the death of sin and the fresh

16. See Steven Lee, *Creation and Redemption in Isaiah 40–55* (Sheffield: Sheffield Academic, 1997) for a full discussion of Isaiah's application of this theme.

creation of heart and spirit. The spirit of the psalmist must be sustained by the *panim* and *ruach* of Yahweh.

In summary, the direct pairing of *panim* and *ruach* can maintain the sense basic to *panim* alone, that of physical presence and protection, as in the case of Ezekiel 39 and Psalm 139. In the case of the latter, we also see introduced the notion of the *ruach*'s abiding presence. In Psalm 51, though, *ruach* lends to the imagery of the psalm the suggestion of an ongoing creative force. Furthermore, it is God's *panim* and *ruach* together which create anew and sustain the psalmist.

The Interplay of Yahweh's *Panim* and *Ruach* in Psalm 104

We have seen an appropriation of the meaning of both *panim* and *ruach* in the poetic language of the Psalter in general and in Psalm 51 in particular that is distinctive, even unique. *Ruach* takes on more the sense of an active agent than an impersonal empowerment. Additionally, three of the five references to God's *ruach* in the Psalter speak directly of his creative activity,[17] a very different emphasis from that found elsewhere in the canon. *Panim* adds to its accustomed function of protection and deliverance the power of blessing that sustains life and delivers from death. With the hiding and shining forth of Yahweh's face, the psalmist draws near to and is lifted up from Sheol.[18]

Structural parallels between Psalm 104 and Genesis 1 have long been observed, so that an implicit reference to the first creation ac-

17. Psalm 33:6 refers to "creatio prima" and Pss 51:9–12 and 104:29–40 to "creatio continua." Psalm 18:7–15 alludes to a theophany of God in which his power is displayed in "the blast of the breath of your nostrils." In Ps 143:10, God's spirit instructs and guides the psalmist in the way of safety.

18. Because of the limits of space, I have chosen not to explore the strong parallels between Ps 104:27–30 and the hymn to the Egyptian sun god, "Hymn to the Aton":

> The world came into being by thy hand,
> According as thou hast made them.
> When thou hast risen they live,
> When thou settest they die.
> Thou art lifetime thy own self,
> For one lives (only) through thee.

The connection of the idea of the sun as sustainer of life is an intriguing one, though scholars find no direct dependence of Ps 104 on the Egyptian hymn. See Bernard W. Anderson, *Out of the Depth: The Psalms Speak for Us Today*, rev. and expanded ed. (Philadelphia, PA: Westminster, 1983) 45.

count has gained general acceptance among commentators.[19] Terrien, for example, asserts that "The eight strophes [which make up Psalm 104] correspond to the eight acts of creation in the Yahwist myth (Gen 1:1–2:4)."[20] Waltner has pointed out that, whereas the focus in Genesis 1 is on the creation, in this psalm it is the creator that is exalted.[21] It should not be surprising, therefore, that commentary on God's maintenance of creation in Ps 104:29–30 focuses on his *ruach*, while frequently overlooking his *panim*. With very few exceptions, commentators all but ignore the role of *panim* in God's ongoing creation, in spite of the clear structural interweaving of *panim* and *ruach*. Schaefer is typical: having acknowledged the three-part structure of 104:27–30 and the dependence of creation on God's provision, presence, and breath, he sees no direct role for *panim* in God's creation.

> God is primarily a provider of food (vv. 20–21, 27–28) for besides being well-ordered and awesome, creation is daily dependent on God's sustenance, presence, and breath. God creates and regulates the pulse of life and death by his *ruah* or "breath" (vv. 29–30; cf. Gen. 2:7; Eccl. 12:7). God breathes, and creatures live; God stops breathing and they die.[22]

Calvin provides a notable exception to this tendency, acknowledging the role of God's *panim* in creation: "by which words he points out, that when God vouchsafes to look upon us, that look gives us life, and that as long as his serene countenance shines, it inspires all the creation with life."[23] Particularly in light of the parallel found in Psalm 51, such ostracism of *panim* in the context of creation is unwarranted.

19. See Anderson, *Out of the Depth*, 158.

20. Samuel Terrien, *The Psalms: Strophic Structure and Theological Commentary* (Grand Rapids, MI: Eerdmans, 2003) 710.

21. James H. Waltner, *Psalms* (Scottdale, PA: Herald, 2006) 502.

22. Konrad Schaefer, *Psalms* (Collegeville, MN: Liturgical, 2001) 258. The majority of commentators that note the role of *ruach* in creation give *no* attention to the function of *panim*, including Kraus, *Psalms 60–150*, 303; Terrien, *Psalms*, 717; Artur Weiser, *The Psalms*, trans. Herbert Hartwell (Philadelphia, PA: Westminster, 1962) 670–71; J. H. Eaton, *Psalms* (London: SCM, 1967) 251; A. A. Anderson, *The Book of Psalms*, vol. 2 (Greenwood, SC: The Attic, 1972) 724; Leslie C. Allen, *Psalms 101–150* (Waco, TX: Word, 1983) 34; James L. Mays, *Psalms* (Louisville, KY: John Knox, 1994) 334–35; and Richard J. Clifford, *Psalms 73–150* (Nashville, TN: Abingdon, 2003) 150.

23. John Calvin, *Commentary on Psalms*, vol. 4, trans. James Anderson (Grand Rapids, MI: Eerdmans, 1949) 167. Walter Brueggemann also notes the role of face along side of his breath as a sustaining force, but without the explicit connection to face

Structurally verses 29–30 so intermingle the two terms that it requires an almost willful act to set one aside in favor of the other. The chiastic structure of these verses serves to underscore the blending of these two expressions of creation and life.

> A When you hide your face, they are dismayed;
>   B when you take away their breath, they die
>   C and return to the dust [*apar*].
>   B´ When you send forth your spirit, they are created;
> A´ and you renew the face of the ground.

Fabry identifies *apar* or "dust" as being among the antonyms in *ruach's* lexical field,[24] and in this context it provides the ideal pivot for the chiasm.

A striking feature of the interplay of *panim* and *ruach* in verse 29–30 is the intimacy established between the divine *panim* and *ruach* and that of his creatures. The hiding of the divine face robs every living creature of breath. The sending forth of God's spirit makes new the face of the ground/man (*adam*) of original creation. Creator and created embrace one another, face to face and breath to breath.

This camaraderie between *ruach* and *panim* in God's sustaining of creation suggests a degree of shared attribution between the two. The *ruach* of God, which has empowered creation and creature alike, is now seen in light of the personal presence of God. The spirit's activity must be ongoing in order for life to be sustained. The divine *panim*, which heretofore has offered Israel their identity as a nation preserved and protected by Yahweh, now takes on a more immediate and personal impulse. Every breath of every creature is a new act of God's creation, an act which is only sustainable before the face of God as he breathes out new life. By drawing them together in this way, the psalmist has extended and enriched the meaning of both expressions of God.

Conclusions

The interplay of *panim* and *ruach* in Ps 104:29–30 suggests a number of preliminary conclusions with regard to our understanding of their role in God's creation.

---

as active agent in creation; see Brueggemann, *The Message of the Psalms: A Theological Commentary* (Minneapolis, MN: Augsburg, 1984) 32.

24. Fabry, "Ruach," 379.

1) Contrary to what might be expected from the preferential focus on *ruach* over *panim* by many commentators on Ps 104:29–30, in the Psalter it is *panim* that is most strongly and regularly associated with both the blessing of renewed life and the threat of death. It is *panim* rather than *ruach* which is the principal expression of God's life-giving activity in the Psalter. For that reason, *panim* should not be seen as an "awkward cousin" in speaking of God's creation. Indeed, in Psalm 104 we see the trajectory set by the "shining of God's face" reach its fullest expression. Life is only sustainable in the continued presence and with the enduring spirit of God.

2) Clear associations of the *ruach* with the creation and sustaining of life appear to be prominent only later in Israel's writings, appearing specifically in the Psalter and the book of Job. While this in no sense negates the participation of the *ruach elohim* in the Genesis creation account, it does point to a development in Israel's thinking with regard to the spirit as creator.

3) The association of *panim* with *ruach* in the affirmation of *creatio continua* in Psalm 104 lends to the latter a sense of being an active agent in creation not found in the Genesis 1 account. The implied and potential participation of the *ruach elohim* in creation becomes for the psalmist an intimate and direct involvement with each creature, breath by breath and heartbeat by heartbeat. Creation happens every moment of every day before the face and through the spirit of Yahweh.

4) The New Testament perspective of the Holy Spirit as a distinct person and active agent, whether one adopts the Trinitarian or Oneness perspective on the Spirit, is nowhere clearly articulated in the Old Testament. The "spirit of God" is more an expression of his activity than his personhood. Having said that, the interplay of the divine *panim* and *ruach* in Psalm 104 suggests a marked progression in Israel's thinking about the *ruach Yahweh*. God's spirit has come to be seen by the worshipping community as an abiding presence, perhaps distinguishable from, but no longer wholly separate from the *panim Yahweh* that accompanies not only Israel, but all of creation.

2

Created for Shalom

Human Agency and Responsibility in the World

R. Jerome Boone

Introduction

The care of creation should be motivated by both love for God and love for neighbor. As love for God, caring for creation recognizes that creation is the work of God. The Creator is honored by the respect we give to the Creator's work. As love for others, caring for creation recognizes the direct relationship between a well-maintained earth and human well-being. A ravaged or polluted earth has devastating results for humankind. My concern in this chapter is the relationship between care for creation and human well-being.

The creation account in Genesis 1–2 reveals two important aspects of how God is at work in creation. First, God transforms chaos into order. Second, God creates humankind with the responsibility to preserve order in creation. These two themes illuminate much about God's purpose and human responsibility for the created world. God structured the world with reproductive power and a cycle for regeneration. However, the structure did not replace God's ongoing involvement in the creation or the need for human agency to control certain forces of nature. Humankind created in the "image of God," was charged with the responsibility for the maintenance of creation even before sin entered the world. The role of sustaining an orderly creation continued to be the responsibility of God's people after the destructive intrusion of sin into history. Evidence of this human responsibility is woven into the fabric of the Torah laws with its concern for land and resources. The goal for human responsibility in the Torah is shalom—well-being—for all of creation. The Torah laws set a trajectory for the rest of the Bible. The inauguration of the Kingdom of God in Jesus of Nazareth comes with a prophetic vision of shalom (Luke 4:18–19). The mission of God is extended to the Church as it seeks to participate in God's redemptive work toward creation within the parameters of human history. This essay will expand on these themes.

Creation of Humankind as an Agent for Shalom

Genesis 1, as a consensus of the polyphonic voices of the Hebrew Bible, declares Yahweh to be the Creator of heaven and earth and all that dwells therein. The account is a theological summary, highly structured in literary form, that addressed Israel's particular context in the Ancient Near East (ANE). It is not possible to date the passage with any certitude but it is commonly understood among Old Testament scholars to have been shaped by the Babylonian Exile (P source) and positioned as a theological preface to the Torah (Pentateuch).[1] Its theological purpose is to claim primacy for Yahweh and to offer a monotheistic account of creation.

The Genesis 1 account reveals how God is at work in the creation. First, God transforms chaos into order, and then God creates humankind with the responsibility to preserve that order in creation. The creation account illuminates much about God and our human role in the world order. God's transformation of chaos into order is evident in the whole of Genesis 1. The opening verses describe the world as "formless and void." The subsequent verses describe the transformation. The form-

---

1. Walter Brueggemann, *An Introduction to the Old Testament* (Louisville, KY: Westminster John Knox, 2003) 30–31.

less becomes formed as land, sea, and atmosphere. The void becomes filled with fish, birds, animals, and human beings. The transformation is completed by the time we reach the end of chapter one. The narrative concludes with God's Sabbath rest (Gen 2:1–3).

Jon Levenson, in his book *Creation and the Persistence of Evil*,[2] has influenced my understanding of the creation account. He rightly points out that the Genesis creation story does not support the doctrine of creation *ex nihilo*. The Genesis account assumes a pre-existent chaos. The very phrase "formless and void," which describes the earth at the start of the creation account, is used elsewhere (Jer 4:23) to describe a chaotic situation that was the result of devastation.

At the end of the creation account order prevails! It not only prevails, order is sustainable! Order is structured with seasons—a cycle that perpetually renews creation. The creation itself is designed with the ability to re-create itself. But the rest of the canon assures us that God did not create the world with sustaining power and then step out of the process.

In conjunction with the transformation of chaos into order at creation, God created humankind to sustain order throughout the parameters of history. The creation narrative is very brief about this provision but also very clear:

> Then God said, "Let us make humankind in our image, according to our likeness; and let them have dominion over the fish of the sea, and over the birds of the air, and over the cattle, and over all the wild animals of the earth, and over every creeping thing that creeps upon the earth." So God created humankind in His image, in the image of God He created them; male and female He created them. God blessed them and God said to them, "Be fruitful and multiply, and fill the earth, and subdue it and have dominion over the fish of the sea, and over the birds of the air, and over every living creature that moves upon the earth" (Gen 1:26–28).[3]

The creation of humankind in the "image of God" is a powerful statement in its ANE context. It is "generally agreed that the image of God

---

2. Jon D. Levenson, *Creation and the Persistence of Evil* (Princeton, NJ: Princeton University Press, 1988).

3. Unless otherwise noted, all biblical quotations will be from the New American Standard Bible.

reflected in human persons is after the manner of a king who establishes statues of himself to assert his sovereign rule where the king cannot be present."[4] Obviously, the imagery has limited application because God is omnipresent. The essence of the narrative is to illuminate the role of humankind in creation. The imagery of the text at once communicates two important truths about humankind: (1) human persons have a unique relationship with God and (2) human persons have a unique relationship to creation.

The personal and moral implications of the image of God in humanity contribute to a better understanding of human responsibility. The "image of God" in humankind has a personal dimension. The image must look like the archetype if it is to be effective. People who see the image must be reminded of the sovereign whom it represents. Therefore, humankind must reflect the character of God in creation. This is in reality one of the ways in which God is present in creation, fragmentary as that may be. The correlation of image to archetype demands a relationship. We are not static statues chiseled in stone or fixed metal images. We are dynamic images that change moment to moment, day to day and year to year. The quality of our role as the image of God is dependent upon our relationship with the triune God. Our responsibility is to allow the character of God to be mediated through us to rest of the creation. Consequently, we hear God's repeated charge to Israel in the Hebrew Bible: "you shall be holy for I am holy" (Lev 11:44–45).

A primary responsibility assigned to humankind in the creation account of Genesis 1 is that of "caretaker" of God's creation. God's command was "be fruitful and multiply, and fill the earth and subdue it; and rule over the birds of the sky, and over every living thing that moves on the earth" (Gen 1:28). What is obvious in this text is that God wanted to fill the earth with God's "image"—men and women. Just as kings and sovereigns in the ANE world set up their images (statues) in every realm of their kingdom, God intended for God's image to be everywhere in the world of God's creation. Divine sovereignty over creation and divine presence in creation would be achieved, in part, through the fulfillment of the command to "be fruitful and multiply."

4. Walter Brueggemann, *Genesis* (Atlanta: John Knox, 1982) 32.

The view of humankind in the Genesis 1 creation account is that of "ruler" over creation, not an autonomous sovereign but a steward with delegated authority. In this role, humankind has the responsibility to maintain order in creation, the responsibility to continue the well-being of the created order for every aspect of creation. The verbs that constitute the command, "rule over and subdue" (Gen 1:28), carry this charge. In a real sense, God has democratized sovereignty over the creation, delegating it to humankind. Human persons as the "image of God" are not inorganic, passive statues of the divine. They are animated and active in the maintenance of world order. They have delegated authority to empower their task. The goal is to ensure "shalom" for every part of creation.[5]

Psalm 8 clearly extols the exalted status of humanity. Human beings are persons of dignity and have a close affinity to God's own self.[6] This status is attached to human persons, quite apart from their performance. It is ontological in nature rather than utilitarian. Consequently, it is a status that remains intact even after the Fall of humankind into sin. It is a status that affects every human person, regardless of gender, skin color, or religious affiliation/non-affiliation.

As "rulers" over creation, both before and after the Fall (Genesis 3), human beings act as God's agents/caretakers for maintaining the creation. The purpose of rulership is to ensure that creation supports shalom for all aspects of creation. But why does God need human agents in order to ensure shalom in creation? The Genesis creation account seems to describe a perfect world, a world in which everything is "good." And yet, it is clear that things cannot operate perpetually without supervision and care. The creation needs "rulers" to "subdue" it. Either this provision anticipates the coming Fall of humankind into sin or something in the primordial world needed an element of control. Quite honestly, the case could be argued either way. Even before the Fall of humankind into sin, Adam was placed in the Garden of Eden as caretaker to "cultivate it and keep it" (Gen 2:15). These verbs indicate that maintenance of creation was necessary before sin entered the world. After sin became a part of the human experience, the creation was subjected to a "curse" (Gen 3:17–19) which intensified the work

---

5. Brueggemann, *Genesis*, 32–33.

6. Elmer A. Martens, *God's Design: A Focus on Old Testament Theology* (N. Richland Hills, TX: Bibal, 1998) 202–3.

of maintenance to a point that made work laborious. The point is that in either interpretation, human agents were needed for the well-being of creation. The question is why? What was there about the nature of creation that made it necessary to set "rulers" over it?

Jon Levenson has an insightful proposal regarding this question. He contends that God's creational activity did not destroy the forces of chaos; it simply pushed chaos to the perimeters of the created world.[7] It is as if one were to establish an orderly community in a chaotic territory. In this model, the forces of chaos are always present, ready to break in upon the created order and overwhelm it. The on-going providence of God and the actions of human persons are the forces that hold chaos in check. It is the omnipotence of God that can always re-establish order when chaos takes over. This is a highly dynamic model of reality that views chaos or evil as pre-existent to the world order.

Whether or not we want to accept the paradigm for chaos offered by Levenson, we must recognize the constancy of the threat of chaos/evil in the creation. The role of humankind as caretakers (rulers) in the created world is directly related to the threatening presence of chaos/evil. In order for shalom to exist for all creation, chaos must be kept away. Divine providence certainly plays the dominant role in this dynamic. Human action also plays a role within the providence of God. Human persons as delegated agents of the Creator socially construct shalom by doing God's will. As human agents pursue justice and benevolence toward others, a world of shalom is created. The work of socially constructing shalom is always difficult and achieved only in fragmentary ways because of the nature of humankind. Chaos wears many masks: abuse, disease, war, poverty, sin, etc. It comes from both wrongful human actions and natural disasters (acts of God). Its goal is always to hurt, maim, and destroy. Its destructive presence in the world is the result of sin (Genesis 3). And where sin abounds, chaos is intensified.

The witness of scripture is that God is at work in universal ways, caring for every part of creation and directing human history toward a pre-determined end—the Kingdom of God. In order to achieve the universal goals of creation, God must work in particular ways in specific aspects of the creation. The nation of Israel is the focus of much of God's particular care in the Hebrew Bible. The Church universal is the focus of the same kind of particular care in the New Testament. God's

---

7. Levenson, *Creation and the Persistence of Evil*, 17.

sustaining care for the creation in the particular work of guiding the destinies of Israel and the Church must interact with human obedience and disobedience. Much of the narrative of the Bible is concerned with this engagement between God and humankind.

Israel as an Agent for Shalom

What role did Israel play in achieving shalom for the world? The Hebrew Bible contains hundreds of statutes and ordinances prescribed for Israel for the purpose of creating shalom. The statutes and ordinances are given in the context of a world under the influence of sin. The divine guidelines reveal God's concern for justice and benevolence. These canonical texts offer insight into God's redemptive work in the world.

These so-called "land laws" of the Hebrew Bible are a fertile area for discerning God's concern for shalom.[8] The "land laws" have an obvious concern for the distribution of resources. Ancient Israel was primarily an agrarian society; land was the primary means of productivity and wealth accumulation. Almost half of the book of Joshua (chapters 13–22) is taken up with describing how the land of Canaan was divided up among the twelve tribes of Israel. The details of the narrative testify to how important land was to Israel's well being.

The land of Canaan was a divine gift to Israel. It was promised to Abraham and his descendants "forever" (Gen 13:15; 2 Chr 20:7). The Jews came to refer to Canaan as the "Promised Land" because of the promissory nature of the place. The promise of Canaan was a gift; it was not earned or merited, it was simply given. The gift was contingent upon obedience to the covenant with Yahweh. Faithfulness to Yahweh ensured occupation of the land of Canaan. Disobedience to Yahweh put the occupation of the land at risk. The contingency of land is well documented in the Torah (Deut 4, 8–11, 27–30).

The divine gift of land to Israel was for the purpose of creating shalom. The land of Canaan is often described as a land "flowing with milk and honey" (Exod 3:8, 17; 13:5; 33:3; Deut 6:3). The fertile land would

8. My attention was first drawn to the significance of the Torah land laws by M. Douglas Meeks in his book, *God the Economist: The Doctrine of God and Political Economy* (Minneapolis, MN: Fortress, 1989). Christopher J. H. Wright is a contemporary scholar who continues to draw attention to the role of the land laws in God's redemptive work in creation; see Wright, *The Mission of God* (Downers Grove, IL: InterVarsity, 2006) ch. 12.

be a place of "blessing." The land would produce the resources needed to sustain life: grain, wine, fruit, animals, and water. It would also be a place of security from famine and homelessness, but also security from the hostile actions of others—Israel's enemies (as the summary statement in Deut 28:1–11 makes clear).

The land of Canaan could only fulfill its divine purpose of "blessing/shalom" if the Israelites maintained the distribution of land among the people. The distribution of land in an agrarian society is the chief means of the distribution of resources for shalom. The opposite is true as well. The loss of land is a loss of shalom. The petition of Nehemiah laments this fact:

> Here we are slaves, to this day—slaves in the land that you gave to our ancestors to enjoy its fruit and its good gifts. Its rich yield goes to the kings whom you have set over us because of our sins; they have power also over our bodies and over our livestock at their pleasure. And we are in great distress (Neh 9:36–37).

Therefore, the "land laws" were initiated as a means of protecting shalom/blessing for the people of Israel.

The "land laws" were linked to the cycle of measuring time in ancient Israel. Instead of the base ten system used in the western to measure time, Israel used a base seven system. Instead of marking time in decades and centuries, Israel marked time in Sabbaths and Jubilees. Every seventh year was a Sabbatical year and every fiftieth year (the conclusion of seven sabbatical years) was a Jubilee year. Many of the "land laws" were correlated with the Sabbatical years and the Jubilee years.

The Jubilee year was commonly known as a year of release. The most unique feature of the Jubilee was that it required all property in Israel to return to the original family/clan that owned it (Leviticus 25). The purpose of the law was to re-distribute resources every fifty years in order to maintain a fairly democratic possession of land and its resources. There was no provision for permanent sale of Israelite land. The best that could be done, at least in theory, was to lease the land for a maximum of forty-nine years. The law allowed entrepreneurial persons to accumulate wealth as a result of their labor. At the same time, the law prevented the accumulated wealth from being passed down to later generations in perpetuity. Beyond this unique element, the Jubilee year shared the same elements inherent in the Sabbatical years.

The Sabbatical years were times of release from debt and servitude (Deuteronomy 15). They also served as periods of benevolence for the poor. The Sabbatical year is discussed in numerous traditions of the Torah. It appears in the "Book of the Covenant" (Exod 21:2, 23:11), the Priestly Code/Holiness Code (Leviticus 25), and the Deuteronomic Code (15:1–15). The Sabbatical legislation mandated a release of all Hebrew slaves. Therefore, slavery for Hebrews was limited to a maximum of six years. Slaves who were released during the Sabbatical year were to be furnished with wine, grain, and livestock (Deut 15:13–14). The provision prevented slaves from being released into poverty—the very reason that many Hebrews were sold into slavery.

The Sabbath year required the forgiveness of all indebtedness between Hebrews. The cancellation of debt amounted to a re-distribution of wealth. The Deuteronomic Code even includes a warning to those who might not want to lend money in the period near the Sabbatical year for fear that the loan would not be repaid (15:9–10). Generosity was encouraged among Hebrews with an assurance that God would be honored.

The Sabbatical year required the land to be fallow or uncultivated. It was a year of "rest" for all, including the land. The impact of a Sabbatical year on an agrarian economy was huge. Nevertheless, it was mandated. The mandate came with a promise that God would provide for Israel during the Sabbatical year. Even though the land was not cultivated, many things grew on their own ability during the Sabbatical year and were dedicated to the poor and anyone in need. All lands were open to all Hebrews for that which grew of it's own accord.

The third-year tithe was another special provision for the poor (Deut 14:22–29). Apparently, every Sabbatical year was subdivided into two cycles of three years each. The tithe in the third year was treated differently than the tithes of years one and two. The third-year tithe was not brought to the central sanctuary. Rather, it was deposited at the "town square" (public place near the main gate). The Levites, the poor, and anyone in need could take from the reservoir of tithes. This is an unusual provision not mentioned in Numbers 18, the text where tithing seems to be codified. From a theological perspective, the provision makes perfect sense. The tithe belonged to the Lord (Mal 3:8–9). The Lord took the Lord's portion and gave it to the poor and disadvantaged. The third-year tithe was simply God's provision for the needy.

A final provision that should be noted is that Hebrews were not allowed to charge interest (usury) on money loaned to other Hebrews (Lev 25:35–38). The principle which underlies the legislation is a concern for the poor and disadvantaged. If a Hebrew were poor enough to need a loan, then charging interest would only acerbate the problem.

Scholars have often raised questions concerning to what degree Israel practiced these Torah laws. We know more about the neglect of the laws than we do about Israel's obedience to them. The prophet Jeremiah contends that Israel's experience of the Babylonian Exile was the result of their repeated failure to observe Sabbatical year laws (2 Chr 36:21; Jer 17:19–27). There is evidence in extra-biblical literature that the Jews observed Sabbatical years after the Exile. Josephus and the book of Maccabees mention the keeping of Sabbatical years in Israel.[9]

The importance of the "land laws" for insight into God's plan for shalom for Israel is not contingent upon Israel's obedience. Regardless of whether or not Israel was faithful, the "land laws" testify to God's concern for a just distribution of resources and God's special concern for the poor and disadvantaged. It is not surprising to discover the trajectory of these concerns expressed in both heirs of the Hebrew Bible: Second Temple Judaism and Christianity. In Judaism, the trajectory led an emphasis on alms giving. Even before the New Testament era, alms giving had come to be one of the three pillars of Judaism, along with prayer and fasting. In Pharisaic Judaism, these were the most important badges of spirituality. Some self-righteous Pharisees, seeking the esteem of others, made public displays of these religious activities. Jesus condemned such self-aggrandizement in Matthew 6. The trajectory of concern for distributive justice and care for the poor is evident in a number of New Testament texts.

Jesus and the Church: Agents of Shalom

The New Testament picks up the vision of shalom as God's goal for creation from the Old Testament. The Torah concept of Jubilee looked forward to restoration for both creation and humanity. The prophetic tradition built on Torah with an expectation of a messianic age in which the "anointed" king would reign in righteousness. The ideal of the pro-

9. David P. Seemuth, "Mission in the Early Church," in W. J. Larkin, Jr., and J. F. Williams, eds., *Mission in the New Testament: An Evangelical Approach* (Maryknoll, NY: Orbis, 2005) 50–60.

phetic tradition is expressed in Isaiah 35 and 61. Both texts anticipate a transformation of the earth and its inhabitants. It is the Isaiah 61 text that Jesus chooses to announce his mission:

> The Spirit of the Lord is upon me, because He anointed me to preach the gospel to the poor. He has sent me to proclaim release to the captives, and recovery of sight to the blind, to set free those who are oppressed to proclaim the favorable year of the Lord (Luke 4:18–19).

Jesus, anointed with the Spirit of God, will "proclaim the favorable year of the Lord" (Jubilee).

Jesus' mission was proclaiming and demonstrating the "good news": help for the poor, release to the captives, recovery of sight to the blind, and freedom to the downtrodden. The mission was about restoration and transformation toward the goal of shalom. The gospel witnesses declare how this was accomplished. Every writer has his own contextualization of the story but the essential mission is consistent in all the gospel accounts. The gospel accounts given by Matthew (28:19–20) and Luke (24:47) conclude with a transfer of Jesus' mission to his disciples. The disciples are instructed to proclaim the good news of God's redemptive work to the nations.

Luke provides a smooth transition from the mission of Jesus to the mission of the early church. The sequel to his gospel—The Acts of the Apostles—begins with the post-resurrection ministry of Jesus. In a pre-ascension event, Jesus instructs the disciples to remain in Jerusalem until they are empowered by the Holy Spirit (Acts 1:8) to carry out their mission to be "witnesses" of the risen Lord Jesus. Jesus' instruction was given in the context of the disciples' confusion over the mission. The messianic and apocalyptic expectations of first century Judaism surely raised questions for the disciples. Even at the point of Jesus' ascension to heaven, the disciples were still trying to comprehend the meaning and implications of Jesus' ministry for their lives.

The promise of the Spirit came on the Day of Pentecost (Acts 2) and transformed the ministry of the apostles. Nevertheless, questions persisted about mission: its scope, its content, and its duration, as David Bosch reveals.[10] The book of Acts and the epistles testify to the pro-

---

10. David J. Bosch. *Transforming Mission: Paradigm Shifts in Theology of Mission* (Maryknoll, NY: Orbis, 1991) 41–46.

gressive unfolding of the church's comprehension of its mission. The apostles endeavored to follow the leading of the Spirit in contextualizing the gospel into new cultural settings in the Greco-Roman world.

Despite the evidence of the early church's struggle to define its own mission in faithfulness to the mission of Jesus, there is clear evidence of continuity. Most obvious is the continued work of evangelism and discipleship. The early church invested great energy and resources in proclaiming the message of Jesus as the prophesied Messiah and the means of salvation for all humankind. The church discipled those who embraced Jesus as savior. Key components of that discipleship included benevolence and social justice.

Benevolence and concern for the poor is an aspect of mission that stands out in Acts and the Epistles. The attempt to have all things in common in the Jerusalem church (Acts 4:32–37) was a policy aimed at helping the poor. The issue over the distribution of food to widows indicates that the early church operated a benevolence program for the needy (Acts 6). The church at Corinth pledged an offering for the church in Jerusalem (2 Cor 8:8–15) in order to provide assistance to the needy. James lists ministering to the needs of widows and orphans as "pure and undefiled religion" (1:27). The apostle John goes so far as to question whether believers even have the love of God in them if they see the needy in distress and refuse to share their resources with the needy (1 John 3:17). These New Testament texts are only a sampling that illustrates the New Testament evidence of God's concern for the poor and disadvantaged.

A concern for justice in the early church is intertwined with benevolence. This is not surprising in view of the ideals of the Old Testament (Mic 6:8, Amos 4, Ps 72:1–4, Isa 58:6). A classical text on justice is Acts 6. Benevolence was already at work in the church in the distribution of goods to widows. The issue of justice presented itself in the conflict between Hebrew widows and Hellenist widows over the amount of the distribution to each. It appears that the distribution of goods was biased in favor of Hebrew widows. The church, when confronted with the injustice, took steps to correct the problem (Acts 6:1–7). The brief pericope gives evidence of the church's commitment to justice. Other key texts (e.g., Jas 5:1–6) offer assurance that the concern was inherent to the nature of the Christian community.

What is clear in the book of Acts and the Epistles is that the "Great Commission" was integrated with the "Great Commandment" (Mark 12:30–31)—love God supremely and love others as yourself. The early church blended these two key aspects of Jesus' mission into a holistic ministry that shaped the community of faith into God's agent for redemption in a fallen world. The early church continued to struggle with the timing of God's consummation of human history in the Second Coming of Jesus (1 Thessalonians, 1 & 2 Peter, Revelation). Nevertheless, the church stayed focused on its mission of evangelism, discipleship, benevolence and justice.

Conclusion

The Bible is clear and uniform in its witness to God as Creator of the heavens and the earth and all that exists. The early chapters of Genesis reveal that God created the world to be an environment which would support well-being (shalom) for all living things. The commission to humankind in Gen 1:26–28 indicates that they are charged with a responsibility to maintain well-being in the world. Humankind, made in the image of God, is to be God's partner in the work of maintaining shalom. The Fall of humankind into sin did not negate the responsibility for shalom; rather, it perverted the focus from all things to self. The self-centered struggle for shalom at the expense of others has characterized human history since the Fall. The people of God are called to transcend the selfishness of sin and to obey God and love others. The transformation from the selfishness of sin to the care for others is the work of the Spirit. The transforming work of the Spirit enables people to return to the role of God's partner in the maintenance of well-being in the world. The task is to recover shalom for all things. The task is part and parcel of God's redemptive plan for creation. It is a work that will reach its ultimate fulfillment at the consummation of history with the Second Coming of Jesus Christ (Rom 8:20–25; Col 1:19–20). In the meantime, it is a task that is achieved in partial and fragmented ways as the people of God strive to be faithful to the mission of God. Faithfulness to the mission includes care for creation as a means of sustaining well-being for others.

3

Revelation and the (New) Creation

A Prolegomenon on the Apocalypse, Science, and Creation

Robby Waddell

An Interdisciplinary Approach to the New Creation

As a child in a Pentecostal church, I heard a lot about heaven, often coupled with its antithesis (hell). Somehow I needed to get to heaven, and thus avoid hell. As far as I knew there was only two ways to get to heaven, either I had to die or be raptured. Option one was not very appealing. I wanted to go to heaven, but I wasn't ready to die to get there. Option two was nebulous and raised a number of questions. Where exactly are we going, and what are we going to do when we get there? An eternal church service promised almost certain, albeit unspoken, boredom. Be that as it may, never-ending ennui seemed far better than the alternative. I suspect that my testimony is not uncommon.

In the final chapters of Revelation, John recounts his vision of a new heaven and a new earth, the first heaven and the first earth have passed away (21:1) and all things are being made new (21:5). Notice that it does not say that God is making *all new things* but making *all things new*. This distinction is of the utmost importance, as I hope to demonstrate in this essay, and has implications not only for a proper understanding of the new creation but for a robust theology of creation which also has significant ramifications for the present life and work of the church.

The description of the new creation focuses on the New Jerusalem, the holy city. Complete with a reference to the pearly gates, this depiction of the golden city has inspired countless paintings, hymns, and even dreams about going to heaven. When North American Pentecostals (or other Christians for that matter) talk about heaven, the conversation often begins with either a longing to see a loved one who has died, hope for a physical healing that seems overdue, or simply a desire to see Jesus. In my opinion, these conversations are perfectly valid and are far better than the materialistically motivated discussions about the streets of gold, or, still worse, individual mansions.[1] Notwithstanding the legitimate hopes for the future, a significant misconception is latent within this greater discussion. Heaven is conceived for the most part as a spiritual (and/or geographical) location in the great beyond, the place where Christians go when they die.

Contrary to the popular evangelical opinion, the New Testament does not support such an idea.[2] In the Gospels, the kingdom of heaven

1. I do not mean to suggest that every Christian who has longed to see streets of gold or enjoy a heavenly mansion is materialistic. I realize that people who have lived economically deprived lives possess a more noble hope of freedom from the oppression of poverty. Nevertheless, large segments of the church are not immune from the consumerism that plagues American culture. In any case, hope for a personal mansion is rooted in a misreading of John's Gospel, "In my father's house there are many rooms [*monaí*]" (14:2).

2. Various texts, when isolated from their contexts, can be cited to support the belief in heaven as a place of eternal bliss or a temporary resting area for Christians who have died and are awaiting the resurrection, e.g., 2 Cor 5:1–10, Col 3:3–4, and Phil 1:19–26. However, an extended study of Paul's teaching on the matter reveals that he has very little to say about the intermediate state, preferring to focus on the resurrection and life thereafter. According to N. T. Wright, a study of the entire Pauline corpus uncovers a consistent emphasis not on life-after-death but rather "life *after* life-after-death." Space does not permit an analysis of Pauline texts, or the Lucan texts such as Jesus' reference to paradise while on the cross (Luke 23:43) and the ever ambiguous "Abraham's Bosom" in the Lucan parable (16:19–31). See N. T. Wright, *The Resurrection of the Son of God* (Minneapolis, MN: Fortress, 2003) 209–398.

(and its verbal equivalent, "kingdom of God") is present on earth, *in-augurated* by the ministry of Jesus.[3] Although the kingdom is presently hidden, it will be fully consummated in the future. Revelation supports this teaching. The final vision of Revelation does not contain an image of humanity being resurrected and going off to the wild blue yonder, but rather of the kingdom of heaven coming down to earth (i.e., the descent of the New Jerusalem). In the new creation, heaven comes to earth and the two become one. The throne of God which was once hidden in the heavenly realm (Revelation 4–5) is now on earth (21:3, 5) thus providing a final consummation of the Lord's Prayer, "Thy kingdom come . . . on earth as it is in heaven."

This scriptural misinterpretation has contributed to a fixation on an anthropocentric eschatology, seeing the future predominantly in terms of eternal life, and thereby not fully appreciating the social, political, and cosmic dimensions of the new creation. While everlasting life is certainly a part of Christian eschatology, an overemphasis on this single aspect potentially distorts other important theological categories. On the one hand, social ministries which address such issues as racial reconciliation, gender equality, injustice, ecological conservation, poverty and war are increasingly popular among a new generation of evangelicals.[4] On the other hand, an emphasis on social action can only be frustrated by a belief system that envisions all of creation, including

3. It should be noted that scholarly opinion is divided in regards to how the kingdom of God should be understood. The various views can be divided into three areas: (1) an apocalyptic kingdom, which expects an abrupt end to the status quo brought about by a radical divine intervention; (2) a realized eschatology, which sees the kingdom being fully present especially in the words and deeds of Jesus; and (3) an inaugurated eschatology, which understands the kingdom to be both already present and not yet fully consummated. The final category, held by most biblical scholars and theologians, is the one that is being assumed here. For the socio-political aspect of the kingdom of God and its significance for Christian eschatology see N. T. Wright, *Jesus and the Victory of God* (Minneapolis, MN: Fortress, 1996) 198–474; *The Challenge of Jesus: Rediscovering Who Jesus Was and Is* (Downers Grove, IL: InterVarsity, IL, 1999) 34–53; and *Evil and the Justice of God* (Downers Grove, IL: InterVarsity, 1999) 101–29. For an especially accessible representation of this idea see Brian D. McLaren, *The Secret Message of Jesus: Uncovering the Truth that Could Change Everything* (Nashville, TN: W, 2006).

4. See Robert E. Webber, *The Younger Evangelicals: Facing the Challenges of the New World* (Grand Rapids, MI: Baker, 2002). The centennial republication of Rauschenbusch's *Christianity and the Social Crisis* does not seem to be generating the same sort of backlash it received from conservative Christianity at its original publication or subsequent reprints. Walter Rauschenbusch, *Christianity and the Social Crisis in the 21st Century*, ed. Paul Rauschenbusch (New York: HarperOne, 2007).

humanity, as transient. The otherworldliness of the eschatology subverts the ecclesiological hope of a transformation in the here-and-now.[5]

A fresh interpretation of the end of John's Apocalypse should help remedy this misreading and provide exegetical support for embracing the whole creation with the love of Christ through acts of service and social transformation as we work, wait, and hope for the new creation. Two prevailing presuppositions pose a challenge to this project, both of which have roots in Christian Fundamentalism.[6] The first is scientific; the second is theological. Science and Christian theology have often been at odds, especially in the more conservative wings of Christianity,[7] the debate of evolution versus creation being a prime example.[8]

5. Eschatological images are vitally important for the contemporary life and ministry of the Christian church, because, "they shape our sensibilities, orient our affections, and inspire our actions"; Amos Yong, *Theology and Down Syndrome: Reimagining Disability in Late Modernity* (Waco, TX: Baylor University Press, 2007) 290.

6. As a label, "Fundamentalism," has been associated almost universally with negative connotations, leading spokesmen of even the most conservative wings of Christianity to abandon the term. Bob Jones II, president of Bob Jones University, prefers the word "preservationist" as a characterization of "Christians with a *fierce* belief in the Bible's literal, inerrant truth" (italics mine). Jones gives the following reason for the change in nomenclature: "Instead of 'Fundamentalism' defining us as steadfast Bible believers, the term now carries overtones of radicalism and terrorism" (see "Campus Seeks to Shed Fundamentalist Label," *Los Angeles Times*, 16 March 2002). Whether it is labeled fundamentalist or preservationist, a hermeneutical theory that purports a strict biblical literalism produces a hermeneutical impasse that inhibits dialogical engagement with both science and a significant portion of Christian theology.

7. Although I highlight points of conflict in this chapter, positive aspects of the relationship between science and Christian theology could also be listed. From the time of the early church fathers through the Middle Ages, Christian thinkers spoke metaphorically of divine revelation being contained in "the Two Books," presumably scripture and nature. On the other hand, Christians have been known (especially those in the fundamentalist genus) to reject findings in science on the grounds of scriptural interpretation.

8. Note the iterative cadence of court cases and school board hearings: Scopes v. Tennessee (1925), McLean v. Arkansas (1982), Epperson v. Arkansas (1987), Edwards v. Aguillard (1987), Kitzmiller v. Dover Area School District (2005), and the Kansas Evolution Hearings (2007). A belief in creation, for many Christians, simply means that God is responsible for creation but that does not categorically rule out an evolutionary process of some kind. In other words, the creation story in Genesis is simply about *who* is responsible for creation and not about *how* it was done. Within evangelicalism there has been an increasing amount of appropriation of evolutionary theories. See Keith B. Miller, ed., *Perspectives on an Evolving Creation* (Grand Rapids, MI: Eerdmans, 2003); and Amos Yong, "God and the Evangelical Laboratory: Recent Conservative Protestant Thinking about Theology and Science," *Theology & Science* 5:2 (2007) 203–11. Cf.

To begin, I want to draw attention to a far less controversial concept. Since the time of Copernicus, basic ideas about the structure of the solar system, though once questioned by the church, have been established. The earth revolves around the sun and not vice versa. Despite common knowledge that would suggest otherwise, the pre-Copernican three tiered view of the universe continues to dominate popular theological grammar. Heaven is up; hell is down; and the earth is in the middle. Testifying to the power of metaphorical language, these spatial metaphors, in my opinion, intensify support for an ancient form of dualism that draws a stark contrast between life in this-world and life in the world-to-come.[9]

Although my knowledge of science is pedestrian,[10] I contend that even a popular understanding of contemporary physics and cosmology is helpful in opening the human imagination to the possibilities of both the origin and development of the first creation and its continuity and discontinuity with the new creation. I am aware that science is limited in the contributions it can make to an exegetical-theological reading of Scripture. The limitation, however, is self-imposed for science observes the physical world only. However, theology seeks to speak about the transcendent as well as the immanent suggesting that the two fields of study are not mutually exclusive. As a primary dialogue partner, I rely mostly on the work of John Polkinghorne, who is both a particle physicist and an Anglican priest. I echo Polkinghorne's sentiment that science cannot "claim to 'prove' Christian eschatology. Proof is an inappropriate cut-and-dried category for the discussion of any kind of metaphysical issue."[11] Nevertheless, a scientific-theological perspective

---

Roland M. Frye, ed., *Is God a Creationist? The Religious Case against Creation Science* (New York: Scribner's, 1983). The authors represent various religious backgrounds, Jewish, Protestant, and Roman Catholic (including Pope John Paul II). The argument follows the basic hypothesis of the "two books" (see footnote above).

9. This sort of dualism bears the marks of a neo-Gnosticism. Cf. Harold Bloom, *The American Religion* (New York: Simon & Schuster, 1992).

10. Science is outside my expertise. I have been involved, nonetheless, in an extended science and religion dialogue, co-directing a local society on faith and science at Southeastern University, FIRST (Further the Integration of Religion, Science and Technology) from 2004–2006, funded by Metanexus and the Templeton Foundation.

11. John Polkinghorne, *The God of Hope and the End of the World* (New Haven, CT: Yale University Press, 2002) xviii; cf. Polkinghorne, *Science and Theology: An Introduction* (Minneapolis, MN: Fortress, 1998).

is helpful in the development of a Christian eschatological hope that is intelligible in the twenty-first century.

The second prevailing presupposition has already been mentioned, namely an apocalyptic eschatology fueled by the popularity of the *Left Behind Series*. Fundamentalist Dispensationalism, which continues to hold sway over the majority of North American Pentecostals, encourages more of a passive resignation towards the present affairs of this world rather than a hopeful anticipation of a renewed and transformed creation.[12] Early Pentecostalism was able to avoid some of these pitfalls, at least temporarily, because it was not yet, in my opinion, thoroughly influenced by fundamentalist Dispensationalism.[13] In recent years

12. The critique of negative effects of apocalyptic eschatology on social ministries and ecological responsibility is by no means new. See Al Truesdale, "Last Things First: The Impact of Eschatology on Ecology," *Perspectives on Science and Christian Faith* 46:2 (June 1994) 116–22. According to Truesdale (a Nazarene) an apocalyptic eschatology "makes it religiously unnecessary and logically impossible to engage in the long-range commitments to the environment" (116). Truesdale also writes, "Until evangelicals purge from their vision of the Christian faith the wine of pessimistic dispensationalist premillennialism, the Judeo-Christian doctrine of creation and the biblical image of stewardship will be orphans in their midst" (118). See Peter Althouse, "In Appreciation of Jürgen Moltmann: A Discussion of His Transformational Eschatology," *PNEUMA: The Journal of the Society for Pentecostal Studies* 28:1 (2006) 28.

In 1967, Lynn White wrote his now famous article "The Historical Roots of Our Ecological Crisis," *Science* 155 (1967) 1203–7. White places the lion's share of the blame for the ecological crisis on Christianity and what he understands to be its anthropocentric nature. White views the utilitarian manipulation and abuse of nature as a logical outcropping of the Christian doctrine that places humanity at the zenith of creation. As a solution, White does not suggest an avoidance of religion, seeing the industrial/technological culture as being morally bankrupt; rather White proposes a revival of Franciscan Christianity, following the lead of its founder, Francis of Assisi. Partially in response to White, Francis Schaeffer articulated a Christian rationale for ecological responsibility in *The Pollution and Death of Man* (Wheaton: Crossway, 1973). In a more apologetic response, Pannenberg commented that the domination of nature by human power corresponded to the time in the eighteenth century "when modern humanity in its self-understanding was cutting its ties with the creator God of the Bible"; Wolfhart Pannenberg, *Anthropology in Theological Perspective* (Philadelphia, PA: Westminster, 1975) 78, previously cited in Douglas J. Moo, "Nature in the New Creation: New Testament Eschatology and the Environment," *Journal of the Evangelical Theological Society* 49 (2006) 449–88.

13. Although eschatology was central for the early Pentecostals, exhibited most conspicuously in the belief that the gift of tongues was a sign of the final outpouring of the Holy Spirit, some in the early Pentecostal movement were nonetheless aware of the social and political consequences of their spiritual renewal. The social transformation is evidenced both from the early literature in the movement as well as the antithetical

Pentecostal theologians have exhibited a significant shift, articulating an eschatological emphasis on the "already/not yet" understanding of the kingdom. The kingdom is already present in the world and therefore "demands our attention and action as Christians in service to the King, but the kingdom itself will break into the world only through a sovereign and free act of God."[14] This shift towards a more transformational eschatology, influenced significantly by Jürgen Moltmann,[15] provides a theological underpinning for the practical engagement of the church with the world.

In *The Coming of God*, Moltmann describes four sub-types of eschatology: personal, historical, cosmic, and divine.[16] These categories are not mutually exclusive but rather serve as organizational loci for his articulation of Christian eschatology. Illustrating each category with a corresponding metaphor, Moltmann links personal eschatology with eternal life, historical eschatology with the kingdom of God, cosmic eschatology with the new creation, and divine eschatology with the glory of God. Such a comprehensive eschatology coalesces nicely with

---

critique which the movement received from the general culture. Within the tradition, there are articles from *The Apostolic Faith* that suggest a significant level of multiracial and multiethnic involvement. An anonymous article in the third issue offers a possible explanation as to why the revival began in a barn. "If it had started in a fine church, poor colored people and Spanish people would not have got it, but praise God it started here. God Almighty says He will pour out His Spirit on all flesh" (*The Apostolic Faith* 1:3 [1906] 1). In reference to multi-nationalism, later in the same article, the author writes, "It is noticeable how free all nationalities feel. If a Mexican or German cannot speak in English, he gets up and speaks in his own tongue and feels quite at home for the Spirit interprets through the face and people say amen. No instrument that God can use is rejected on account of color or dress or lack of education. This is why God has so built up the work." In addition to the issues of race and culture, the empowerment of women also took a step in the right direction, evidenced by the significant numbers of female leaders and participants in the revival. See Estrelda Alexander, *The Women of Azusa Street* (Cleveland, PA: Pilgrim, 2005).

14. Althouse, "In Appreciation of Jürgen Moltmann," 29. See also Peter Althouse, *Spirit of the Last Days: Pentecostal Eschatology in Conversation with Jürgen Moltmann* (Edinbugh: T. & T. Clark, 2003) especially chapter 4.

15. Moltmann's contributions to the dialog between faith and science and his ubiquitous influence on Christian eschatology makes him the perfect resource for my rereading of Revelation 21–22. Be that as it may, my theological expertise outdistances my knowledge of science only slightly. For this reason, I will be following closely the Pentecostal appropriation of Moltmann produced by Peter Althouse, cited above. Misappropriations are my own.

16. Jürgen Moltmann, *The Coming of God: Christian Eschatology* (Minneapolis, MN: Fortress, 1996).

John's vision of the new creation which includes the future not only of humanity and the kingdom of God but of all creation: "Behold, I make all things new" (21:5). Although a reading of Revelation could benefit from insights from each of these categories, such a project is beyond the bounds of this essay. Therefore, I have chosen to focus on cosmic eschatology because it offers the most potential for points of connection with science. Moltmann writes, "Christian eschatology cannot be reduced to human eschatology, and human eschatology cannot be brought down to the salvation of the soul in heaven beyond. There are no human souls without human bodies, and no human existence without the life system of the earth, and no earth without the universe."[17] Scientific-theologians, like Polkinghorne, and systematic-theologians, like Moltmann, share in common a view of the future that entails both continuity and discontinuity with the present and the past. This shared theme governs much of the discussion that follows. To offer such an interdisciplinary reading is a daunting task and requires one final qualification. The analysis is not a traditional verse by verse exegesis. Instead, I focus on key verses where the three disciplines of science, theology, and biblical studies converge.

John's Vision of the New Creation

When John sees the new heaven and the new earth, he also specifies that the first heaven and the first earth had passed away (21:1). John's enigmatic phrase, "passed away," is notoriously difficult to interpret. On the surface, John's language, in agreement with a number of Jewish apocalyptic texts,[18] seems to suggest a radical end to the world as we know it, an annihilation of the cosmos, and a totally new creation.[19]

17. Jürgen Moltmann, *Science and Wisdom* (Minneapolis, MN: Fortress, 2003) 71. Richard Bauckham echoes a similar sentiment, "We recognize that, in continuity with the Old Testament (the New Testament) assumes that humans live in mutuality with the rest of God's creation, that salvation history and eschatology do not lift humans out of nature but heal precisely their distinctive relationship with the rest of nature"; Richard Bauckham, "Jesus and the Wild Animals (Mark 1:13) A Christological Image for an Ecological Age," in Joel B. Green and Max Turner, eds., *Jesus of Nazareth: Essays on the Historical Jesus and the New Testament Christology* (Grand Rapids, MI: Eerdmans, 1994) 4.

18. E.g., *1 En.* 72:1; 91:16; *2 Bar* 44:12; *Sib. Or.* 3:75–90; and Pseudo-Philo, *Liber Antiquitatum Biblicarum* 3:10.

19. Grant R. Osborne, *Revelation* (Grand Rapids, MI: Baker, 2002) 730. Margaret Barker, *Revelation of Jesus Christ* (Edinburgh: T & T Clark, 2000) 367, speaks of the

The origins of this idea can be found in the Hebrew prophets. Isaiah writes, "The heavens will vanish like smoke, the earth will wear out like a garment" (51:6).[20] It is not uncommon to see the theme of total destruction linked with the image of the final judgment. Revelation 20:11 is a prime example, "the earth and the sky fled away from the presence of him who sat on the great white throne and no place was found for them."[21] Perhaps the most vivid depiction of such an event appears in 2 Pet 3:10–12, "the day of the Lord will come like a thief, and then the heavens will pass away with a loud noise, and the elements will be dissolved with fire, and the earth and the works that are upon it will be burned up . . . the heavens will be kindled and dissolved, and the elements will melt with fire."

Allusions to this sort of catastrophic imagery have inspired apocalyptic imaginations for millennia. Regrettably the prospect of an impending annihilation of human life has become an increasingly possible reality as the scientific prowess of humanity, both industrially and technologically, has reached unprecedented proportions. Human life faces a real threat of destruction from nuclear weapons, global warming, and perhaps a new disease that is resistant to all forms of treatment. A more sober assessment suggests that while these threats may significantly reduce human life, they will probably not end it all together. Additionally, these threats to the future of humanity, while possible, are by no means certain.

On the other hand, there are cosmic threats to all life, not just humanity, which are certain. I am not referring to the possibility of an earth-killing asteroid or the explosion of a super nova, but rather to the cosmic future of the universe. The universe is presently expanding as a consequence of the big bang; however, a worthy competitor to this expansion, gravity, is attempting to draw all things together. Neither one

---

new heaven and new earth as "beyond time and matter." See Tertullian's comment, "The belief that everything was made from nothing will be impressed upon us [also] by the ultimate dispensation of God that will bring back all things to nothing. For 'the very heaven shall be rolled together as a scroll'; no, it shall come to nothing along with the earth itself, with which it was made in the beginning"; Tertullian, "Against Hermogenes," in Alexander Roberts and James Donaldson, eds., *Ante Nicene Fathers* (Buffalo, NY: Christian Literature, 1885–1896) 3:496–97.

20. See also Isa 34:4; Joel 2:10. Cf. Ps 102:26.

21. Similar images can be found in Rev 16:20, "every island fled away, and no mountains were to be found."

of these forces is strong enough to bring the universe to its end any time soon, but the struggle cannot last forever. If expansion wins the day (the most popular opinion among cosmologists) the universe will die a slow and cold death of decay, the inevitable effects of thermodynamics. If gravity ever gets the upper hand, the universe would start a long process of constriction, ending in a cosmic implosion, the inverse of the big bang, which Polkinghorne calls "the big crunch."[22] In the words of William Stoeger, "if we are to take the truth discovered by the sciences seriously, denying the . . . accounts of eventual life-ending and earth-ending catastrophes is really not an option."[23] The scientific view of the future seems to support the cataclysmic predictions of the dooms-day prophets. The natural sciences lack the resources to respond to what seems like a meaningless universe. Theology, aided with the resources of the biblical texts, may respond to this despair "because theology bases its post mortem hope on a reality inaccessible to scientific investigation, the faithfulness of a living God."[24]

The good news is that there is more than one way to read an apocalypse.[25] The fears associated with the apparent references to the

22. Polkinghorne, *The God of Hope and the End of the World*, 9. I have been following Polkinghorne very closely. He is not advocating the theory that gravity will win out over expansion; rather he is simply highlighting the inevitability that "however fruitful the universe seems today, its end lies in futility."

23. William R. Stoeger, "Eschatology: Some Questions and Insights from Science," in John Polkinghorne and Michael Welker, eds., *The End of the World and the Ends of God* (Harrisburg, PA: Trinity, 2000) 19.

24. Polkinghorne, *The God of Hope and the End of the World*, 10.

25. Apocalyptic literature resists conformity to modern standards of lucidity and coherence, being akin more to the poetic character of myth than the principles of Aristotelian logic. John Collins writes that "apocalyptic literature provides a rather clear example of language that is expressive rather than referential, symbolic rather than factual"; John J. Collins, *The Apocalyptic Imagination: An Introduction to Jewish Apocalyptic Literature* (Grand Rapids, MI: Eerdmans, 1998) 17. This seems especially to be the case with the closing chapters of Revelation, where even the symbolic language reaches its limits. The images, symbols, and modes of thinking which are used to describe the new creation are part of the original creation. "Strictly speaking," according to Richard Bauckham and Trevor Hart, "language belonging to the here-and-now is not fitted to speak of anything more than the here-and-now"; Richard Bauckham and Trevor Hart, *Hope Against Hope: Christian Eschatology and the Turn of the Millennium* (Grand Rapids, MI: Eerdmans, 1999) 81. Bauckham and Hart reject the idea that an appeal to revelation is helpful on this point because revelation, in order to transform, must be relatable to humans in some meaningful manner. Even so, Christian eschatology must utilize the human imagination, the ability to "transcend the limits of the given in one way or another" (85).

annihilation of the cosmos may be tempered by other texts that speak about the transformation of the world.[26] In other words, annihilation is not the only legitimate interpretation of the phrase, "passed away." A closer look at the story of the new creation at the end of Isaiah (65:17–35) is a good place to begin, given that it serves as a primary source for most, if not all, of the accounts of the new creation in Jewish apocalyptic literature, not to mention Revelation. The Hebrew verb for "create," *bârâ'*, is used three times in the first two verses, emphasizing the creative activity of God; however, the description of this new creation is so continuous with the former life of Israel that to believe in it requires hardly any eschatological imagination. Although the infant mortality rate will be zero (v. 20) and the standard life expectancy will be considerably lengthened ("those dying at a hundred years will be considered youth"; v. 20),[27] the life of the people seems strikingly similar to their former way of living. They live in Jerusalem, build houses, plant vineyards, enjoy the fruits of their labor, and provide a secure future for their children and grandchildren. The discontinuity lies not in the kind of life which they live, full of peace and hope, but the prevalence with which they live it, no longer in a partial or threatened way but to the fullest extent. The first hint that life in the new creation represents a radically different ecosystem comes in the final verse with references to the domesticated lifestyle of wolves, who will feed not on the sheep but with the sheep, and lions, who will eat straw like the oxen (v. 25). "What the prophet does in this passage, then, is to evoke a vision of

26. A number of apocalyptic texts speak about transformation, for example *1 En.* 45:5; *Jub* 1:29; *2 Bar.* 32:6; and *4 Ezra* 7:75. The earliest commentaries on the Apocalypse of John adhere to a transformational interpretation of this text. For example, Andrew of Caesarea writes, "This passage does not speak of the obliteration of creation but of its renewal into something better . . . The renewal of that which has grown old does not involve the annihilation of its substance but rather indicates the smoothing out of its agedness and its wrinkles"; Andrew of Caesarea, "Commentary on the Apocalypse," in Franz Zaver Seppelt, Joseph Pascher, and Klaus Mursdörf, eds., *Münchener Theologische Studien, Historische Abteilung* (Munich: Karl Zink, 1950) 1:232–33. See also the commentary of Oecumenius, "They do not say this as though heaven and earth and sea are destroyed and pass into nonexistence and that other things come into being in their place. Rather, they mean that the present realities have cast off their corruption and become new, putting off their filth as though it were an old and dirty garment"; Oecumenius, "Commentary on the Apocalypse," in *Traditio Exegetica Graeca* (Lovain: Peeters, 1991) 8:265–66.

27. Extraordinary long life, while remarkable, would not have been totally foreign for the Israelites given the life span of their patriarchs as recorded in Genesis.

God's future which is rooted thoroughly in Israel's familiar world, but which modifies it substantially by replacing lack with plenty, chaos with order, and conflict with peace."[28]

As always John is not captive to earlier texts but rather weaves various word pictures together into his own unique creative whole. John explicitly contradicts Isaiah by describing life in the new creation as everlasting, "death will be no more" (21:4). Bauckham and Hart draw attention to John's combination of the image of the new creation from Isaiah 65 with the image of a complete eradication of death found earlier in Isa 25:7–8, "And he will destroy on this mountain the shroud that is cast over all peoples, the sheet that is spread over all nations; he will swallow up death forever. Then the Lord God will wipe away the tears from all faces, and the disgrace of his people he will take away from all the earth." Pressing on the very limits of eschatological imagination, a new reality without death, mourning, crying, or pain practically defies belief. Bauckham and Hart ask,

> Can this strange world really be identical in any sense with the world which we know? The images in which it is depicted are scarcely inhabitable. It provides no coherent pattern in terms of which we might make sense of its various contents. The sense of dislocation is thus far more acute (than Isaiah 65). The vision draws us out of our present world in the direction of another and makes us aware in the process that it points beyond itself to something which is, strictly speaking, unimaginable.[29]

The inability to even imagine the complete composition of the new creation should not deter from the most important fact that John's vision points toward a new eschatological life that will exist beyond the threat of death. The former things that pass away are death, sorrow, and pain. The death of death, to a large extent, is what makes the new creation new, i.e., different.

The principal prototype for imaging the eschatological human life is the resurrection of Jesus Christ. The post-Easter descriptions of Jesus are the only examples available from which to construct a hypothesis

28. Baukham and Hart, *Hope Against Hope*, 97. Acknowledging the strong tenor of continuity, Bauckham and Hart insist, nevertheless, that "the prophet expects us to read the whole passage as an account of what will follow the fashioning of new heavens and a new earth. This is not, in other words, a political vision of Israel's historic future, but a genuinely eschatological hope"(98).

29. Bauckham and Hart, *Hope Against Hope*, 99–100.

about the nature of life after the resurrection. Though other humans may have died and come back to life, whether by medical resuscitation or miraculous intervention, only Jesus has died and come out on the other side of death, hence the proclamation, "I have the keys to Death and Hades" (Rev 1:18).[30] The assorted depictions of the post-resurrection accounts notwithstanding, the crucial point is that Jesus was bodily resurrected. He could eat (Luke 24:43); he could be touched (John 20:17); and apparently he could vanish (Luke 24:31). Perhaps the most significant characteristic of Jesus' resurrected body for the present discussion is that it retained the scars from his life on earth (John 20:27).[31] In the pictorial language of Revelation, the resurrected, though scared, body of Jesus is depicted as "a Lamb standing, as though it had been slain" (5:6). Given the presence of scars on Jesus' resurrected body, it is safe to say that it was not annihilated and then replaced but transformed.

According to Revelation, the eschatological transformation is not limited to the physical bodies of humans but also includes a social transformation as well, exhibited in the fact that the nations continue to exist, bringing their glory into the city of God (21:24) and receiving healing from the leaves of the tree of life (22:3). The socio-political transformation is also portrayed in terms of God coming and dwelling with humanity. John hears, for only the third time in Revelation, a voice come from the throne,[32] proclaiming, "Behold, the dwelling of God is

30. Note the second line of the third stanza of Charles Wesley's hymn, "Christ the Lord has Risen Today":

> Vain the stone, the watch, the seal,
> *Christ hath burst the gates of hell*:
> Death in vain forbids his rise,
> Christ hath opened Paradise.

31. The fact that the text does not actually say that Thomas touched the scars is irrelevant to the present discussion. It is enough that Jesus identified his scars for Thomas.

32. A number of later manuscripts read "out of heaven" as opposed to "from the throne." The former seems to be a late scribal correction to make 21:3 conform to 21:1. John hears a voice from the throne for the first time in 16:17; the voice declares, "It is done," indicating the end of the series of judgments. In a manner similar to a responsive reading, John hears a voice from the throne for a second time in 19:5–6, saying: "Praise our God, all you his servants, you who fear him, both small and great!" And a great multitude responds in unison, "Hallelujah! For the LORD our God the Almighty reigns." It is difficult to tell whether the following three hortatory subjunctives in 19:7 are spoken solely by the multitude or if the voice from the throne is also included. A third possibility is that the voice from the throne speaks alone in 19:7a, announcing

with people, and he will dwell with them, and they will be his peoples, and God himself will be with them as their God" (21:3). Coupled with the references to the nations (21:24; 22:3) the use of the plural, "peoples" (*laoí*),[33] which diverges from the standard Hebrew formula, "They will be my people, I will be their God,"[34] further supports the notion that the old social orders, not unlike the individuals that comprise them, are not annihilated but transformed.[35]

The inclusiveness of the transformation does not stop with individuals or socio-political systems but extends ultimately to the whole creation. It is very rare in Revelation for John to hear speech directly from God. In fact, there are only two clear cut examples.[36] The first occurrence comes at the end of the prologue: "'I am the Alpha and the Omega,' says the Lord God, 'who was and is and is to come, the Almighty'" (1:8).[37] The last time John hears directly from God is none

---

a litany of exhortation, "let us rejoice; and let us exult; and let us give Him the glory, for the marriage of the Lamb has come," to which the multitude responds in 19:7b–8, "And His Bride has made herself ready; it was granted her to be clothed with fine linen, bright and pure."

33. The manuscript evidence is divided, but the plural reading is the *lectio difficilior* given that the singular conforms to the Old Testament norm. The United Bible Society (UBS) third edition gave the plural reading a "D." However, the UBS fourth revised edition gives the plural reading a "B," thus proving the ubiquity of the problem of grade inflation.

34. So Lev 26:12; Ezek 11:20, 37:27; Zech 2:11, 8:8.

35. Bauckham writes, "The combination of particularism (reference to the covenant people) and universalism (reference to the nations) in the account of the New Jerusalem . . . brings together the Old Testament promises for the destiny of God's own people and the universal hope, also to be found in the Old Testament, that all the nations will become God's people"; Richard J. Bauckham, *The Climax of Prophecy: Studies on the Book of Revelation* (Edinburgh: T. & T. Clark, 1993) 312–13. Cf. Moltmann, *The Coming of God*, 315–17.

36. Twice the voice coming from the throne speaks about God in the third person, and therefore is clearly not an example of divine direct speech (19:5; 21:3). The comment in 16:17 (*gégonen*) which speaks of divine judgment may be directly from God or may be a statement from Christ. In the final statement from God (21:5–8) a similar announcement, "they are done" (*gégonan*), refers to the renewing of all things. John hears a number of other voices throughout Revelation including various angels, the martyrs, the altar (?), the four living creatures, and the seven thunders. Numerous times John hears a voice from heaven, but the speaker is often unclear (10:4, 8, 11; 11:12; 14:13; 16:1; 18:4). While exact identification of the heavenly speakers is not possible, none of these statements seem to be coming directly from God.

37. The red-letter edition mistakenly identifies this phrase as the words of Jesus.

other than the commencement of the new creation, "Behold, I make all things new" (21:5). Similar to the story in Genesis where God speaks the first creation into existence, the new creation likewise comes into existence by means of the spoken words of God. The biblical narrative forms an inclusio, opening and closing with the creative speech of God. Although clear allusions are made to the first creation (21:1) and to Eden, i.e., the tree of life (22:3), it would be, nevertheless, incorrect to simply equate the new creation with a return to a restored Eden.

A return to the beginning, *restitutio in integrum*, is problematic both theologically and scientifically. The idea that the new creation is simply paradise regained begs the question of the possibility of a second Fall, and to deny the possibility of a second Fall begs the question of the quality of human freedom in the new creation. In other words, are humans going to be less free in the new creation than they are now because they can no longer choose to sin? On the one hand, a possible answer to this philosophical conundrum is to redefine freedom not as the principle of alternative possibilities but as the freedom to act as a one wishes.[38] On the other hand, it is not necessary to jettison the principle of alternative possibilities in order to avoid a repeat of the Fall. Being perfected in love, people in the new creation will act accordingly. They will be patient and kind, not jealous or boastful, not arrogant or rude, not insisting on their own way, not irritable or resentful, rejoicing in the right (1 Corinthians 13). Humanity will experience a new transformed freedom in the new creation, a freedom that has been liberated from sin. This sort of eschatological freedom is analogous to the freedom of

38. Harry Frankfurt coined the phrase "principle of alternative possibilities" (PAP) to represent a longstanding and seeming irrefutable philosophical opinion that a free moral agent could only be held responsible for a decision if an alternative option could have been chosen. Frankfurt challenged the validity of PAP by arguing that a decision which is freely chosen based on personal desire could still be understood to be free even if an outside force predetermined the choice. Frankfurt's repudiation of PAP has been utilized by philosophers who wish to maintain a compatibilist view of determination and moral responsibility. Harry Frankfurt, "Alternate Possibilities and Moral Responsibility," *Journal of Philosophy* 66 (1969) 828–39. Contrariwise, philosophers of a libertarian sort have questioned the veracity of Frankfurt-style cases. See especially the Dilemma Defense of David Widerker, who argues that Frankfurt-style counter-examples to PAP cannot logically exist. David Widerker, "Libertarianism and Frankfurt's Attack on the Principle of Alternative Possibilities," *Philosophical Review* 104 (1983) 247–61. See also Carl Ginet, "In Defense of the Principle of Alternative Possibilities: Why I Don't Find Frankfurt's Argument Convincing," *Philosophical Perspectives* 10 (1996) 403–17.

God, a freedom unfettered from sin with limitless possibilities to express beauty and love.

If this is the case, the question could be asked, "Why did the original Fall occur? Were the original people not also perfect? And were they not living in a perfect world?" The best answer to the latter two questions seems to be "No." As opposed to seeing the Garden of Eden as a perfect world with perfect people who made a conscious decision to disobey God, Irenaeus understood the first humans to be in a young stage of innocence, not knowing the difference between good and evil. For Irenaeus, the initial stage of innocence is a necessary condition for finite creatures. In his work, *Against Heresies,* Irenaeus writes,

> Now it was necessary that man should in the first instance be created; and having been created, should receive growth; and having received growth, should be strengthened; and having been strengthened, should abound; and having abounded, should recover [from the disease of sin]; and having recovered, should be glorified; and being glorified, should see his Lord . . . . For it was necessary, at first, that nature should be exhibited; then, after that, that what was mortal should be conquered and swallowed up by immortality, and the corruptible by incorruptibility, and that man should be made after the image and likeness of God, having received the knowledge of good and evil.[39]

The process which Irenaeus identifies beginning with innocence and ending with glorification does not deny in any way the seriousness of sin nor the necessity of redemption. However, by connecting the end of the story (glorification) with the beginning of the story (innocence) Irenaeus is able to disprove his theological nemesis, Gnosticism, which would have argued instead for an annihilation of the physical world and the future of a purely spiritual world.

Irenaeus' theological project intuitively presupposes a dynamic process of development to which the creation narratives attest. According to Genesis, the world emerges "from out of primordial chaos through processes of division, distinction, and particularization, beginning with the separation of light from darkness and continuing in the separating out of species of plant and types of animals."[40] The process presupposes

39. Irenaeus, *Against Heresies* 38:4, in Alexander Roberts and James Donaldson, eds., *Ante-Nicene Fathers* (Peabody, MA: Hendrickson, 2004) 1:522.

40. Yong, *Theology and Down Syndrome*, 159–60.

the presence of time. In other words, "Creation in the beginning is simultaneously the creation of time," and "if God made creation to be the kingdom of his glory, then it was he who gave it movement and set it in motion, at the same time lending it an irreversible direction."[41] For Moltmann, creation is best understood in three parts, creation in the beginning, continual creation (which understands God not only as creator but sustainer),[42] and the consummation of creation.[43] Adding to this discussion, Pannenberg writes, "Thinking of creation as incomplete at the beginning corresponds more fully to the Christian conception of God's action in history as culminating in Jesus Christ."[44] This dynamic view of creation, rather than a doctrine of a perfect, self-sufficient equilibrium,[45] aligns far better with cosmological and evolutionary theories of development. Based on cosmological predictions about the age of the universe (billions of years old) not to mention at least some form of evolutionary theory, whether Darwinian progressivism or punctuated

41. Jürgen Moltmann, *God in Creation* (Minneapolis, MN: Fortress, 1993) 207.

42. See Ps 104:27–30: "These all look to you to give them their food at the proper time. When you give it to them, they gather it up; when you open your hand, they are satisfied with good things. When you hide your face, they are terrified; when you take away their breath, they die and return to the dust. When you send your Spirit, they are created, and you renew the face of the earth."

43. Moltmann, *God in Creation*, 206.

44. Wolfhart Pannenberg, "Theology and Science," *Princeton Seminary Bulletin* 13 (1992) 302. Other theologies of creation must grapple with the charge that the cross and resurrection are reactions taken to remedy the fact that the original plan for humanity had been thwarted by human sin. Irenaeus' theory of innocence is not vulnerable to this critique for creation has operated as planned and the cross and resurrection were part of the plan from the beginning, the means by which the creation would be transformed.

45. The alternative, though most prevalent, view is of a perfect world which was subsequently ruined by human sin. Although a number of Christian apologists have attempted to respond to the issue of theodicy based on a belief that the Fall was the origin of all human suffering, contemporary cosmology and biology would insist that death has always been a part of life. Furthermore, the notion that human sin is the cause of natural disasters such as earthquakes, volcanoes, and tsunamis seems most unlikely. To the contrary, the true effect of the Fall is a spiritual death, a withdraw from God into the self (Romans 5). The universality of sin is not an inherited part of physicality (contra Augustine). "The truth of original sin means that all human beings find themselves caught up through socialization in such a cycle of violence and injustice and each one of us perpetuates this reality to ourselves, one another, and our descendants even as we suffer from its effects"; Yong, *Theology and Down Syndrome*, 165.

equilibriums (*á la* Stephen Gould), the time era of primordial humanity represents many things but paradise is not one of them.

The dynamic quality of the creation suggests a corollary for the new creation. If the creation was originally not static but dynamic so that finite beings could exists and develop, then the new creation must also have this dynamic quality given that finitude is constitutive to being human. In other words, the infinity of God and the finitude of humanity requires that in the new creation, human beings will be in a continual state of growth and development, "being changed into his likeness from one degree of glory to another" (2 Cor 3:18). As Amos Yong observes, the theory of continual growth in the afterlife was developed thoroughly by Gregory of Nyssa. Yong writes,

> Gregory's doctrine of *epectasis* (the soul's perpetual journey) is framed within a metaphysics of divine infinity that includes within it the Platonic theory of the soul's ascent to God. From a theological perspective, Gregory adds that the divine infinity includes the divine perfections that transform human creatures so that they are able to participate in the divine life (deification, or *theosis*) . . . . Building on the Pauline claim "I do not consider that I have made it my own; but this one thing I do: forgetting what lies behind and straining forward to what lies ahead" (Phil 3:13), Gregory suggests it is the desire of the heart transformed by God that drives us deeper and deeper (or further and further) into the apophatic reality of God.[46]

Irenaeus' theory of innocence, on the one hand, and Gregory's theory of *epectasis,* on the other, suggests that a dynamic ongoing relationality is an essential characteristic of both the first creation and the new creation. From beginning to end, human beings are creatures in relationship. The dynamic relationship of the Trinity (*perichosis*) serves as the template on which all creation has been modeled. However, this relationality is not limited to humanity but extends to all of creation. Contrary to a Newtonian view of closed-system universe, contemporary science advocates a more open, holistic, and relational model, exhibited in Einstein's theory of general relativity where time, space, and matter are all tied together into an integrated whole. Likewise, "Quantum theory has shown that once two subatomic entities have interacted with each other, they remain mutually entangled . . . It appears that even the sub-

46. Yong, *Theology and Down Syndrome*, 275.

atomic world cannot properly be treated atomistically."[47] Polkinghorne includes chaos theory as an additional example of a theory in science that supports the concept of relationality. "Chaos theory has revealed the widespread existence of systems exquisitely sensitive to the finest details of their circumstances, and this implies that entities of this kind can never be treated in isolation from the effects of their environment."[48] The relational quality found in the Trinity, in humanity, and in the rest of creation lends further support to the conclusion that the new creation is a transformation of the first creation.

The vision of a transformed creation found in Revelation and supported on both theological and scientific grounds resonates with Paul's eschatological hope in Romans. Linking the new creation not only with human destiny but also with a cosmic destiny, Paul writes,

> For creation waits with eager longing for the revealing of the children of God; for the creation was subjected to futility, not of its own will but by the will of the one who subjected it, in hope that the creation itself will be set free from its bondage to decay and will obtain the freedom of the glory of the children of God. We know that the whole creation has been groaning in travail until now; and not only creation, but we ourselves, who have the first fruits of the Spirit, grown inwardly while we wait for adoption, the redemption of our bodies (Rom 8:19–23, NRSV).

In the End—The Beginning[49]

Although I have emphasized the transformational aspects of the new creation, I would be remiss to casually overlook the metaphors of annihilation in Revelation. The new creation cannot be all it is promised to be if a significant portion of the first creation is not purged, e.g., death and sin. As Moltmann writes, "What will be annihilated is Nothingness, what will be slain is death, what will be dissolved is the

---

47. Polkinghorne, *The God of Hope and the End of the World*, 16.

48. Polkinghorne, *The God of Hope and the End of the World*, 16–17.

49. Jürgen Moltmann adapted this phrase from T. S. Eliot's poem, *East Coker*, which concludes with the words, "in my end is my beginning." Moltmann used the adapted version as a title for a wonderfully accessible book, which might best be described as "Moltmann for Beginners"; see Moltmann, *In the End—The Beginning: The Life of Hope* (Minneapolis, MN: Fortress, 2004) ix.

power of evil, what will be separated from all created beings is separation from God, sin."[50]

To summarize, the rationale in Revelation for a transformational eschatology goes as follows: (1) Jesus, who is "the first born of the dead" (1:5), is the one and only example of a person who has been resurrected and all indications are that his body was transformed; (2) the ultimate future for humanity is not life after death but life after the resurrection,[51] an everlasting life which is available because death has been defeated, cast into the lake of fire (20:14); (3) the socio-cultural systems appear to be a part of the new creation evinced by the presence of the nations and the kings of the earth having access to the New Jerusalem (21:24);[52] and (4) the earth is renewed (21:5), *renovatio omium*, a renewal of all things.[53]

Biological life does not end in an eschatological equivalent of primordial ooze with all humanity assimilating into a singular consciousness; rather each person remains an integrated whole with all the individual diversity of race, sex, culture, and nationality. Paul's declaration that "there is neither Jew nor Greek, slave nor free, male nor female, for you are all one in Christ Jesus" (Gal 3:28) is not an endorsement of a raceless, sexless, and classless homogeneity, but a statement on equality, acceptance, and love.

According to Moltmann, "We do not die into the eternal Nothingness or infinite silence; we die into the eternally bounteous God and the wide space of his creative love."[54] In this creative love, sins are not erased but forgiven, sorrows are not forgotten but redeemed, life is not restarted but renewed, and creation is not destroyed but transformed. It is to this transformational creation, full of hope, that the eschatological Spirit in tandem with the Bride of the Lamb say, "Come . . . come . . . come" (22:17).

---

50. Moltmann, *In the End—The Beginning*, 145.

51. Life after the resurrection is another way of referring to life *after* life-after-death, or life after the death of death.

52. Cf. Rev 15:4: "All nations will come and worship you, for your judgments have been revealed."

53. Moltmann, *The Coming of God*, 265. See also John Polkinghorne, *The Faith of a Physicist* (Princeton, NJ: Princeton University Press, 1994) 167.

54. Moltmann, *In the End—The Beginning*, 139.

The Spirit-inspired church at the end of Revelation ought to serve as the model for the Spirit-inspired church of the Pentecostal movement, inviting "everyone who hears, everyone who is thirsty, and everyone who wishes to take the water of life" to come. The invitation is extended to all to come and participate in the newly transformed creation. As a scholar in the Pentecostal tradition, my hope is that the future generations of Pentecostal believers will be able to shake loose from the shackles of the Fundamentalist Dispensationalism which dominated the inchoate theological grammar of my childhood and embrace a transformational eschatology, thoroughly informed by the scientific academic disciplines.

PART TWO

Historical Elaborations

4

Cautious Co-belligerence?

The Late Nineteenth-Century American Divine Healing Movement and the Promise of Medical Science

Bernie A. Van De Walle

Introduction

The late nineteenth century was a time of monumental change. It witnessed a cyclone of transformation and progress rivaling, at least, that of any preceding era. Not surprisingly, it was a time of key advances in medical science. This era was home to Pasteur, Röntgen, Lister, and a number of lesser known, but still significant, medical pioneers. These inventors and their discoveries radically reshaped and significantly advanced the practice of medicine. New advances seemed to be dawning with every new day. At the end of the nineteenth century, the promise of medical science seemed unlimited.

At the same time, the late nineteenth century also saw religious change. There was the emergence of the Divine Healing movement, a loosely associated group of religious teachers and practitioners who sought to promote and practice the healing power of the indwelling and resurrected Christ over that of natural means. This movement gained tens of thousands of adherents in a significantly short span of time. Key figures in this group included people from a wide-variety of denominations, men and women, ministers and physicians. Furthermore, this movement played an essential role in the birth of Pentecostalism,[1] the greatest religious movement of the twentieth century.

Therefore, there rose simultaneously on the American landscape at least two significant approaches to health and healing in the late nineteenth century, each with its own biased and ardent champions and devotees. Yet, the opinion of the late nineteenth-century Divine Healing teachers did not, as one might expect, thoroughly dispense with the value and goodness of physicians, their diagnoses, and medical treatment. While they did not completely dismiss the advances, usefulness, and propriety of medical science, they did assert that it was, at best, a deficient approach to the gravity, complexity, and depth of human disease. While they believed that physicians and their medical treatments may be gifts from God, they were convinced that medical science was fundamentally unable to bring to humanity the kind of health and life intended for them by God and found solely in the redeeming work of Jesus Christ.

This chapter will explore those common and key responses—both the affirmations and the denials—of the late nineteenth-century Divine Healing proponents to the growing popularity and use of medicine, remedies, and physicians.

Divine Healing Affirmations of Medical Science

Almost to a person, Divine Healing advocates readily granted that doctors and many of their treatments exist by the providence of God. A. B. Simpson, founder of The Christian and Missionary Alliance, noted that physicians and their medical treatments are "among God's good gifts" to humanity.[2] Charles Cullis, the renowned Boston homeopath and

1. See Donald W. Dayton, *Theological Roots of Pentecostalism* (Metuchen, NJ: Scarecrow, 1987).

2. Albert Benjamin Simpson, *Earnests of the Coming Age and Other Sermons* (New York: Christian Alliance, 1921) 98–99; Albert Benjamin Simpson, *The Old Faith and the New Gospel* (New York: Christian Alliance, 1911; repr., Harrisburg, PA: Christian, 1966) 59.

father of the Divine Healing movement in the United States noted the "valuable" role that doctors and their treatments may play and continued his own homeopathic medical practice in harmony with his ministry of Divine Healing.[3] Carrie Judd Montgomery, one of the Divine Healing movement's more celebrated authors, speakers, and founder of the "Home of Peace" in Oakland, California, granted the skill of those physicians that worked with her during her own infirmity.[4] One lesser-known figure, Kenneth McKenzie, a member of Simpson's Christian and Missionary Alliance and author of no fewer than two significant texts on the theology and practice of Divine Healing, noted that only those with an immature theology of Divine Healing and "extremists" would deny that there is good in doctors and medicine.[5] Furthermore, the fact that most Divine Healing proponents continued to refer to physicians as "Dr." shows that only by caricature could one assert that Divine Healing movement saw absolutely no good or use in consulting with physicians and implementing their prescriptions.[6]

These affirmations of physicians and medical treatment by Divine Healing proponents, however, were not blanket endorsements. Rather, as we will see, they were limited to particular and specific arenas. What is particularly interesting is the seeming unanimity of the Divine Healing proponents in regard to those particular areas that they affirmed in regard to medical science. Almost universally, the Divine Healing teachers affirmed three separate but related aspects of the goodness of physicians and medical science: 1) the recent and substantial advances in medical science, 2) the physicians' ability to diagnose the physical cause of disease, and 3) the physicians' occasional ability to alleviate symptoms of disease.

Affirmed the Recent and Substantial Advances in Medical Science

The nineteenth century, as noted earlier, was a time of significant progress in the realm of medical science—advances not always appreciated

3. Charles Cullis, *Faith Cures; Or, Answer to Prayer in the Healing of the Sick* (Boston, MA: Willard Tract Repository, n.d.) 6.

4. Carrie F. Judd, *The Prayer of Faith* (Chicago: Revell, 1880) 12.

5. Kenneth Mckenzie, *Divine Life for the Body* (New York: Christian Alliance, 1926) 1–2.

6. Judd, *Prayer of Faith*, 85.

by the religious establishment. The Divine Healing proponents were not so biased, however, as to deny that there were any real and worthy developments. Observing that the general progress in knowledge was a fulfillment of Daniel's prophecy,[7] Simpson also noted, "The progress of medical science in the past half century has been phenomenal. No fair-minded person can refuse to concede its value, notwithstanding all its limitations, counterfeits, and failures."[8] On another occasion, he called recent scientific progress "radical and astounding."[9] Cullis, in defending to the local authorities his establishment and placement of a "Cancer Home" in Boston, cited the recent progress in medical science as that which made the presence of such a home no real threat to the surrounding population.[10] These advances, though, were not without scrutiny and criticism. One of the advances, for example, that Simpson questioned was the developing medical science of eugenics that alleged that disease in all of its manifestations could, at the very least, be significantly limited by the legislated and selective breeding of humanity to do away with "the imperfect product." He described such a program as "foolishness with God."[11]

Affirmed the Physicians' Ability to Diagnose the Physical Cause of Disease

Second, the Divine Healing teachers affirmed physicians' ability to often accurately diagnose the physical cause of disease. This affirmation, though, was more often implicit than explicit. R. Kelso Carter, a noted professor, author, and composer (he wrote the hymn "Standing on the Promises of God"), while eventually pursuing an avenue of physical restoration other than medicine, at no point doubted that the diag-

---

7. Simpson, *Earnests of the Coming Age*, 5.

8. Albert Benjamin Simpson, "Divine Healing," *Living Truths* 3:4 (October 1903) 172.

9. Albert Benjamin Simpson, *Life More Abundantly* (New York: Christian Alliance, 1904) 38.

10. W. H. Daniels, ed., *Dr. Cullis and His Work: Twenty Years of Blessing in Answer to Prayer. The Hospitals, Schools, Orphanages, Churches, and Missions Raised Up and Supported by the Hand of the Lord through the Faith and Labors of Charles Cullis, M.D.* (Boston, MA: Willard Tract Repository, 1885) 224–25.

11. Simpson, *Life More Abundantly*, 38.

nosis his doctors gave him of "incurable heart disease" was accurate.[12] Montgomery never questioned that she suffered from spinal fever as her physicians had diagnosed.[13] Cullis often relied on his own medical training and expertise to identify the particular physical distress of those who came to him and trusted implicitly the diagnosis of others in the medical profession.[14] A. J. Gordon, noted author, educator, and pastor of the Clarendon Street Baptist Church in Boston, asserted that physicians are those who have the "ability to interpret . . . the laws of health to the sick" and implies that they are right to do so and may do so rightly.[15]

One example of particular interest is found in Simpson's discussion of the cause of the death of Jesus Christ. In order to make a theological point, Simpson appealed to the opinion of contemporary physicians, diagnosing across the centuries and relying on the biblical accounts, regarding the cause of Jesus' death. He noted that many physicians attributed the death of Jesus, medically, to a "rupture of the heart. He did not die from the ordinary causes incident to crucifixion, but He died from a spasm that caused His heart to burst."[16] Simpson not only leaned on the diagnosis of contemporary physicians of an event centuries previous but cited them as authoritative and accurate on an issue as theologically significant as the crucifixion.

AFFIRMED THE PHYSICIANS' OCCASIONAL ABILITY TO ALLEVIATE SYMPTOMS OF DISEASE

Third, the Divine Healing proponents affirmed the medical community's ability to occasionally alleviate, if not eliminate, symptoms of disease. In his later retraction of one aspect of his earlier Divine Healing

12. Russell Kelso Carter, *The Atonement for Sin and Sickness: Or, A Full Salvation for Soul and Body* (Boston: Willard Tract Repository, 1884; repr., New York: Garland, 1985) 19.

13. Carrie Judd Montgomery, *Under His Wings: The Story of My Life* (Oakland, CA: Office of Triumphs of Faith, 1936) 50.

14. Cullis, *Faith Cures*, 16.

15. Adoniram Judson Gordon, *The Ministry of Healing: Miracles of Cure in All Ages* (Chicago: Revell, 1882) 144.

16. Albert Benjamin Simpson, *The Lord for the Body*, rev. ed. (Camp Hill, PA: Christian, 1996) 79; Albert Benjamin Simpson, *Discovery of Divine Healing* (New York: Alliance, 1903) 117.

assertions, Carter noted that the actual practice of the key proponents of Divine Healing shows that, while their rhetoric may seem to leave no room for the use of natural means, each of them both prescribed and practiced the use of natural means.[17] Such is most evident in the life of Cullis who never relinquished his medical practice and continued to think of and identify himself as a member of the medical community with a practice, at least to a great degree, founded on the use of natural means.[18] Montgomery, speaking about the malady from which she was eventually divinely healed, did note that often her grandmother's "old-fashioned home remedies" afforded her some level of comfort and relief as did the medication provided by physicians.[19] Gordon affirmed the "recuperative forces of the natural world."[20] Even Simpson, who so strongly warned against the use of medicine, granted its "limited value" and cautious employ.[21] The Divine Healing proponents noted that, by divine providence, there was woven into the very fabric of creation some level of medical relief. The goal and practice of physicians was to identify these recuperative, "mechanical" powers of nature and apply them to those in need.[22] Some of the proponents called the employment of this recuperative power of nature which existed by the purposeful, beneficent, and creative power of God, the *vis medicatrix naturae*.[23] As it was part of the providential structure of creation, it should not be

17. In chapters 7 and 8 of his measured retraction of previous doctrinal convictions, Carter points out how leading figures in the Divine Healing Movement all "practically" used medical means personally or referred others to them. These figures include but are not limited to Cullis, Simpson, Gordon, Montgomery, and Dowie. Russell Kelso Carter, *"Faith Healing" Reviewed after Twenty Years* (Boston: The Christian Witness Company, 1897; repr., New York: Garland, 1985). Carrie Judd Montgomery acknowledges that they all had been inconsistent in their treatment of faith and medicine (*Prayer of Faith*, 80).

18. Paul G. Chappell, "The Divine Healing Movement in America" (PhD diss., Drew University, 1983) 141; Cullis, *Faith Cures*, 5–6.

19. Montgomery, *Under His Wings*, 50.

20. Gordon, *Ministry of Healing*, 144.

21. Albert Benjamin Simpson, *The Gospel of Healing*, rev. ed. (Harrisburg, PA: Christian, 1915) 70.

22. Daniels, *Dr. Cullis*, 348; Gordon, *Ministry of Healing*, 144.

23. Simpson, *Earnests of the Coming Age*, 26, 98; A. J. Gordon uses a slightly different name, the *"vis medicatrix"* (Gordon, *Ministry of Healing*, 186).

rejected, as far as it went, and may have been the best help that some could obtain.[24]

It should be noted that one of the internal debates between the Divine Healing proponents concerned whether or not one could legitimately ask God to give his blessing to the use of means. Implicitly, the very discussion shows that, to varying degrees, each side admitted that natural means may bring about some measured effects, at least. If there were no effects, the question of blessing is, at the very least, much less pressing.

Denials and Critiques of Medical Science

Certainly, however, the endorsement of physicians and medical treatment by those involved in the Divine Healing movement was cautious and limited. While they affirmed the recent real progress made by medical science and affirmed its ability to diagnose and alleviate the physical cause of disease, they also made some stark denials that set them clearly at odds with the medical community. While some of the promoters of Divine Healing had critiques that were peculiar to themselves, there were five critiques they all held in common and that were, for each of them, the central critiques of medical science.

DENIED THERE IS EITHER SCRIPTURAL PRECEDENT OR PRESCRIPTION TO CONSULT PHYSICIANS OR TO USE MEDICINE

First, the Divine Healing promoters denied that there is either scriptural precedent or divine prescription to utilize medicine, remedies, or to consult physicians. Simpson asserted that nowhere in Scripture did God prescribe medicines or remedies for his people.[25] When medical means are mentioned in Scripture, he noted, "such 'means' are referred to in terms not at all complimentary."[26] There is no mention of God's institution or blessing of the medical profession. When the people of God are sick, Montgomery noted, they are not to turn to the created

24. Simpson, *Gospel of Healing*, 41, 70, 114, 183.
25. Simpson, *Gospel of Healing*, 67.
26. Simpson, *Gospel of Healing*, 68.

order for relief. Instead, they are to seek God alone.[27] The only prescription found in Scripture for the sick is to turn to God in faith to be their healer,[28] to be *Jehovah Rophi*. In the New Testament, in particular, the only means the sick are to follow is found in James 5, to call upon the elders of the Church, whose credentials do not lie in their ability to manage the *vis medicatrix naturae* but in their being full of the Holy Spirit able to exercise the prayer of faith.[29] Given the absence of any other divinely prescribed means of dealing with sickness, Simpson asserted that to turn to medicine, remedies, and doctors is not only unwise, it is, simply, both dangerous and impertinent.[30]

DENIED CESSATIONIST THEOLOGY

Second, they all denied the doctrine of *cessationism* that affirmed that, upon the establishment of the Church, the age of miracles came to an end.[31] Simpson asserted that the lack of the historic manifestation of Divine Healing, which he did not deny, was based on the promotion of a theology of cessation and the consequential lack of belief in its possibility, rather than on a change in the character or ministry of God in Christ.[32] Montgomery asserted that unbelief in the continuation of the miraculous was the reason that most people, both Christian and non-Christian, did not bother to pursue Divine Healing.[33] Gordon argued that, with the establishment and rule of a cessationist theology, average Christians who might otherwise assume the ongoing exercise of the supernatural were bullied into submission and unbelief.[34] They all noted

27. Judd, *Prayer of Faith*, 82.

28. Simpson, *Gospel of Healing*, 45; Albert Benjamin Simpson, *Genesis and Exodus*, Christ in the Bible 1 (New York: Word, Work, and World, 1888) 205.

29. Carrie Judd, "The Lord Our Healer," *Triumphs of Faith* 5:12 (December 1885) 272.

30. Simpson, *Gospel of Healing*, 44, 70.

31. Gordon noted that the opinion of the Divine Healing figures is at odds with the greatest majority of Christians on this issue. Gordon, *Ministry of Healing*, 3; Carter, *Atonement for Sin and Sickness*, 23.

32. Simpson, *Gospel of Healing*, 10–11; Albert Benjamin Simpson, *Messages of Love; Or, Christ in the Epistles of John* (Nyack, NY: Christian Alliance, 1892) 76; Simpson noted that unbelief resulted in a lack of healing in Jesus' day and it continues in the same way (*Gospel of Healing*, 19).

33. Judd, *Prayer of Faith*, 26.

34. Gordon, *Ministry of Healing*, 3.

that cessationism could not be sustained by Scripture.[35] Gordon wrote, "[Jesus] made no provision for the arrest of the stream of divine manifestations which he had started, either in the next age or in a subsequent age."[36] To those who would want to limit the miraculous gifts to the founding era of the Church, he wrote, "[A]ntiquity has no monopoly of God's gifts, and ancient men as such had no entrée into God's treasure-house which is denied to us."[37] He also showed how cessationism in regard to Divine Healing could not be sustained by a thorough study of Church history.[38] For these teachers, the ministry of God in Christ did not change from one era to another.[39] In one of his more famous hymns, Simpson reminded people that the Jesus who walked the Earth and healed was the same Christ "Yesterday, Today, Forever," and his ministry did not significantly change either.[40]

The Divine Healing practitioners credited the new instances of Divine Healing that were being manifest in their day to the renewed faith of some not only in the power of Christ but in the subsistence of the miraculous. That is, a more scriptural theology, or as Gordon called it, "primitive faith," was reemerging in the church and, consequently, so was a more scriptural practice and manifestation.[41] This resurrection of a more scriptural theology, though, was not understood to be merely

35. Judd, *Prayer of Faith*, 26.

36. Gordon, *Ministry of Healing*, 54.

37. Gordon, *Ministry of Healing*, 37.

38. Gordon, *Ministry of Healing*, 1–15 and 58–86. Gordon also appealed to the Church Fathers who identified the ongoing role of the miraculous in their own day, a time past that when a cessationist theology would say that miracles had ended (*Ministry of Healing*, 59–62).

39. Carrie Judd, "The Name of Jesus," *Triumphs of Faith* 4:5 (March 1881) 34.

40. Particularly verse three:

> Oft on earth He healed the sufferer
>   By His might hand;
> Still our sicknesses and sorrows
>   Go at His command.
> He who gave His healing virtue
>   To a woman's touch
> To the faith that claims His fullness
>   Still will give as much.

Albert Benjamin Simpson, "Yesterday, Today, Forever," *Hymns of the Christian Life*, rev. and enlarged ed. (Harrisburg, PA: Christian, 1978) 119.

41. Gordon, *Ministry of Healing*, 64.

coincidental. It was, rather, part of the restoration of biblical Christianity that they believed would precede the return of Jesus Christ.

> With a reviving faith, with a deepening spiritual life, with a more marked and Scriptural recognition of the Holy Spirit and the Living Christ, and with the nearer approach of the returning Master Himself, this blessed gospel of physical redemption is beginning to be restored to its ancient place, and the Church is slowly learning to reclaim what she never should have lost.[42]

DENIED THE LEGITIMACY OF MEDICAL SCIENCE'S EXCLUSIVE NATURALISM/MATERIALISM

Third, they denied the legitimacy of the late nineteenth-century medical community's predominant and excessive, if not exclusive, "materialism."[43] Such a perspective believes that people are nothing more than bio-mechanical/physical beings and, therefore, cure is a strictly secular and physical affair. Consequently, the training of physicians occurred in a purely naturalistic way, biasing, if not blinding, them from the spiritual aspect of human being and certainly dismissing any chance of a psycho-somatic unity. If humanity is a purely physical being, then disease is understood as being purely physical as well. The supernatural, in general, and the spiritual aspect of humanity, in particular, is not only largely ignored in such a perspective, it is practically denied. The Divine Healing advocates noted that the very ideas of the miraculous, spiritual, and supernatural were illegitimate to the medical community and that "any *anti-miraculous*" theory was automatically favored.[44] Simpson noted that manifestations of Divine Healing had not subsided (certainly not to the same degree) in those countries, cultures, or eras that were less "modern" in their worldview and that expected the involvement of

42. Simpson, *Gospel of Healing*, 10–11; Albert Benjamin Simpson, *Leviticus to Deuteronomy*, Christ in the Bible 2 (New York: Word, Work, and World, 1889) 119.

43. Albert Benjamin Simpson, *The King's Business* (New York: Word, Work, and World, 1886) 71; Albert Benjamin Simpson, *The Present Truth* (South Nyack, NY: Christian Alliance, 1897) 106; Kenneth Mckenzie, *Our Physical Heritage in Christ* (New York: Revell, 1923) 17, 53.

44. Carter, *Atonement for Sin and Sickness*, 23; Gordon, *Ministry of Healing*, 4; Charles Cullis, M.D., introduction to *Dorothea Trudel; Or, The Prayer of Faith, Showing the Remarkable Manner in Which Large Numbers of Sick Persons Were Healed in Answer to Special Prayers*, 3rd and enlarged ed. (Boston: Willard Tract Repository, 1872) 18.

the supernatural in the whole of one's being. He wrote, "It is not surprising, therefore, that [Divine Healing] comes natural [*sic*] to our simple-hearted converts in heathen lands, who know no better than to trust the Lord for both body and soul."[45]

DENIED MEDICAL SCIENCE'S ABILITY TO DIAGNOSE THE ULTIMATE CAUSE OF DISEASE

The Divine Healing proponents, consequently, denied medical science's ability to diagnose the central root and cause of all disease. For them, no physical aspects of disease are foundational but are, instead, always consequential and symptomatic. At the most foundational level, the cause of all sickness and disease is sin. Medical science's excessive, if not exclusive, naturalism and its understanding of sickness and disease solely as a chain of physical causes and effects prejudiced it from considering this option. This is medical science's fatal flaw. For the Divine Healing proponents, sin is the ultimate cause of all human suffering, including human disease.[46] Sin, as a force in the cosmos, has led to the disruption of the good created order and has resulted in the move to chaos and the disintegration of the created order of which human disease is but one manifestation. Therefore, medical science and its exclusive naturalism, at best, can only identify the symptoms of disease and can never get to the heart of the human predicament. "The doctor's eyes are often more at fault than his hand," wrote A. J. Gordon; he continued, "He cannot cure because he cannot comprehend the cause of our plague."[47] Kenneth Mckenzie granted that medical science may make accurate diagnoses, to a degree. It fell short, however, since the heart of the human predicament is supernatural. Science may see the "fruitage" of human sickness, but "the roots of sickness . . . are spiritual."[48] Given medical science's naturalistic presuppositions, the Divine Healing promoters asserted that it cannot diagnose the cause of human disease at its most fundamental level. It is not that the human dilemma is "contranatural" but that it is supernatural.[49] Therefore, if medical science hoped to accurately

45. Simpson, *Discovery of Divine Healing*, 11.

46. Simpson, *Gospel of Healing*, 30; Judd, *Prayer of Faith*, 66.

47. Gordon, *Ministry of Healing*, 191.

48. Mckenzie, *Divine Life for the Body*, 103.

49. Gordon, *Ministry of Healing*, 44.

diagnose the cause of disease, it must lay aside its exclusive natural-istism. The understanding of sin—a supernatural entity—requires the supernatural means of revelation and illumination.[50]

DENIED MEDICAL SCIENCE'S ABILITY TO TREAT THE ULTIMATE CAUSE OF DISEASE

Consequently, the Divine Healing proponents also denied medical science's ability to provide a cure suitable to the cause of humanity's ills. By nature, medical science was only interested in the physical treat-ment of humanity. Consequently, medicine could never be a "sufficient remedy"[51] to the root and breadth of human disease. As such, it was an "imperfect institution"[52] and must be content with being symptomatic, at best.[53] Alleviation is within its grasp, for a time. The finality of cure, however, is not. It may address, to a degree, pain and discomfort but it cannot address and eliminate the root of the disease.[54]

Sin is ultimately a supernatural matter and, therefore, it demands a supernatural response.[55] Like many in the medical profession, the Divine Healing proponents assumed that only "like cures like."[56] The nature of the cure must be of the same kind as the disease. The cause of disease, while manifesting itself physically, is in essence supernatural. Therefore, its cure must be supernatural, too. For the promoters of Divine Healing, only one remedy is suitable to the address both the supernatural aspect and the breadth of the diseased human condition. Only in Jesus Christ can one find relief from consequences of the onslaught of sin. "Christ is the remedy for the Fall, for sin and, therefore, for disease which is

50. Daniels, *Dr. Cullis*, 345; Simpson, *Lord for the Body*, 101.

51. Albert Benjamin Simpson, "Question Drawer," *Living Truths* 4:3 (March 1904) 179.

52. Judd, *Prayer of Faith*, 81

53. Simpson, *Gospel of Healing*, 30.

54. For this reason, Simpson cautioned against seeing medical means as cure. He wrote, "It is no use to apply your medical treatment to mere symptoms and try invigo-rating air and good nourishment so long as that cancer or ulcer is feeding on the vital organs. Get the root of evil removed, then your hygiene will be of some value"; Albert Benjamin Simpson, *Practical Christianity* (New York: Christian Alliance, 1901) 108.

55. Simpson, "Divine Healing," 172.

56. Richard Harrison Shryock, *Medicine in America: Historical Essays* (Baltimore: Johns Hopkins University Press, 1966) 171.

the result of sin."[57] Faith in the "Great Physician"[58] is not only the only appropriate response to sin, it "is *God's remedy* for disease as well as sin" (emphasis added).[59]

As important as physical healing is for the Divine Healing teachers, it is not the priority. The need for regeneration and sanctification—the spiritual blessings of Christ's work—is more fundamental. Consequently, the healing homes and retreat centers operated by some of these individuals focused their work on these essential items early in their regimen.[60] In addition, and prior to the exercising of an explicit ministry of healing, these homes sought to ensure that its guests had experienced the regenerative work of Christ and had, subsequently, experienced the sanctifying work of Christ, as well.[61] This would often occur through a routine of spiritual therapy that had as its base careful Bible study, pastoral counsel, and the exercise of the "Prayer of Faith" according to James 5. Charles Cullis wrote that his own practice was "to get [those under his care] to give themselves to the Lord Jesus first, and then . . . to pray for them [for healing]."[62] As a result, while many found the healing that they sought, many more would find spiritual blessing, even if they were not ultimately physically healed. Cullis boldly reported that while not all who came to his homes were physically healed, "none died until [their] soul [was] healed."[63] This was not seen as underperformance of any measure. Rather, they reported that such was an even greater blessing than the healing that was pursued. In Cullis' homes, which were exclusively reserved for those who had been pronounced "incurable" by their own physicians, this spiritual restoration far outnumbered the cases of physical healing. Cullis reported that both host and guest considered such a success.[64] Those who were

57. Simpson, *Discovery of Divine Healing*, 18; Judd, *Prayer of Faith*, 66.

58. Gordon, *Ministry of Healing*, 191.

59. Simpson, *Lord for the Body*, 19; Judd, *Prayer of Faith*, 66

60. Simpson, *Old Faith and the New Gospel*, 60.

61. Daniels, *Dr. Cullis*, 347; Simpson, *Old Faith and the New Gospel*, 61.

62. Charles Cullis, *Tuesday Afternoon Talks* (Boston, MA: Willard Tract Repository, 1892) 24.

63. Cullis, *Faith Cures*, 30.

64. Daniels, *Dr. Cullis*, 19, 344.

fortunate enough to be physically healed also had "as great a blessing . . . come to the soul as to the body."[65]

The Notable Exception: John Alexander Dowie

Those acquainted with the late nineteenth-century Divine Healing movement will note the conspicuous absence of one leading figure. John Alexander Dowie, the founder of the International Divine Healing Association, the Christian Catholic Apostolic Church, and the settlement of Zion, Illinois, was one of the best-known, if not notorious, figures in the late nineteenth-century Divine Healing movement.[66] Dowie echoed many of the denials made by the other Divine Healing advocates. He, like the others, denied, that there was scriptural precedent or prescription to employ medical science.[67] He staunchly opposed the assertion that the age of miracles was past.[68] He believed, too, that the root of disease was ultimately spiritual[69] and that science's excessive naturalism disqualified it from being able to diagnose the ultimate cause of sickness and disease.[70]

65. Cullis, *Faith Cures*, 31. The proponents of Divine Healing also noted that there were many Christian doctors who would in their private practice operate in much the same manner. In their consultation with patients, they would ascertain their spiritual condition and proceed accordingly (Simpson, *Gospel of Healing*, 81).

66. Kenneth Mckenzie noted that Dowie, along with Cullis and Simpson, constituted the "three great figures [that] loom against the sky-line of the last quarter of the nineteenth century" when it comes to Divine Healing. In particular, Mackenzie called Dowie "the apostle of healing in his day" (McKenzie, *Physical Heritage in Christ*, 17, 20).

67. John Alexander Dowie, "Prayer and Testimony Meeting," *Leaves of Healing* 1:6 (October 5, 1894) 84; John Alexander Dowie, "Doctors and Medicines," *Leaves of Healing* 1:4 (September 21, 1894) 61; John Alexander Dowie, "Zion's Onward Movement," *Leaves of Healing* 2:25 (April 10, 1896) 389.

68. John Alexander Dowie, "The Opening of the Beautiful Gate of Divine Healing," *Leaves of Healing* 1:1 (August 31, 1894) 5.

69. "Disease, the foul offspring of its father, Satan, and its mother, Sin, was defining and destroying the earthly temples of God's children, and there was no deliverer"; John Alexander Dowie, "He Is Just the Same To-Day," *Leaves of Healing* 1:22 (February 15, 1895) 341.

70. The only thing that Dowie seemed to affirm in medical science was its intermittent ability to diagnose the physical cause of human sickness. Like the others, Dowie would cite the diagnosis of physicians approvingly and without question while at the same time denying their ability to either understand it fully or do anything about it.

Dowie is distinct from the other figures, however, in his outright and vitriolic rejection of even the limited good of medicine and the medical profession.[71] First, he strongly and repeatedly denied that there was anything that could legitimately be called "medical science."[72] Quoting numerous figures within the medical community for support,[73] Dowie claimed that medical practice had no scientific method and was nothing more than an on-going and disconnected series of guesses on the part of the practitioner.[74] There was no real science to it. Consequently, the concept of medical advance was an "ILLUSION" established by the medical community solely to establish its own reputation and power.[75] The whole business was, actually, an "infamous humbug."[76]

Dowie also denied that medical "science" could alleviate symptoms. He believed that there is no cure in medical science[77] and that it was, therefore, of "no value."[78] Rather, Dowie asserted that the means employed by medical "science" did far more harm than good. He labeled

71. Dowie's writings on the medical profession must be read in light of the persecution he faced, especially during the mid-1890's, at the hands of the Chicago medical community, who brought Dowie and his Healing Homes under the scrutiny of the Chicago press, Health Department, Building Department, Police Department, and, even, the local Post Office.

72. "Where is the science in medicine? There is none. There are no physicians of any standing to-day in any department of medicine who will declare it to be a science" (Dowie, "Opening of the Beautiful Gate," 5). "There is no science in medicine; not the first atom of foundation for science in medicine" (Dowie, "Zion's Onward Movement," 390).

73. Dowie, "Opening of the Beautiful Gate," 5; Dowie, "Doctors and Medicines," 61–63.

74. Dowie, "Zion's Onward Movement," 390.

75. "THE ALLEGATION THAT DOCTORS AND SUREGEONS ARE IN THE POSSESSION OF A FORMULA OF A WELL ESTABLISHED SCIENCE, IS AN ABSOLUTE LIE" (Dowie, "Zion's Onward Movement," 390). Note that all capitalizations in Dowie quotations in this section are original to Dowie.

76. Dowie, "Zion's Onward Movement," 393.

77. "I believe, and I can prove it, that doctors and medicine do not heal" (Dowie, "Prayer and Testimony Meeting," 84). "The alleged cures are not cures, and the patent poisonous drugs are shams and lies" (Dowie, "Zion's Onward Movement," 394). The abandoned crutches, braces, etc., that were displayed at the front of the tabernacle show Dowie's belief that Divine Healing is powerful and effective and that medical science is impotent. These appliances were aids, at best, and never cures.

78. Dowie, "Zion's Onward Movement," 389.

the drugs administered by physicians "poisons"[79] and surgical proce-
dures "butchery."[80] Hospitals were "murderous vivi-section holes from
which the victims rarely escaped with either money or life," and were
institutions wherein physicians practiced "prolonged and nameless tor-
tures."[81] Most, if not all, medical patients were worse off after their treatment than they were before. Worse still, Dowie charged that medical
practice was responsible for "hundreds of thousands of deaths,"[82] more
than "WAR, PESTILENCE AND FAMINE COMBINED."[83] Not only
were people physically poorer than they were before, Dowie contended
that many were driven into poverty paying their medical bills, as well.[84]

It will come as little surprise, then, that Dowie denied that physicians and medicine were in any way manifestations of the grace of God.
Rather, Dowie boldly alleged that their source was diabolical. Physicians,
"AS A PROFESSION, ARE DIRECTLY INSPIRED BY THE DEVIL"
and, in their medical practice, are the Devil's servants.[85] Dowie described
these "MONSTERS" as worse than either Herod, who killed the children
of Bethlehem, or the pagan Druids, who offered up virgin sacrifice.[86] The
diabolical character of the medical community was manifest in the performing of abortions, the murder of patients, the doctors' addiction to
drugs, and their insincerity regarding the legitimacy of their practice.[87]
The diabolical nature of the practice of medicine, however, is most clearly seen in its desire to stop the practice of Divine Healing, attempting
to remove Christ from his rightful place as the Healer.[88] Consequently,

79. Dowie, "Doctors and Medicines," 61.

80. Dowie, "Zion's Onward Movement," 390; John Alexander Dowie, "A Letter to
the Friends of Zion Tabernacle," *Leaves of Healing* 1:22 (February 15, 1895) 337.

81. John Alexander Dowie, "Divine Healing and the Chicago Doctors: A New
Attack on the Divine Healing Homes," *Leaves of Healing* 1:36 (June 14, 1895) 563.

82. Dowie, "Prayer and Testimony Meeting," 84.

83. Dowie, "Zion's Onward Movement," 392.

84. Dowie, "Zion's Onward Movement," 389.

85. Dowie, "Zion's Onward Movement," 390.

86. Dowie, "Zion's Onward Movement," 390, 393.

87. Dowie, "Zion's Onward Movement," 393–96.

88. "Men were doubtless willing then, as they are now, to give glory to one another,
and account for Divine Healing in every way but the right way." Dowie, though, is also
sure to note that many within the Church are accomplices in this move. "They declare
that medical science has taken the place of Divine Healing, and that no longer do we go
to Christ but to the doctor. This is the teaching of a great part of the church concerning

Dowie would contend "DOCTORS AND DRUGS ARE NECESSARILY THE FOES OF CHRIST AS THE HEALER."[89]

The Popular Reputation of Late Nineteenth-Century Medical Science

From an early twenty-first century perspective, we can see that the late nineteenth century, undoubtedly, was a time of great and monumental change in medical practice. The late nineteenth century saw the advancement of microbiology under Louis Pasteur, the vast improvements to an antiseptic surgical context resulting from the work of Joseph Lister, and the development of x-ray technology by Willhelm Röntgen. The implementation of these advances vastly improved not only medical diagnosis and practice but, perhaps more importantly, the chances of full recovery from medical and surgical procedure. Despite these very significant advances, however, medical science and medical practitioners in the late nineteenth century were held in low esteem by the general public and the denigration of the American physician was common.[90]

Scholars of the history of medicine have pointed out no fewer than four separate though related reasons for this low view of medicine in late nineteenth-century America. First, during this period, the licensing requirements of government for those practicing medicine was rather low.[91] This afforded various practitioners no level of civic endorsement and, consequently, no level of civic respect. Practically, many physicians operated on the fringes of society and were, for the most part, not accountable to the magistrate or anyone else for their methods.

Related to this idea is the second reason for the low level of esteem: the relative lack of formal education that most physicians of the day had received.[92] Prior to the late nineteenth century, the training in

---

Divine Healing to-day" (Dowie, "Opening of the Beautiful Gate," 5; Dowie, "Zion's Onward Movement," 393).

89. Dowie, "Zion's Onward Movement," 394.

90. Shryock, *Medicine in America*, 150–51. John Duffy notes "while individual physicians were admired, the profession collectively continued to have little public respect"; Duffy, *From Humors to Medical Science: A History of American Medicine*, 2nd ed. (Urbana, IL.: University of Illinois Press, 1993) 167.

91. James H. Cassedy, *Medicine in America: A Short History* (Baltimore, MD: Johns Hopkins University Press, 1991) 67.

92. Shryock, *Medicine in America*, 152.

the practice of medicine was usually limited to an apprenticeship. New candidates would receive their training at the hands of an older practitioner and, consequently, be limited in their training by the opinions, practices, and resources of that particular mentor. Given this method of training, many of the great advances taking place in the wider medical community were not known, endorsed, or widely practiced, in some cases, for decades. Physicians and their apprentices simply continued to use those methods that had held sway for decades, which they knew best, or those that they personally felt were most effective and appropriate. While medical schools were present and enrolled large numbers of students, the quality of both the schools and students was suspect. Most medical schools of the day, since they did not need any type of sanction, were little more than "diploma mills."[93] Furthermore, it was possible, in those days, for one to be admitted to a medical school when that same person would not meet the most basic requirements of a good liberal arts school.[94] The curriculum at most of these medical schools "required attendance at only two four-month lecture sessions. There was generally no clinical training sessions, no laboratories, and, for that matter, no admissions requirements. Even as late as 1870, only a very small percentage of medical students had earned a bachelor's degree."[95] It was not until the 1890's when American medicine would begin to come of age.[96]

A third reason that the medical community was held in low esteem in the public eye was due to the medical community's constant, public, and often vitriolic internal disagreements on both the diagnoses and, consequently, the method of treatment of almost any illness.[97] Part of the reason for this stems from the medical "doctrine that there was one cause and therefore one cure of disease."[98] Post-enlightenment

93. Duffy, *From Humors to Medical Science*, 167.

94. Shryock, *Medicine in America*, 152.

95. Robert C. Fuller, *Alternative Medicine and American Religious Life* (New York: Oxford University Press, 1989) 16.

96. The men who would bring about this change "were [not only] far better educated than their predecessors, [but] nearly all of them had studied [outside of America] in Vienna, Paris, and other European medical centers" (Duffy, *From Humors to Medical Science*, 192).

97. Shryock, *Medicine in America*, 151.

98. Shryock, *Medicine in America*, 171.

healers, following the lead of Isaac Newton, sought to understand the single "fundamental force or principle responsible" for disease in all of its manifestations. This would lead to the various "sectarian" schools of medical science such as mesmerism, Grahamism, hydropathy, etc."[99] Disagreement, of course, rose over the nature of this singular and rudimentary cause of disease. Consequently, there were equally divergent opinions and practices concerning the mode of effective treatment. Having put all of their proverbial eggs in one diagnostic basket meant that if one were to disagree with a practitioner on any level, it would be understood to be a lethal attack on the whole of that practitioner's medical understanding and ability. Such attacks could not be taken lightly if one wished to continue practicing medicine and attracting patients as the competition for business was great. This led to constant internal yet very public sniping and "professional quarrels."[100] This level of division did little good for the reputation of physicians or to instill the confidence of a watching public.

Finally, the unpleasant, strange, and often fatally ineffective methods of many physicians did not help the profession's reputation. "Bleedings, sweatings, blistering, and the use of drugs aimed at inducing vomiting or diarrhea were the most common therapeutic techniques."[101] Mercury, now widely known for its deathly effects, was used to treat a variety of diseases in the nineteenth century including tuberculosis, constipation, and headache. "Those hardy patients who did not die in the course of these largely futile endeavors were at the very least weakened by the ordeal."[102] The terms "butchery" and "stupendous humbug" were words used in the secular media to describe the medical profession.[103]

No single case brought more attention to the inability of medical science in the late nineteenth century than that of President James Garfield. The well-publicized and closely-watched case of Garfield's ultimately ineffective medical care showed the inability of, assumedly, the nation's best doctors and latest techniques to deal with something

99. Fuller, *Alternative Medicine and American Religious Life*, 13.

100. Shryock, *Medicine in America*, 155.

101. Fuller, *Alternative Medicine and American Religious Life*, 14; A. J. Gordon lists these as well, showing not only their ineffectiveness but their barbarism (*Ministry of Healing*, 176).

102. Fuller, *Alternative Medicine and American Religious Life*, 14.

103. Shryock, *Medicine in America*, 151.

as straightforward and as common as a gunshot wound. Garfield suc-
cumbed to his wound after a number of days despite round the clock
medical care. The failure of the nation's leading physicians and their
"medical science" to restore him shone clearly and brightly in the
spotlight.[104]

Conclusion

Though it may come as a surprise to some, the view that the Divine
Healing proponents held of medical science was not at all out of step
with that of American society. The American public, in general, held
medical science and medical practitioners in low esteem. The vicious
attacks of John Alexander Dowie were not necessarily the isolated rant-
ings of an extremist. The secular media was just as likely to use the
words "poisons," "butchers," and "murderers" when talking about contemporary medical practice and practitioners. On balance, the Divine
Healing practitioners actually appear to have been more gracious than
many in the secular press when it came to discussing the promise and
possibilities of medical science. They cited medicine and physicians as
providential. They believed that creation was divinely and intentionally
endowed with properties that could assuage human suffering. The mandate of medical science, they said, was to discover these and to apply
them appropriately.

Still, the Divine Healing proponents suggested only a limited appropriation of the offerings of medical science. While the Divine Healing
proponents did not completely dismiss the advances, usefulness, and
propriety of medical science, they did assert that it was, at best, a deficient approach to the gravity, complexity, and depth of human disease.
Therefore, they encouraged only the guarded employ of these "scientific" means and methods. Their reasons for doing so were numerous.
First, they realized that much of what was promoted as medical science
had not been well-proven and may have had side-effects as distressing
as the disease itself. Second, they were convinced that medical science's
anthropology and hamartology were both myopic and, therefore, its

---

104. Duffy, *From Humors to Medical Science*, 190. Simpson pointed to the Garfield
case, and that of President McKinley, as well-known examples of the ineffectiveness of
physicians and medical treatment; Simpson, *Lord for the Body*, 131; Albert Benjamin
Simpson, "The Doctors and the Lord," *Living Truths* 1:6 (December 1902) 307.

means to relieve human distress were short-sighted and deficient as well. Finally, they realized that there was a tendency for the advances and successes of medical science to usurp the primary and necessary, if not exclusive, role of Jesus Christ as Healer. This, above all, was intolerable for the Divine Healing proponents.

The champions of Divine Healing argued that Christians, especially, should seek their healing, not from a deficient medical science, but from the omnipotent and unchanging Christ directly and alone. In addition to those cautions listed previously, they argued that such an approach was the sole and repeated prescription of Scripture. Therefore, it was the only sanctioned course for the believer. Second, they believed that Christ alone was the only appropriate and adequate solution to the depth and breadth of human disease. Humanity's disease was more than just physical. It affected the totality of the human condition. Only the atoning work of Jesus Christ was able to deal with the destructive effects of sin on humanity, in its depth and in all of its manifestations—spiritual and physical.

Both medical science and the practice of Divine Healing have had long histories. Each saw momentous growth and popularity in the late nineteenth century as part of the larger and wider interest in holism and health. It is of no surprise, then, that key figures related to these movements would interact with the nature and developments of the other. They did, after all, seek to address the same human needs even if from two different perspectives. While both medical science and the Divine Healing movement sought to combat the problem of human disease, they did have fundamental disagreements about how it ought to be pursued and the legitimacy of the other perspective. Therefore, their relationship could be described as a cautious co-belligerence, at best.

5

Creation Revealed

An Early Pentecostal Hermeneutic

David S. Norris

Introduction

Almost fifty years after the 1859 publication of Darwin's *Origin of the Species* the Azusa Street revival propelled Pentecostalism onto the world stage.[1] Pentecostals were "Johnny-come-latelys" to the evolution/ creation controversy and typically had little or nothing to say on the subject. For them the facts were self-evident. The Bible is true. Evolution is wrong. End of discussion. Still, there were a few Pentecostals who addressed the issue of creation and the age of the earth. Most notable are Charles Parham, George Floyd Taylor, and G. T. Haywood. For these men, a correct understanding of creation was a part of broader interest in eschatological concerns, the theological ordering of the cosmos from the creation to the eschaton.

1. See Cecil M. Robeck, Jr., *The Azusa Street Mission and Revival: The Birth of the Global Pentecostal Movement* (Nashville, TN: Nelson, 2006).

Oneness Pentecostal G. T. Haywood[2] enhanced his theological treatise on creation by couching it in terms of "revelation." The book that most fully articulates both Haywood's theory of origins and his perspective on revelation is *Before the Foundation of the World: A Revelation of the Ages.*[3] G. T. Haywood's concept of "revelation" largely centers on God's illumination of scripture and is connected with prayerfully seeking God's voice. This language of revelation is captured in Haywood's prefacing remarks about his study of Genesis chapter one. He offers that biblical illumination occurred for him as he was engaged in both "a prayerful and careful study of the Word of God"; at first it was as if Haywood was seeing "through a glass darkly" but ultimately "the veil began to lift like a fog disappearing before the brilliant rays of the rising sun."[4]

While this sort of language may strike today's reader as a bit odd, Haywood's writings represent a high tide of a certain kind of speaking and thought woven into the fabric of Pentecostalism and its predecessors that was in itself an argument. In this context, let us analogously think of correct theological interpretation as being made possible by a recipe that calls for specific key ingredients and a dash of this or that. This essay seeks to demonstrate the way in which "illumination of the Spirit," or what we are calling "revelation," served as an ingredient that was added with increasing spoonfuls to the theological interpretive mix at the inception of the Pentecostal movement. Further, the place for "church tradition" as a substantial ingredient in this same theological recipe arguably decreased more or less in proportion to the increased emphasis on revelation, and for a brief time tradition was not a significant ingredient all.

2. On the history of G. T. Haywood, see Paul Dugas, *The Life and Writings of Elder G. T. Haywood* (Stockton, CA: Apostolic, 1968); Douglas Jacobsen, *Thinking in the Spirit: Theologies of the Early Pentecostal Movement* (Bloomington and Indianapolis, IN: University of Indiana, 2003); Morris Golder, *Before I Sleep: A Narrative and Photographic Biography of Bishop Garfield Thomas Haywood* (Indianapolis: n.p., 1976). On Haywood's place in the Oneness movement, see Daniel L. Butler, *Oneness Pentecostalism: A History of the Jesus Name Movement* (San Gabriel Cerritos, CA: n.p. 2004); and James Tyson, *The Early Pentecostal Revival: History of Twentieth-Century Pentecostals and The Pentecostal Assemblies of the World, 1901–1930* (Hazelwood, MO: Word Aflame, 1992).

3. G. T. Haywood, *Before the Foundation of the World: A Revelation of the Ages* (Indianapolis, IN: Christ Temple Book Store, 1923).

4. Haywood, *Before the Foundation*, 9.

Perhaps more than any other from this first generation of Pentecostals, G. T. Haywood displayed a tremendous curiosity about scientific discoveries, exhibiting a genuine respect for science. Haywood was familiar with solutions offered by conservative Christians to harmonize the biblical text with the scientific claim for the antiquity of the earth. He was aware of both the "day-age theory" and the "pre-Adamic gap" theory as solutions to reconcile the Bible with science. But his interests went beyond propping up the biblical text or simply finding a useful polemic to pummel evolutionists. His greater concern was in mining the Bible for truth.

This essay will explore G. T. Haywood's hermeneutic, not only in the context of first-generation of Pentecostals, but over against nineteenth century conservative Christians as well. In this context, we will suggest ways in which challenges of Darwinism coalesced with eschatological concerns to give rise to nineteenth century dispensational premillennialism, an interpretive system useful to first generation Pentecostals. We will show how G. T. Haywood was empowered by nineteenth-century philosophical underpinnings that decried "theories" generally, particularly the theory of evolution, and how such an attitude led to his inductive study of scripture to arrive at ultimate answers. Most importantly, we will work to demonstrate how Haywood's theological understanding of revelation arose out of a specific historical impulse. That is, while G. T. Haywood could speak in terms of God revealing answers to him related to the age of the earth, this kind of speaking can best be understood when considering the place of revelation in a kind of chronological trajectory leading up to the Pentecostal Movement, one that can be readily traced all the way back to John Wesley.

John Wesley and "Experience"

While "experience" has meaning for a larger Protestant audience, Pentecostals generally track their theological appreciation of experience to John Wesley. Wesley did not differ from Calvinists of his day in allowing experience to inform his theology, but in many ways he was more intentional about its place.[5] Wesley regularly attempted to spiritually discern

5. On John Wesley, see Donald A. D. Thorsen, *The Wesleyan Quadrilateral: Scripture, Reason and Experience as a Model of Evangelical Theology* (Grand Rapids, MI: Zondervan, 1990); Stephen Tomkins, *John Wesley: A Biography* (Grand Rapids, MI:

God's specific direction for his own life. A single example will suffice. In one instance, when George Whitefield invited Wesley to come to Bristol to join him in preaching outdoors to thousands of people, Wesley consulted Scripture for personal wisdom. The biblical text that offered him direction was, "Son of man, behold I take from thee the desires of thine eyes with a stroke"; in ways that we cannot entirely understand from this historical distance, this Scripture confirmed to Wesley that he should go to be with Whitefield.[6] Interestingly, John Wesley thought that the meaning of the biblical text was that he would be martyred by traveling to meet his friend. Still, he willingly chose to embrace what he deemed to be the Spirit's guidance in his personal life (what we are categorizing as revelation). Fortunately, Wesley lived to tell the tale.

This same sort of illumination regularly functioned for Wesley to offer corporate guidance as well. As we have suggested, John Wesley allied with Whitefield in evangelistic efforts, even though the latter was a Calvinist. It worked because, as one author notes, "they had agreed to let sleeping dogmas lie."[7] Calvinism continued to be a moot point for Wesley until a letter from another quarter challenged his own Arminianism, and Wesley felt compelled under the direction of the Spirit to speak against predestination. The written record states that he prayed aloud spontaneously, imploring that if his view on free will were correct, then God should send a sign. Wesley writes,

> Immediately the power of God fell upon us. One and another, and another, sunk to the earth. You might see them, dropping on all sides, as thunderstruck. One cried out aloud. I went and prayed over her, and she received joy in the Holy Ghost. A second falling into the same agony, we turned to her, and received for her also the promise of the Father.[8]

Wesley regarded this phenomenon as the confirmation of the Spirit, in part a revelation of the rightness of his doctrinal position. Thus, the door was left open, not merely for the Spirit informing his own personal

Eerdmans, 2003); Robert Tuttle, *John Wesley: His Life and Theology* (Grand Rapids, MI: Zondervan, 1971).

6. Tomkins, *John Wesley*, 68–69.
7. Tomkins, *John Wesley*, 71.
8. Tomkins, *John Wesley*, 72.

life, but as well for God to either corroborate or repudiate a doctrinal position by revelation.

Interestingly, academics do not emphasize revelation as a principle source of Wesley's theology. Since the late 1960s, Albert Outler's "Wesleyan quadrilateral" has been utilized to describe four sources for Wesley's theology: Scripture, tradition, reason, and experience.[9] But caution is needed. That it took two hundred years of reflection to deduce such a paradigm ought to suggest that this approach is more of a heuristic model than a concrete template. While on the face of it, Wesley has no room specifically for "revelation" on this matrix, that the Spirit would guide him was a given for Wesley. Some may subsume Wesley's spiritual illumination under the category of experience, yet Wesley's revelations also interfaced with scripture and on a certain level with reason. Further, if one takes tradition to mean applying the normative beliefs from the first centuries of the church,[10] Wesley's understanding of tradition was interwoven as well with spiritual illumination in his continuing to jettison Augustine in favor of "free will."[11]

The Holiness Movement and Revelation

A century after John Wesley and George Whitefield, a similar understanding of illumination was still at play in informing theology. Allied with Arminians from the Holiness Movement were revivalists, particularly those with Keswick theology. While these groups may have debated the theological meaning of the Spirit's working as either cleansing or empowerment, what was not debated was their shared emphasis on experience and a corollary expectation of spiritual illumination in ways not dissimilar to what we have already read in John Wesley.

---

9. Albert Outler's use of the term "quadrilateral" is in some sense unfortunate, for he did not intend a geometric model. He chose the term "Wesleyan quadrilateral" as an analogue to a term already used by Anglican and Episcopal Churches, the "Lambeth Quadrilateral" (*Thorsen Wesleyan Quadrilateral*, 21).

10. Donald Dayton, *The Theological Roots of Pentecostalism* (Metuchan, NJ: Scarecrow, 1987) 41; Dayton notes that "the shape of Wesley's primitivism was then in this sense somewhat more historically nuanced than the biblicistic appeal of Pentecostalism to the Book of Acts."

11. Thorsen, *Wesleyan Quadrilateral*, 155. Wesley was particularly attracted to the ante-Nicene fathers and took them as very profitable for both life and theology.

These same groups were also affected by a sizable nineteenth-century cultural shift that challenged their understanding both of the "beginning" and the "end" of human history. In terms of "the beginning," Darwinians disputed the validity of the Genesis narrative of creation. In terms of "ending," increasing social and cultural ills critiqued the theological presupposition that America would Christianize the world, thus, bringing the return of Christ. That is, because America was getting worse and not better, postmillennial optimism seemed unfounded.

In seeking answers to the challenges, conservative Christians began looking towards premillennial dispensationalism. It was advantageous because while on the one hand, dispensationalism worked to harmonize Genesis with science, on the other hand, it addressed social upheaval by framing it in terms of expected crises anticipating the return of Jesus. That is to say, prophecy, as it was rightly understood, demonstrated that the world would not get better but worse, and rescue would occur imminently when Jesus Christ would break in, rapture his Bride, and subsequently judge the world.

Although acceptance of such a system was uneven at first, it would be universal in those who would later become a part of the Pentecostal Movement at the turn of the twentieth century. Further, as the pendulum swung towards embracing premillennialism, a kind of intuitive logic was set in motion. That is, if in fact Jesus were revealing new understanding about His anticipated return, the Lord was necessarily providing revelation to believers who would receive it. Accordingly, the revelation of new truth began to cast doubt on whether or not one could with any certainty trust received church tradition.[12] Confirming such a

---

12. See chapter 4: "The Formation of Pentecostal Thought," in D. William Faupel, *The Everlasting Gospel: The Significance of Eschatology in the Development of Pentecostal Thought* (Sheffield: Sheffield, 1996). Faupel historically demonstrates that at the close of the nineteenth century, there was at the same time a conversion to a premillennial perspective and an anticipation of the restoration of the apostolic church in connection with the empowering the church to do missionary work in preparation for the return of Christ. Robert Mapes Anderson, *Vision of the Disinherited: The Making of American Pentecostalism* (New York: Oxford University Press, 1979) 45–46, delineates the way in which denominal dissatisfaction led to an exodus by certain groups. This exodus propelled acceptance of new experiences and doctrines. A further contribution to this religious milieu is what George M. Marsden was nineteenth century American culture itself, which lacked "strong views about the nature and authority of the church"; see Marsden, *Fundamentalism and American Culture: The Shaping of Twentieth-Century Evangelicalism, 1870–1925* (New York: Oxford University Press, 1980) 70.

position was the suspicion that the American religious establishment was more or less complicit with a culture deemed to be headed in the wrong direction. Thus, in a revised "recipe" for theological truth, a few more spoonfuls of revelation were now required for a correct mix while at the same time a few cupfuls of tradition were removed as ingredients fundamentally required for correct biblical interpretation. To understand the way in which the implications of this epistemological shift found its full flowering in the Pentecostal movement, we must focus on the specific historical factors creating the eschatological necessity to explain origins and endings.

Issues of "Origins"

While a crisis had been brewing for some time, the 1859 publishing of Charles Darwin's *The Origin of the Species* tipped the scales toward broader acceptance of a naturalistic theory of origins. Although the dominant Protestant response came to "sanctify" scientific opinions that tended towards evolution,[13] conservative church leaders felt betrayed not only by scientists but as well by clergy who endorsed any form of evolutionary thought. Upon the discovery of dinosaurs, new theories about fossils, and an increased acceptance of evolutionary thought, revivalist Dwight L. Moody complained of scientists who "dug up old carcasses . . . to make them testify against God."[14] But Moody did more than complain. He functioned as a catalyst to promote conferences and gather a coalition of conservative Christians to actively advocate a worldview that upheld the veracity of the biblical text. It was in this context that Moody and others promoted a dispensational meta-narrative that worked to elevate biblical principles into absolute laws that were capable of defining both the past and the future in arguably scientific ways.[15]

Although a full presentation of dispensationalism is complex, at its core, its method is fairly simplistic: it advertizes that prophecy is literal and is governed by certain laws that anyone can understand. Such an

13. Michael Ruse, *The Evolution-Creation Struggle* (Cambridge: Harvard, 2005) 157.

14. Ronald L. Numbers, *The Creationists* (New York: Knopf, 1992) 14; Numbers is citing the words of Moody in William G. McLoughlin, Jr., *Modern Revivalism: Charles Grandison Finney to Billy Graham* (New York: Ronald, 1959) 214.

15. On Moody's reception of John Nelson Darby's dispensationalism, see Anderson, *Vision of the Disinherited*, 32–40.

approach appealed readily to the American psyche. Philosophically, Francis Bacon was highly regarded, mediated through Scottish Common Sense Realism,[16] and this cultural orientation confirmed the place for pragmatic biblical interpretation. God was not theoretical but practical. Theories were bad. Facts were good. The Bible could be readily understood by a common sense approach to the text where people could dig out answers for themselves.[17] Because dispensationalism had the feel of being scientific, and because it functioned as a whole system, it was a bulwark against Marxism, Darwinism, and suspect theologians from Germany. R. A. Torrey explained, "The methods of modern science are applied to Bible study—through analysis followed by careful synthesis."[18] For Torrey, real science was defined by utilizing proper methods of induction, offering a method easily applied in interpreting the biblical text.

While C. I. Scofield was not alone in calling dispensationalism a scientific system,[19] one of the real difficulties for Scofield and those of his ilk was to reconcile Genesis with the scientific claim that the earth very, very old. With regard to the Genesis narrative, Evangelicals offered two different methods whereby Genesis 1 could allow for the antiquity of the earth. The first solution was to read each of the days of creation in Genesis as "ages." This "day-age" approach recognized each day stood as an epoch of time, thus allowing enough time for the Bible to be reconciled with science. A second alternative, and one that was ultimately popularized by the dispensationalism of C. I. Scofield, suggested that between Gen 1:1 and 1:2 there existed an incredible expanse of time. This "pre-adamic gap" still allowed for a literal seven-day creation while

16. The influence of Scottish Common Sense Realism on early Pentecostalism was indirect but pervasive throughout the North American movement; for discussion, see Marsden, *Fundamentalism*, 16–18, 55–56.

17. Raymond A. Eve and Francis B. Harrold, *The Creationist Movement in Modern America* (Boston: Twayne, 1990) 14. Associated with this was a kind of "Baconian" method, distrusting words like "theory" and "hypothesis" and emphasizing that a collection of facts about the natural world would lead to scientific conclusions.

18. Eve and Harrold, *Creationist Movement*, 60, citing R. A. Torrey, *What the Bible Teaches: A Thorough and Comprehensive Study of the What the Bible has to say Concerning the Great Doctrines of Which it Treats*, 17th ed. (1898; reprint, New York: Revell, 1933) 1.

19. Scofield contrasts his work with previous "unscientific system"; Marsden, *Fundamentalism*, 60, citing *The Scofield Reference Bible* (1909; reprint, New York: Oxford University Press, 1917) Introduction, page 2i.

acknowledging the antiquity of the earth. Further, as one proponent argued, the gap allowed enough time "for all of the geologists of the ages to have floundered in primeval mud until they had worked out all the problems concerning which they now can but theorize and guess."[20] While the day-age theory was prominent among a number of more highly educated Princeton theologians and was propagated by millions of copies of the *Fundamentals*, the pre-Adamic gap theory too had its adherents, popularized by the notes in Scofield's Reference Bible, of which the 1909 edition sold two million copies.

Issues of "Endings"

Since the time of the Mayflower Compact, there were those who settled America in hopes of establishing the Kingdom of God. The underlying motivation for numbers of Protestant Calvinists who migrated to America was to Christianize America so that America could Christianize the world.[21] While such motivation was in part secularized and became a part of the American psyche, nineteenth-century Protestantism still held on to the broad eschatological notion that upon the completion of America Christianizing the world, Jesus Christ would return. Yet, as we have begun to suggest, a series of historical eruptions challenged such a position. The tension that preceded the Civil War brought an end to a number of religious coalitions.[22] The Civil War itself was a terrible travesty and the carnage did little to suggest that Christian civilization was advancing. At the same time, American shores welcomed an influx of immigrants whose presence challenged the forward advance of Protestant Christianity. Further, what were once conservative church denominations were sliding towards liberalism: numbers of churches

20. Numbers, *Creationists*, 15, citing Robert Patterson, *The Errors of Evolution: An Examination of the Nebular Theory, Geological Evolution, the Origin of Life and Darwinism*, 3rd ed. (Boston, MA: Scriptural Tract Repository, 1893) ix–x.

21. For a narrative approach as to how such a sense of American purpose evolved, see Peter Marshall and David Manuel, *The Light and the Glory* (Old Tappan, NJ: Revell, 1977).

22. Dayton is correct when he catalogs the significance of a number of events, including the Civil War, replacing the broad optimistic religious and cultural feeling with a kind of apocalypticism (*Roots*, 76).

were admitting members with no true conversion experience.[23] Finally, Marxism had reared its head as a competing philosophical system.[24]

Once again, dispensational premillennialism explains just why there was such a crisis in the first place. In terms of world-view, the principle difference between a postmillennial and premillennial system is the apocalyptic nature of the latter. That is, a premillennial understanding offers a more pessimistic telling of the human story. Because continued depravity functions in making the world worse and worse, Jesus Christ must necessarily break into the affairs of humanity to rescue His church, after which He will cleanse the earth through judgment.

There was no natural propensity among Holiness believers to accept dispensational premillennialism. Wesleyans were typically not given to take a stand on prophecy, and as we have suggested, Calvinists historically had come to eschatology in more culturally progressive terms. Still, there was no doubt that the religious and cultural crisis was real enough. Additionally, such a crisis could only make sense if what had been believed before were incorrect. Consequently, a premillennial proclamation fell on ears that were ready to hear it. At first, it was largely Calvinists who accepted and promoted dispensationalism, but eventually even Wesleyans in the Holiness Movement adopted the system as well.

Once this eschatological shift began, it propelled an increasing faith in revelation. William Faupel establishes this link between eschatology and increased anticipation of the unfolding plan of God. The logic of this change is that if in fact God were revealing new light on prophecy *just because* it was the end of the age, the implication was that He would reveal His end-time purpose in other ways as well. In part, this expectation laid the ground work for the Pentecostal Movement. As Faupel suggests, "As the movement neared the turn of the century, expectations arose that God was about to restore apostolic authority and power to the church to enable it to accomplish his end-time purposes."[25]

The notion of revelation that Pentecostals inherited from the Holiness Movement operated within specific limits. It could not violate the

23. Anderson writes, "In the last quarter of the nineteenth century, the identification of Protestantism with middle class culture was almost complete" (*Vision of the Disinherited*, 30). Standards for membership in congregations were lowered and church discipline was largely abandoned.

24. Marsden, *Fundamentalism*, 64–65.

25. Faupel, *Everlasting Gospel*, 114.

biblical text; indeed, revelation was understood as God making known the clear meaning of scripture. Further, while it is correct to acknowledge that it was God who was revealing His plan through scripture, His was not a one-sided project. An Arminian approach to the Bible suggested that although God could sovereignly give revelation, it would likely come through prayer and study. Thus, people experienced revelation by studying the Bible inductively and mining it for the correct meaning. This coincided with the confidence provided by premillennial dispensationalism: God's plan was revealed through scripture in a biblically "scientific" way. In this way, revelation was confirmed by reason but largely over against tradition.

Pentecostalism and Revelation

The trajectory that had begun among adherents to Holiness/Keswick theology found fuller expression in Pentecostalism. If tradition was bad before, it became doubly bad in a Pentecostal gestalt. If new revelation had begun before, then anticipation only increased for the full restoration of the apostolic doctrine and praxis prior to the return of Christ. Thus, when Pentecostals received the baptism of the Holy Spirit in a way expressed differently than before, they came to believe that not only was this experience part of the full restoration of the church; this experience would as well empower them to receive further revelation.[26]

Charles Parham was one of the few Pentecostals to reflect broadly about eschatology. Parham, arguably the theological founder of the Pentecostal movement, created an elaborate taxonomy that encompassed the whole sweep of cosmos, from the "original creation to the final consummation."[27] While Parham certainly believed in the spiritual illumination, what the Spirit necessarily illuminated was the biblical text. Indeed, the declared method at Parham's Bethel Bible School in Topeka was that the "the only textbook was the Bible [and] its only object was in obedience to the commandments of Jesus."[28]

26. Haywood writes, "it is no marvel to see the 'mysteries that have been hid for the ages' being 'made manifest to the saints,' who are being baptized with the Holy Ghost according to Acts 2:4; 10:45; 19:6"; *Ezekiel's Vision* (Indianapolis, IN: Christ Temple Books Store, n.d.) 2.

27. Jacobsen, *Thinking in the Spirit*, 16.

28. Charles Parham, *Kol Kare Bomidbar: A Voice Crying in the Wilderness* (1902; reprint, Baxter Springs, KS: Apostolic Faith Bible College, n.d.) 32.

Further, the illumination of the Spirit married biblical understanding with scientific knowledge. With reference to creation, Charles Parham believed that for the most part "science and the Bible agree beautifully."[29] Parham had no problem breaking with the perspective that the earth was created in six literal twenty-four hour days, allowing that this perspective was given up by everyone except those with very narrow "moss covered" minds. Parham taught a kind of "day-age theory" that had been popularly offered by certain Princeton theologians. Regarding the seven days of creation in Genesis one he offered, "these were God's days, reckoned from the standpoint of eternity, computed by the Mind . . . and with whom a day is as a thousand years and thousand years as one day."[30]

Further, while for Parham there was the possibility of genuine revelation, there could be what were in his reckoning "false revelations" as well. Competing theological systems were for Parham relegated to this category. Like other Pentecostals, Parham felt strongly about his own convictions and didn't hold kindly to contrary opinions. He writes of men "whose so-called 'divine revelations' are vain as mad man's dreams, the unction of overwrought imaginations of self-exaltation and esteem."[31]

In contrast with Charles Parham, Pentecostal George Floyd Taylor harmonized the Genesis narrative with the antiquity of the earth by utilizing the already formulated pre-Adamic gap theory. [32] Interestingly, Pentecostals after Parham felt little compunction to incorporate either his understanding of creation or his very elaborate taxonomy for the end-times. Pentecostals were thus not only exercising their Baconian right of biblical discovery through inductive study; they also exercised their inheritance to receive illumination directly from the Spirit. Consequently, if their conclusions were different than what had been

29. Parham, *Kol Kare*, 81.

30. Parham, *Kol Kare*, 81.

31. Parham, *Kol Kare*, 25.

32. Taylor was introduced to Pentecostalism through G. B. Cashwell. Taylor's writings about prophecy include *The Spirit and the Bride*. The preface dates the book to 1907, though it came out in 1908; cf. his books *The Second Coming of Jesus* (1916) and his *The Rainbow* (1924). For Taylor, there was a "long process of creation" and that the earth "was a result of the workings of God in his laboratory for millions of years." At the end of the day, he allows for a kind of pre-Adamic world while retaining a six day literal creation.

offered before, this was hardly an issue. Such an approach became even more normative as the perceived value of church tradition continued to slide. Consequently, while Pentecostals might rely on hermeneutical systems received from a previous generation,[33] tradition itself was a potential hindrance in determining truth.

G. T. Haywood and Creation Revealed

Garfield Thomas Haywood was celebratory in his use of the language of revelation, utilizing it to fully undergird his interpretation of Genesis chapter one. Haywood was an African American indebted to both Baptist and Methodist influences before he received the baptism of the Holy Spirit at an Indianapolis mission in 1907.[34] In 1909, he took over that same mission and built a thriving church. When in 1915 G. T. Haywood accepted the Oneness message and was baptized in Jesus' name, four hundred and sixty five members of that same church were baptized with him. Compared to his Pentecostal peers in ministry, there was nothing exceptional about Haywood's educational background.[35] Still, his intellectual interests went far beyond most Pentecostals. For example, Haywood was current with the most recent discoveries of dinosaurs. In the decade prior to his writing, there had been so many discoveries of fossils of dinosaurs, that it has been called a "Dinosaur Rush," and Haywood was keenly interested in finding a place in the biblical text for these prehistoric creatures.[36]

33. Though one can't be certain, it may well be that something like the "Law of Seven" influenced Taylor's construct of how the Spirit works. For Taylor, there were seven actions of the Spirit, offices and administrations performed by the Spirit in an individual's life. See Jacobsen, *Thinking in the Spirit*, 90.

34. Dugas, *Haywood*, 7.

35. Garfield Thomas Haywood was a song writer, an artist, a writer, a preacher, and most notably, a Bible teacher. Theologically, Haywood reflected on a broad range of topics. Although Haywood possessed only a high school education, this was consonant with most of his Pentecostal contemporaries. On this, see Anderson, *Vision of the Disinherited*, 101.

36. Related to this, see http://www.ucmp.berkeley.edu/diapsids/dinodiscoveriesna. html.internet. While there had been what has been termed a "Dinosaur Rush" related to discoveries of parts of dinosaurs in the 1850s, the Second Great Dinosaur Rush took place in the badlands of the Red Deer River in southern Alberta in 1910. As noted in below, note 45, he cites a number of references related to the subject. So intriguing was this question that Haywood supplies pictures of dinosaurs on pp. 37, 41, and 43 of his *Before the Foundation*.

Though G. T. Haywood was familiar with both the "day-age theory"[37] and a "pre-Adamic gap theory,"[38] he utilized neither in his attempt to unravel the Genesis narrative. Confident that God would reveal secrets in the last days, Haywood worked inductively to understand Genesis chapter one, beginning with a kind of dispensational template. Following the dating scheme of others, Haywood accepted the Old Testament to be four thousand years long, and believing that the church age would be no more than two thousand years in length, he calculated human history to be roughly six thousand years. Haywood then added a thousand years for the millennium to achieve God's seven thousand year plan for humanity.[39]

Only then did Haywood appeal to a kind of "day-age theory," building a system based on three connecting assertions: first, each "day" in Genesis chapter one represented not twenty-four hours but a significant period of time; second, when it says that humanity was created on the "sixth day," Genesis is really describing not a literal day but an age, a period of some seven thousand years in length (humanity's day); third, because of how the Genesis narrative is constructed, it follows that each "day" in Genesis is the same length as this sixth day. Thus, because the "sixth day" is seven thousand years in length,[40] the earth is some forty-one thousand years old.

37. The day-age theory was propagated through *The Fundamentals*, printed and distributed while Haywood was pastoring. It cannot be proven that Haywood got his hands on the *Fundamentals*, but given his bent towards reading broadly, it is likely, for it was said to have been sent to "every pastor, evangelist, missionary, theological professor, theological student, Sunday School superintendent, Y.M.C.A. and Y.W.C.A. secretary in the English speaking world, so far as the addresses of all these can be obtained"; A. C. Dickson, L. Meyer, and R. C. Torrey, eds., *The Fundamentals: A Testimony*, 12 vols. (Chicago: Testimony, 1910–1915) 1:4.

38. The Scofield Reference Bible is advertized in some of the publications with which Haywood is associated. Along with the main tenets of dispensationalism, it taught the pre-Adamic gap theory. So prominent was the Bible and its notes that Scofield is said to have canonized premillennialism by its publication.

39. While the dating of the creation at 4000 BC goes back to Bishop James Ussher, it was the dispensational formulation of "sevens" stemming from nineteenth century exegetes such as Nathaniel West to whom Haywood is most indebted. On Haywood's dependence on a hermeneutic similar to West, see below.

40. Haywood offers, "Since the sixth day of Creation is seven thousand years' duration, then it is evident that the other 'days' before it contained the same number of years, for 'the Law of the Lord is perfect'" (*Before the Foundation*, 14).

Waxing even a bit more speculative, G. T. Haywood placed dinosaurs on the earth during the fifth "seven thousand year day." This Haywood deduced because the Genesis narrative says that it was on the fifth day that fowls and other creatures were created from the sea. In Haywood's telling, the fifth creative day is the age of reptiles, and because scientists had speculated as to the relationship between birds and dinosaurs, Haywood, made this connection. He projected that during this period there were "winged fowls many times larger than the 'inhabitants of the air' of our day"; Haywood paints a picture of birds larger than airplanes "pinioning their way to some prehistoric water brook to clumsily nestle among their young."[41]

On the face of it, G. T. Haywood's system was one produced whole cloth out of "revelation."[42] It certainly didn't have much to recommend it, for it did not answer the question of how to reconcile Genesis 1 with the antiquity of the earth. It didn't satisfy those conservative Christians who felt that any attempt to tinker with the Genesis "seven day creation" to satisfy scientific dating was unnecessary. Nor did it satisfy more progressive Christians who had already had in place systems meant to harmonize science and the Bible. Haywood's system did not allow enough time to reconcile Genesis 1 with the apparent antiquity of the earth. Haywood seemed to have ignored all hermeneutical laws in his revelatory leap to create a not-too-useful interpretive scheme.

Yet, while one may challenge how Haywood's system "solves" the issue of reconciling the Genesis narrative with the antiquity of the earth, Haywood's argumentation and his incorporation of revelation demonstrates a surprising affinity with the more rational theological gestalt of conservative Evangelicals of the late nineteenth century. Further, as we suggested above, it was not merely that Haywood had no concern for science. Like John Wesley,[43] Haywood had keen interest in things

41. Haywood, *Before the Foundation*, 34.

42. For Haywood, this understanding was not available to "the natural man" (1 Cor 2:14) but the Lord "will reveal [these things] to His saints, for the 'secret of the Lord is with them that fear Him' (Psalm 25:14)" (*Before the Foundation*, 4).

43. Wesley had broad interests and was fascinated with experiments that had been conducted with electricity by Benjamin Franklin and Richard Lovett; he even published a book extolling its likely health benefits. Thorsen, *Wesleyan Quadrilateral*, 58, citing Wesley's "The Desideratum: Or Electricity made plain and useful. By a Lover of Mankind, and of Common Sense," from *Works of Rev. John Wesley*, Thomas Jackson, ed., 3rd ed. (Grand Rapids, MI: Baker, 1978) 14: 241–44.

scientific and read as broadly as he could.[44] Indeed, like other conservative Christians of the nineteenth century, Haywood could offer, "True
science and the word of God are in perfect harmony, but we are warned
against the 'oppositions' of science, and not science in itself (1 Tim
6:20–21)."[45]

We must recall that Haywood was also the inheritor of a confidence in inductive reasoning which had been "scientifically" applied
to the biblical text by those just prior to the turn of the century. He accepted dispensationalism as "science," and though he was not above tin-
kering with it as a received system, he utilized its method. For instance,
Haywood employed "the Law of Sevens," in order to intuitively tease out
his own presentation of Genesis 1. Prophecy teacher Nathaniel West
had previously said that the "Law of Seven" was as sure "the Law of motion in gravitation, in Astronomy which Kepler and Newton discovered,
or the law of division and integration which gave rise to the systems of
Hegel and Spencer all their vitality."[46] In utilizing West's methodology,
Haywood created multiple systems of seven that framed first a "day" of
seven thousand years; then, these days formed an eschatological week.
Thus, Haywood was following what was for that time, at least, approved
hermeneutical principles.[47]

Although G. T. Haywood was a bit conjectural in his approach, his
motive was in part pastoral. When explaining his teaching, he offered
this defense: "It answers the skeptics, infidels, scientists, and higher
critics of the Bible . . . it inspires faith in the word of God, and feeds

44. While in his *Before the Foundation*, G. T. Haywood refers indirectly to a number of sources, it is clear that he was fascinated by the correlation between science
and scripture. Haywood cites *The Literary Digest*, Dec. 29, 1917, with reference to the
evidence derived from the ocean floors. *The Literary Digest* was a kind of general interest reading, forebear of the time magazine into which it finally merged in 1938.
He then cites from the more scholarly *School Science and Mathematics Journal* (*Before
the Foundation*, 23–24). Further, Haywood is conversant with dinosaurs both through
popular literary sources and trips to the museum.

45. Haywood, *Before the Foundation*, 35–36.

46. Nathaniel West, *The Thousand Years: Studies in Eschatology in Both Testaments*
(1889; reprint, Grand Rapids, MI: Kregel, 1993) 339, 343–44.

47. West declares, "Ever since God rested from His creative work, the number 7 has
not only borne a sacred Sabbatic value, but has been a measure of exact time, and the
septennial division of time has been the peculiar characteristic of sacred history and
prophecy, alike, and continues repeating itself down to the sounding of the seventh
trumpet" (*The Thousand Years*, 103).

the souls of His anointed; it shows the age of the earth and silences wild speculations."[48] Haywood was aware that his system did not satisfy scientists and in the end did not answer the question of the antiquity of the earth. But this did not matter. For Haywood, what God demonstrated from the biblical text must be the ultimate source of truth, no matter if contradicted science or not. In retrospect, even though Haywood's system was little more than a historical footnote even for Oneness Pentecostals, what can be said of G. T. Haywood is this: in him we find the full flowering of the language of revelation in the context of a specific biblical hermeneutic consonant with the time period.

The Decline of "Revelation" as Theological Source

Historically, "revelation" as a normative part of the interpretive recipe would soon be eclipsed and "tradition" added back into the mix for coming to theological truth. It was not so much that G. T. Haywood's view of the creation of the earth that was so offensive. Rather, what drew the ire of others was his critique of the creedal affirmation of "Persons in the Godhead" and his insistence that the biblical formula of Jesus' name baptism be practiced. Though the vocabulary of revelation was a common currency among Pentecostals at the time of Haywood, because Oneness Pentecostals utilized the language of revelation as an explanation for how they came to biblically reinterpret the Godhead, such speaking became a lightening rod for critics. Just as many in the Holiness Movement felt that their own language was being used against them when Pentecostals appropriated it, [49] so many in the Pentecostal circles felt Oneness adherents were employing the language of revelation as a kind of argument in and of itself.

Critics of the Oneness position responded by working to reframe the definition of revelation to mean something extra-biblical or contrary to received understanding. Because of this turn, the vocabulary of "revelation" quickly went out of use. Nor was it the language alone that was altered. As part of a larger reactionary response to the Oneness construal, tradition, which in the last twenty years had largely been

---

48. Haywood, *Before the Foundation*, 1–2.

49. On the way in which the emerging Pentecostal movement was able to control the language, see Wolfgang Vondey, "The Symbolic Turn: A Symbolic Conception of the Liturgy of Pentecostalism," *Wesleyan Theological Journal* 36:2 (Fall 2001) 223–47.

viewed as a blight on Christianity, was now rehabilitated to be a significant source for truth. Certainly by the year 1920, Pentecostals began unwittingly returning to an interpretive approach that was not too different from the so-called Wesleyan quadrilateral.

Even Oneness Pentecostalism has largely left the language of revelation behind, in part because of the way in which the vocabulary became polarized. Further, it has been almost a hundred years now since the formation of a Oneness Pentecostal movement, and this movement, too, has a tradition. Oneness proponents insist that the only really important tradition is the one that can be found in the first century church; certainly they have little use for church history. Still, the writings of G. T. Haywood have themselves become an important part of Oneness Pentecostal tradition. Although Haywood's construct of Genesis 1 is studied more historically than theologically, much of Haywood's christological proclamation remains theologically significant. Given then the development both of Trinitarian and Oneness Pentecostalism, it is only with intentionality that one can discern the place of revelation in Haywood's theological method. For although one finds in Haywood a full flowering of a particular hermeneutical inheritance, because his was an understanding of revelation current over just a few decades of dynamic change, a clear understanding of Haywood's hermeneutic is one that has largely faded from our historical memory.

Conclusion

During the years leading up to the twentieth century, conservative Christians worked at reconciling the Bible with the purported antiquity of the earth. While the "day-age theory" was promoted in *The Fundamentals*, the "pre-Adamic gap theory" was popularized in the *Scofield Reference Bible*. This latter effort at harmonizing Genesis with science was typically allied with a premillennial dispensationalist understanding of the cosmos, a meta-narrative believed by its adherents to be scientific and useful for providing interpretive rules for inductive biblical study. Conservative Christian responded to Darwinian evolution with cosmogonies that, although adhering to certain interpretive rules, allowed for a certain kind of freedom of expression informed by a kind of underlying Baconian system.

Of the Pentecostal responses to questions of origins, arguably the most creative was offered by G. T. Haywood. Douglas Jacobsen rightly notes that the vocabulary of revelation is more prominent in Haywood than with any other Pentecostal. Yet, Jacobsen goes on to allow that Haywood puts "more trust in scientific insight than any other early pentecostal thinker."[50] That said, we have attempted to demonstrate that it was neither his understanding of revelation nor his study of science that most informed Haywood's presentation; it was Haywood's received hermeneutic that treated the Bible as containing ultimate scientific truth with the further understanding that this truth could be determined inductively. Further, while Bible study was accomplished prayerfully, particular aspects of dispensational numerology had already been suggested to Haywood methodologically. Thus, while we regard as significant G. T. Haywood's claim that issues of creation were revealed to him, it is a claim that makes particular sense during the time in which it was made, for it embodies a concept of revelation that can only be appreciated in its historical and theological context.

50. Jacobsen, *Thinking in the Spirit*, 197.

6

Evolving Paradigms

Creationism as Pentecostal Variation on a Fundamentalist Theme

Gerald W. King

Introduction

"As Vinson Synan has observed," to quote Ronald Numbers, "the most outspoken defamers of Darwin during the Scopes trial 'were not the "Holy Rollers on Shinbone Ridge," as H. L. Mencken implied, but the Presbyterians, Baptists and Methodists in the Courthouse.'"[1] In other words, Pentecostals were not at the forefront of the evolutionary controversy which took place at the "monkey trial" in Dayton, Tennessee, in the summer of 1925. And yet neither were they completely oblivious to the events or their implications. While Numbers, a science historian, limits the role of Pentecostals in the Creation-Evolution dialogue, law

---

1. Vinson Synan, *The Old-Time Power* (Franklin Springs, GA: Advocate, 1973) 187, cited in Ronald L. Numbers, *Darwinism Comes to America* (Cambridge, MA: Harvard University Press, 1998) 119.

historian Edward J. Larson in his account of the Scopes trial implies that the contribution of Pentecostals was at least potentially legion. Together with holiness adherents, "Both brought to the antievolution crusade an army of loyal foot soldiers ready to fight any public-school teachings that threatened to undermine the religious faith of their children."[2] Yet just how far involved Pentecostals were in this fundamentalist fight has been little documented. Were they rabid antievolutionists or apathetic bystanders? This essay seeks to find the place of Pentecostals in the evolution debate prior to World War II.

Evolution as a Fundamentalist Theme

Evolution was predominantly a fundamentalist concern. Fundamentalism arose primarily as a conservative response to modernism which had encroached upon the mainline churches, particularly the northern branches of both the Presbyterian and Baptist denominations.[3] As such, their initial target had been biblical higher criticism with evolution being a comparatively minor issue. Taken together, higher criticism undermined the divine origin of Scripture while evolution undermined the divine origin of man.[4] Everywhere God's and consequently the churches' authority in society were crumbling. Many fundamentalists were not so much ruffled over the theory of evolution itself, as B. B. Warfield, James Orr, and others could admit of a limited role for it in creation, as they were over the place of man in God's order.[5]

Darwin's *Origin of Species* (Britain 1859, America 1860) did not have as much initial impact on the religious world as it did upon the scientific, and even then not until the after-effects of the Civil War had subsided.[6] Asa Gray, a botanist at Harvard University, became one of the earliest proponents of theistic evolution. Other scientists either

2. Edward J. Larson, *Summer for the Gods* (Cambridge, MA: Harvard University Press, 1997) 33.

3. George M. Marsden, *Fundamentalism and American Culture* (Oxford: Oxford University Press, 1980) 4.

4. This essay will use "man" in its early twentieth century context to describe "humankind" in the contemporary sense.

5. Mark A. Noll, *The Old Religion in a New World* (Grand Rapids, MI: Eerdmans, 2002) 193.

6. See Ronald L. Numbers, *The Creationists* (Berkeley, CA: University of California Press, 1992) 4–13; David O. Beale, *In Pursuit of Purity* (Greenville, SC: Unusual Publications, 1986) 80–81.

challenged Darwin's assumptions or adopted them in varying degrees. The religious significance of Darwin's theory was felt primarily after the publication of *The Descent of Man* (Britain 1870, America 1871), in which Darwin made anthropologically explicit what had been implicit in *Origin of Species*, namely that man had evolved from a lower order of primate. Princeton theologian Charles Hodge responded in 1874 with a short book which asked in its title *What is Evolution?* and answered in its pages, simply, "It is atheism."[7]

Having had their faith in biblical authority already eroded by higher criticism, and now confronted by the mounting scientific evidence for Darwinian thought, theistic evolution would come to typify the views of the emerging modernist worldview up to the turn of the century. Harry Emerson Fosdick, the arch-heretic of modernism, announced to his father one day while on break from Brown University that he had discarded his Sunday school faith in Adam and creation.[8] Books by leading theologians Henry Ward Beecher (*Evolution and Religion*, 1885) and Henry Drummond (*The Ascent of Man*, 1897) placed a progressive and hopeful spin on the evolutionary story. But for dedicated premillennialists like A. T. Pierson such remarks were indicative of the sad state of the church.[9] Dispensationalism in particular predicted the drifting away of an apostate church prior to the second coming of Christ. By the end of the century, premillennialists and postmillennialists held two competing visions of Christianity, one which expected the world to get better through education, the advancement of science, and the civilizing effects of religion, and the other which expected the world to get worse through the apostasy of the church and deteriorating moral conditions.

Fundamentalism coalesced around these premillennial and higher critical themes in the prophecy movement, which had two leading venues, Niagara (1880–1899) and the sporadically produced International Prophecy Conferences (1878–1918).[10] The events of World War I con-

---

7. Cited in Marsden, *Fundamentalism*, 19.

8. Harry Emerson Fosdick, *The Living of These Days: An Autobiography* (London: SCM, 1957) 252; George Dollar, *A History of Fundamentalism in America* (Greenville, SC: Bob Jones University Press, 1973) 93.

9. A. T. Pierson, *Many Infallible Proofs* (Chicago and New York: Revell, 1886) 213.

10. See Beale, *Pursuit*, 23–33, 47–67. The International Prophecy Conference (IPC) was originally known as American Bible and Prophecy Conference.

firmed fundamentalists' predictions relating to the demise of civilization, but more importantly to the movement, exposed the moral threat
which evolution and atheism posed.[11] At the beginning of the war
evangelicals were overwhelmingly pacifists who believed a Christian
America had no right to participate in a degenerate European war
that anticipated the coming of the antichrist. Further, German atroci-
ties reported in the American press provided ample verification that
evolution and skepticism would result in moral collapse. German ag-
gression was attributed to Nietzsche and his avowed evolutionary and
anti-Christian views. Where, after all, did higher criticism first appear
but in Germany and where but there had nihilism taken root?[12] Social
Darwinism had been played out on a national scale to devastating effect. Fundamentalists were alarmed that American culture was headed
in the same direction, and the fight to ban evolution from teaching in
public schools became their leading crusade. In the summer of 1918
leaders from the May 1918 Philadelphia IPC met in the conference
home of R. A. Torrey in Montrose, Pennsylvania, and planned their
assault in the form of a World's Christian Fundamentals Conference
for May 1919, also held in Philadelphia, which later birthed the World's
Christian Fundamentals Association (WCFA).[13]

Former Democratic presidential candidate William Jennings
Bryan led the charge against evolution, supported by Baptist leaders
William Bell Riley in Minneapolis and J. Frank Norris in Dallas. Their
efforts ultimately helped Tennessee pass the first antievolutionary ban
of its kind in the United States in 1925. They were less successful in
rallying the Southern Baptist Convention, which met in Memphis that
year, to endorse their views.[14] However, nearly half of the adult population in Tennessee identified themselves as Baptists, many of whom
did support passage of the law.[15] Methodists in the state tended to be
modernists, including their main educational institution, Vanderbilt

11. Timothy Weber, *Living in the Shadow of the Second Coming* (New York: Oxford
University Press, 1979) 105–8.

12. R. A. Torrey, *What the War Teaches; or, The Greatest Lessons of 1917* (Los
Angeles: Biola Book Room, 1918) in Joel A. Carpenter, ed., *Conservative Call to Arms*
(New York: Garland, 1988) 11.

13. Weber, *Shadow*, 161.

14. Larson, *Summer*, 97–99.

15. Larson, *Summer*, 48.

University. Pentecostals had established three denominations in the state, the Church of God in Christ in Memphis, the Church of God (CG) in Cleveland, just over twenty miles from Dayton, and a splinter group, the Church of God of Prophecy, also in Cleveland.

Pentecostals Enter the Fray, 1906–1930

Evolution was a little discussed topic for Pentecostals both before and after Scopes. However, when they spoke up, it was always on the side of fundamentalism. The earliest reference I could find to "evolution" came from William Durham in 1910, embedded in an attack upon modernism. "Instead of telling of the quickening power of faith in the Blood of Christ," he charged, "the ministers are preaching evolution; instead of preaching the Bible doctrine of regeneration, and calling men to repentance, they preach reform, and advise men to come under the moral influence of the church."[16] Elizabeth Sexton, editor of the *Bridegroom's Messenger* in Atlanta, was similarly perturbed. Referring to a number of scientific experts from Berlin to America, she predicted that evolution would "soon be swept away forever" along with all other theories and doctrines that, unlike Scripture, lacked a "firm foundation."[17]

Evolution received little press until the 1920s when Bryan began his campaign against it. At the 1920 General Council of the Assemblies of God (AG), Aimee Semple McPherson quipped, "When I was at high school I found that the books of physical geography were filled with the theory of evolution. My observation is that far more men become monkeys than monkeys men."[18] Jethro Walthall, prompted by a "man of skeptical trend of mind," defended the Bible's veracity at a conference in Wesson, Arkansas, on 31 December 1921. His discourse was partly dependent upon the Creation story, which could account for the "chaos" of pre-history that scientists stumbled to resolve.[19] An unsigned 1921 article in the *Pentecostal Evangel* complained of modernists who decried Noah's Flood as an act of God's judgment, notwithstanding

16. William Durham, "The Great Crisis Number Two," *Pentecostal Testimony* 1:5 (1 July 1910) 2.

17. Elizabeth Sexton, "Man's Work Made Manifest," *Bridegroom's Messenger* 4:75 (1 December 1910) 1.

18. "Council Crumbs," *Pentecost Evangel* 364–365 (30 October 1920) 3.

19. W. J. Waltham, "What Proof Have We that the Bible Is the Word of God," *Pentecostal Evangel* 440–441 (15 April 1922) 6.

the "conflicting theories of evolution" which they used to discredit Scripture as myth.[20] Professions supporting creationism increased in 1924. David McDowell had labelled Pentecostals as "fundamentalists plus," to which the editor, Stanley Frodsham, added, "None of us have the slightest sympathy with the Modernist's unproved and unprovable theories regarding the evolution of man."[21] Similar pronouncements on the "unprovability" of evolution had been made by fundamentalist lawyer Philip Mauro, whose *Evolution at the Bar* had been available through Gospel Publishing House of the AG since 1922.[22]

AG minister Frank Boyd, ever keen on current events, was clearly annoyed at Unitarian minister Charles Francis Potter's barrage upon fundamentalism after he erected a statue of a man emerging from a gorilla in front of his church. Theistic evolution was inconceivable to Boyd, who suggested such proponents be given the moniker "Mangorites"—short for "man-gorilla"; "It takes more blind credulity to believe such nonsense than it does to believe the simple statement, 'God created man in His own image.'"[23] The first full article dedicated to evolution was copied from a Toronto periodical, *The Evangelical Christian*, titled "Plants and Evolution," which proved that the un-evolved flax of today was identical in structure to flax found in a mummy's tomb from 1300 B.C.E.[24] Except for a long paragraph from C. J. Minter, the *Pentecostal Evangel* did not give space to the topic again until after the Scopes trial.

Despite its proximity to Dayton, the CG took little notice of the events. In 1919 an article had run in the *Church of God Evangel* in which an anonymous author declared that it did not matter to him whether man evolved from mud or monkey, either way it was a miracle—hardly

20. Anonymous, "A Just God and a Saviour," *Pentecostal Evangel* 422–423 (10 December 1921) 11.

21. [Stanley H. Frodsham], "'Fundamentalists Plus,'" *Pentecostal Evangel* 554 (12 July 1924) 4. Frodsham iterated that pentecostals stood "one hundred per cent" with those who taught inerrancy.

22. Philip Mauro, "Evolution at the Bar," *Pentecostal Evangel* 468–469 (28 October 1922) 5. Mauro was a 1920s version of modern antievolutionary lawyer Philip Johnson and assisted the prosecution in the Scopes trial; see Gordon Gardiner, *Champion of the Kingdom* (Sterling, VA: Grace Abounding Ministries, 1961) 65.

23. Frank Boyd, "Current Events and Topics of Interest," *Pentecostal Evangel* 554 (12 July 1924) 6.

24. Anonymous, "Plants and Evolution," *Pentecostal Evangel* 564 (20 September 1924) 6–7.

a fundamentalist approach.[25] The article was introduced with a caveat from Tomlinson that they ran it because some Pentecostal members could not avoid encountering "higher criticism" in their daily business. The *Church of God Evangel* again gave attention to evolution in June 1925 as the trial loomed a month away. An untitled piece likened the process of squaring Scripture and evolution through ignoring Genesis to that of discarding the foundation of one's house to make an airplane (i.e., having the house float in mid-air).[26] An excerpt on the same page suggested that those who accepted the doctrine of evolution had the same common sense as that of a monkey.

J. S. Llewellyn gave a tribute to Bryan following his death in Dayton five days after the trial ended. "The nation bows its head in mourning on account of the decease of one of the greatest men it ever produced," he commented.[27] Llewellyn had sat spellbound on the platform when "Col. Bryan" spoke on the Bible in Nashville the year before, calling books on evolution fit for the humour section of the library.[28] Llewellyn declared Bryan the "victor" in his latest battle against "infidelity under the guise of Evolution" and admonished believers to carry on his legacy: "On the battlefield where this noble hero fell let a mighty host assemble and make an offensive attack against those who would make our nation a nation of infidels."[29] Bryan's "martyrdom" at the hands of Clarence Darrow, as it was widely perceived, stirred the sympathy of millions of believers.

At the Scopes trial itself, however, the only appreciable Pentecostal presence came from the black Church of God in Christ, which had a small contingent camped near town. Darrow took time one weekend

25. Anonymous, "Opposition of Science Falsely so-called," *Church of God Evangel* 10:26 (28 June 1919) 1–2, quoted in Ronald L. Numbers, "Creation, Evolution, and Holy Ghost Religion: Holiness and Pentecostal Responses to Darwinism," *Religion and American Culture* 2:2 (Summer 1992) 134–35.

26. "[Untitled]," *Church of God Evangel* 16:24 (13 June 1925) 2.

27. J. S. Llewellyn, "The Nation Mourns," *Church of God Evangel* 16:31 (1 August 1925) 1.

28. W. J. Bryan, *Is the Bible True?* (Chicago: Bible Institute Colportage Association, 1924) 17. This was an address given at Ryman Auditorium, 24 January 1924, and made into a 28-page booklet by Moody Bible Institute. Llewellyn mistakenly calls it Rymer Auditorium. Bryan was a colonel during the Spanish-American War.

29. Llewellyn, "The Nation Mourns," 1.

to observe their worship and found them "better than Bryan."[30] The
Pentecostal Holiness Church virtually ignored evolution until George
Taylor wrote a series of articles on the first three chapters of Genesis
in the early 1930s.[31] A week after Bryan died the *Pentecostal Evangel*
ran a two-part series of an address he had given at Moody Church in
Chicago, hailing him as a "sturdy champion of the faith."[32] Here, Bryan
challenged any professor at any tax-receiving institution to explain away
Creation as set forth in the Bible.[33] His concern, the anxiety of many a
believer, he explained in quoting a hypothetical parent, "I sent my boy
or my girl [to college] a Christian and they came back an atheist."[34] This
attitude was similar to that of Mauro: "It is high time for parents to be
awakened out of sleep as to the dangers to which their children are exposed in our modern schools."[35] To Mauro, the halls of education were
filled with more peril than the streets of mean cities.

The *Latter Rain Evangel*, published by the AG-affiliated Stone
Church in Chicago, was aware of Bryan's campaign by at least 1923. His
sermon "Moses vs. Darwin," delivered at Moody Church, was reprinted
in two parts.[36] It was in fact the same speech printed in the *Pentecostal
Evangel* in 1925 as "Contending for the Faith" but in its full-form.
Editor and publisher Anna Reiff expressed the feeling of many when
she wrote:

> We know that our readers do not need this [sermon] for them-
> selves, but those who are sending their children to school need
> to be informed of what they are being taught, for we learn that

30. Larson, *Summer*, 142, 184.

31. Numbers, *Darwinism*, 119.

32. W. J. Bryan, "A Defense of the Faith once Delivered to the Saints," *Pentecostal Evangel* 608 (1 August 1925) 2.

33. Bryan championed the rights of the majority of taxpayers to dictate what ought to be taught in schools with their money—see Larson, *Summer*, 103–4. The article was copied from *Moody Church News*.

34. W. J. Bryan, "A Defense of the Faith once Delivered to the Saints," *Pentecostal Evangel* 609 (8 August 1925) 3.

35. Philip Mauro, *Evolution at the Bar* (1922; reprint, Swengel, PA: Reiner Publications, 1972) 72

36. W. J. Bryan, "Moses vs. Darwin," *Latter Rain Evangel* 15:5 (February 1923) 2–6; *Latter Rain Evangel* 15:6 (March 1923) 2–7.

even in the grades the pupils are taught by their instructors that the Bible is not true.[37]

Reiff offered a three months subscription for twenty-five cents for worried readers to send to their friends and family. "You may save them from being wrecked on the shoals of infidelity and help them to become established on the Rock of Ages," she implored; she also commended Byran's *In His Image* as the "greatest rebuttal of Darwinism ever written," although in fact relatively little of it assaulted evolution.[38]

A month after Bryan's homily appeared in the *Latter Rain Evangel*, German Pentecostal pastor C. B. Fockler railed against evolution in the Civic Auditorium of Milwaukee. He began his sermon where Bryan had, "In the beginning, God," but attributed his inspiration to a revelation he had received.[39] In response to a query from his son (who had learned about the evolution of the cosmos in school), "Where did the atom come from?" Fockler replied that if he stuck to that mode of inquiry he would not go far astray. His meditations fixed upon the grandeurs of creation (beginning with Crater Lake in Oregon) and the Fall and the restoration of humanity through the Cross, stating, "I do not like to think of my Heavenly Father looking anything like an ape or a monkey."[40] Reiff would echo Bryan's sentiments for parental control of school curriculum in 1924, blaming the increase in crime on the lack of moral and religious education in schools. "Filling the school-room with child experts in biology, zoology and geology does not train the children to honesty, trustworthiness and integrity," she opined.[41]

Evolutionary laws became a regional contest in the next five years with Arkansas, Louisiana, and Texas following Tennessee while Riley suffered a resounding defeat in Minnesota.[42] Few Pentecostals took a

37. A. Reiff, "A Solemn Warning," *Latter Rain Evangel* 15:5 (February 1923) 14.

38. Reiff, "Solemn Warning," 14. W. J. Bryan, *In His Image* (New York and Chicago: Revell, 1922) was advertised several times in *Pentecostal Evangel*. The book was taken from a lecture series at Union Theological Seminary.

39. C. B. Fockler, "In the Beginning It was Not So," *Latter Rain Evangel* 15:8 (May 1923) 18–20; address given March 25.

40. Fockler, "In the Beginning," 19.

41. [A. Reiff], "The Need of Religious Instruction," *Latter Rain Evangel* 16:5 (February 1924) 11.

42. Larson, *Summer*, 221–22; William Vance Trollinger, Jr., *God's Empire: William Bell Riley and Midwestern Fundamentalism* (Madison, WI: University of Wisconsin Press, 1990) 50–51.

lead in opposing evolution with the exception of McPherson, whose own faith had been challenged in high school over the issue.[43] Bryan had spoken at her Angelus Temple twice, inspiring her to lobby for legal curtailment in California in 1926. Her petition however was hampered by a civil trial over her mysterious disappearance to alleged Mexican drug traffickers that summer.[44] She later revived her efforts by debating atheist Charles Lee Smith in the early 1930s, asserting that evolution bred atheism.[45] She clung to the "gap theory" of Genesis promoted in the *Scofield Reference Bible*.[46] McPherson biographer Matthew Sutton depicts her as a mainstream Pentecostal reflecting the resurgence of fundamentalism in America—but in fact McPherson was in many ways an atypical Pentecostal.[47] After all, what other Pentecostal consulted with Charlie Chaplin for theatrical advice on sermon illustrations?

William Bennett used the trial in order to compare agnosticism with liberal Christianity. Indeed, theistic evolutionists had cooperated with Darrow's defensive manoeuvre to humiliate Bryan on the stand and defend intellectual freedom in the classroom. Bennett exposed this relationship to his best ability, seeing little demarcation between the outright scepticism of Darrow and the doubts of Potter.[48] One denied the possibility of human salvation through the Cross while the other denied its necessity. Soon after the trial ended, the *Pentecostal Evangel* promoted *A Scientific Man and the Bible* by Howard Kelly, a Johns Hopkins medical professor who appeared as the only scientist of credential on the list of potential witnesses for the prosecution of Scopes.[49]

43. Numbers, *Darwinism*, 119.

44. Matthew A. Sutton, *Aimee Semple McPherson and the Reconstruction of Christian America* (Cambridge, MA: Harvard University Press, 2007) 122.

45. Ronald L. Numbers, ed., *Creationism in Twentieth-Century America*, vol. 2, *Creation-Evolution Debates* (New York and London: Garland, 1995) 467.

46. Remember the "gap theory" attributed the old age of the earth to an unknown time gap between Gen 1:2 and 3. The "day-age theory" equated each day of creation as a long period of time.

47. Matthew Sutton, "'Between the Refrigerator and the Wildfire': Aimee Semple McPherson, Pentecostalism, and the Fundamentalist-Modernist Controversy," *Church History* 72:1 (March 2003) 159–88. Sutton contrasts her political differences with pentecostal leaders like AG head Ernest Williams demonstrating that her attitude was often at odds with mainstream pentecostals (*McPherson*, 215).

48. William Bennett, "The Dayton Affair Again," *Pentecostal Evangel* 615 (19 September 1925) 13.

49. Howard A. Kelly, "A Scientific Man and the Bible," *Pentecostal Evangel* 614

Physician W. S. Manners quoted a litany of scientists who denounced evolution, any number of which could have been pulled from popular books by Bryan, Mauro, George McCready Price's *The Phantom of Organic Evolution* (1924), or John Horsch's *Modern Religious Liberalism* (1920), the latter two of which became available to Pentecostal readers shortly after Scopes.[50] The doctor however chastised fundamentalists for thinking they could change the public's mind through legislation. "Evolution is here to stay!" he declared; employing a typical dispensationalist argument, he continued, "Evolution and its concomitant [sic] theories is [sic] the great final apostasy from 'the Christian faith once for all delivered to the saints', as foretold by Christ and His apostles."[51] While short on analysis, Manners could be long on praxis.

Charles Robinson, lawyer-turned-pastor-turned-assistant editor at *The Pentecostal Evangel*, writing under his pen-name "Rajoma," began his campaign against evolution in April 1926. He insisted that his "purpose in writing these words is to jar the minds of parents whose children are being taught evolution at school. Don't think it doesn't matter much."[52] Robinson appealed to the notorious case of Leopold and Loeb, two university students who murdered an innocent to see if they could commit the perfect crime. The pair had been represented by Darrow, who saved them from the death penalty on the grounds of psychological determinism—they were conditioned to kill because of their evolutionary convictions.[53] Evolution and Christianity were opposing philosophies, Robinson chided, and if children accept the one they will reject the other—Leopold and Loeb were proof positive.

For the most part, articles lambasting evolution in Pentecostal periodicals were reprinted from fundamentalist papers or were brief excerpts based on the same.[54] One article by a Pentecostal, identified only

(12 September 1925) 15; Larson, *Summer*, 130–31. See also Howard A. Kelly, *A Scientific Man and the Bible: A Personal Testimony* (Philadelphia: Sunday School Times, 1925).

50. W. S. Manners, "Evolution," *Pentecostal Evangel* 621 (7 November 1925) 4–5; "Good Books," *Pentecostal Evangel* 608 (1 August 1925) 15 [Price]; "Good Books," *Pentecostal Evangel* 625 (5 December 1925) 24 [Horsch].

51. Manners, "Evolution," 5.

52. [C. E. Robinson], "Some Logical Results of a Belief in Evolution," *Pentecostal Evangel* 643 (17 April 1926) 3.

53. Bryan used Darrow's arguments against him at the Scopes trial.

54. E.g., P. M., "The Bee's Knees: A Challenge to Evolutionists," *Pentecostal Evangel* 650 (5 June 1926) 4–5, from *Bible Champion*; Anonymous, "Another Hoax Exposed,"

by the initial "C."—possibly Charles Robinson—took a virulent jab at
Darwin and his supporters, lining up the usual evolutionary naysayers
of Agassiz, Lord Kelvin, and "Frieshmann" [sic].[55] The writer surmised
that the priests of Baal had been evolutionists as they had worshipped
the god of nature; thus, modern science was little better than ancient
heathenism. Missionary Mrs. Watt in Central Africa reported how the
tribesmen laughed when her husband told them that some white men
believed humans were derived from apes.[56] The natives considered the
monkey much less cunning than jackals and knew they did not inter-
breed to produce hybrid species as the theory implied. They were no
fools, she noted with confidence.

The first sustained decrial of evolution in the *Pentecostal Evangel*
came from Dr. A. P. Gouthey, a Presbyterian evangelist from Seattle who
frequently preached in AG churches and gave the 1928 Baccalaureate
address at Central Bible Institute.[57] Gouthey delved into the inability
of proponents to agree on a definition of evolution and their failure to
explain either the origins of the universe or the origins of life. "All hail
Nothing!" he mocked. "Thou didst lay the foundations of the universe
upon nothing, using nothing as thy building material, and out of thy
nothingness . . . thou hast created the multiplied millions of stars."[58]
Gouthey accepted an old earth but noted the apparent lack of intermediary life forms in the geological record.[59] Citing three surveys regarding the paucity of Bible knowledge among the day's youth, he sounded
the fundamentalist trumpet-blast over declining morals with an im-
passioned plea for his listeners to purge their churches of modernist

---

Pentecostal Evangel 751 (9 June 1928) 5, from *Alliance Weekly*; A. I. Brown, "The Story
of the Apis," *Pentecostal Evangel* 771 (3 November 1928) 4, from *The King's Business*.

55. C., "The Evolution Fable," *Pentecostal Evangel* 739 (17 March 1928) 3;
"Frieschmann" is probably Albert Fleischmann, who taught zoology at the University
of Erlangen.

56. Mrs. Watt, "Not so Foolish as to Believe in Evolution," *Pentecostal Evangel* 755
(7 July 1928) 13.

57. Frank Boyd, "Another Wonderful Year at C.B.I.," *Pentecostal Evangel* 751 (9 June
1928) 6; C. E. Robinson, "The Big Fish Story," *Pentecostal Evangel* 754 (30 June 1928) 3.
Gouthey's CBI address was titled "The How of Best Living."

58. A. P. Gouthey, "Is Evolution an Established Fact?" *Pentecostal Evangel* 756 (21
July 1928) 7.

59. A. P. Gouthey, "Is Evolution an Established Fact?" *Pentecostal Evangel* 757 (28
July 1928) 4.

ministers (hardly a problem among Pentecostals) and petition schools and politicians to curb the teaching of evolution.[60] There is no indication in the periodicals that they heeded his advice on political activism, however.

CG Overseer F. J. Lee told the story of creation in April 1926, contrasting the two competing theories appertaining to man's origins: "the genuine Christian belief" of special creation versus "evolution by dead force."[61] Lee's treatment of evolutionary claims was painted in the broadest of strokes, summarized in five paragraphs, touching upon the progression of life through the geological ages with man emerging from "a hairy quadruped." He attacked evolutionists *ad hominem*: "the greater part of them smoke, chew, take the name of the Lord in vain, and many of them drink, and practice many other things contrary to the Word of God." He preferred to trust a man like Paul who revered Christ than infidels who didn't. According to his Syriac Bible, Paul urged Timothy (1 Tim 6:20) to avoid profane babblings and "the opposition of false science," which Lee applied to evolution—a satanic ploy to dupe the world. Alluding to theistic evolution, he remarked that God did not throw out an atom into space and say, "Make something of yourself." God would not have received honor in it, and honor is what Satan would steal from Him. In sum, the debasing story of evolution was far inferior to the noble story of creation in Genesis in which man stood at the pinnacle.

Franklin Bowles provided a long but crude exposé of evolution in July. Bowles adhered to the "flood geology" of G. M. Price, proposing that the various species were suddenly fossilized in the strata, evidence of a catastrophic worldwide deluge. Starting his defense with an inerrantist view of Scripture, he wrote, "Those who accept the literal translation of the Bible, [sic] have no great difficulty in accepting the Genesis account of creation."[62] A strict interpretation brokered no room for compromise; either Moses and the Bible or Darwin and evolution were right. In the second half of the article, he exploited the gaps between species and ridiculed the "descent of man" theory. The ancestors of evo-

---

60. A. P. Gouthey, "Is Evolution an Established Fact?" *Pentecostal Evangel* 758 (4 August 1928) 6–7.

61. F. J. Lee, "The Story of Creation," *Church of God Evangel* 17:13 (3 April 1926) 1–2; the rest of the Lee quotes in this paragraph are from p. 1 of this article.

62. F. Bowles, "God, Science, Evolution, and the Bible," *Church of God Evangel* 17:29 (24 July 1926) 1.

lutionists may have hung from trees, but so far as he knew his may have only hung from a rope about the neck, he joked.[63] Quoting evolutionist William Bateson, Bowles denied that the variation within species proved the evolution of species. His attempt to debunk evolution was anything but systematic. Aside from a brief mention in March 1928 of evolution as one of several signs of the end of this age, the *Church of God Evangel* abandoned the topic until 1934.[64]

Pentecostal Variation, 1930–1940

In the 1930s, while fundamentalism retreated from society, the AG stepped up its effort to combat evolution. Stanley Frodsham presented the fight in his regular news column, successively titled "The Editor's Notebook," "The Passing and the Permanent," "The Outlook and the Uplook," and "The Dying World and the Living Word." These tidbits of current events, culled from newspapers and evangelical magazines, demonstrate how closely Frodsham followed the dispensationalist view of the world then dominant in fundamentalist circles. Communism, the League of Nations, Mussolini, the Federal Council of Churches, and the virtual dictatorship of President Roosevelt were all indications that the end was drawing nigh. Evolution appeared some twenty times in his columns during the decade, usually from single paragraphs to a printed column in length.

German-born AG evangelist Otto Klink churned out a 51-page booklet titled *Why I am not an Evolutionist* in 1931.[65] He supplied four objections that the theory could not account for: the origin of life, the origin of the various species, the gaps in the geological record, and the differences between mankind and the brute. Klink was well-educated and read widely, reciting a variety of contemporary sources and scientific authorities. He was however no scientist and relied on secondary knowledge for his arguments. Klink found no evidence that man had

63. F. Bowles, "God, Science, Evolution, and the Bible," *Church of God Evangel* 17:30 (31 July 1926) 1.

64. E. J. Boehmer, "Some Signs of the Last Days: We are Living in the Saturday Evening Age of Time," *Church of God Evangel* 19:9 (3 March 1928) 1–2.

65. Otto Klink, *Why I am not an Evolutionist* (Springfield, MO: Gospel Publishing House, 1931). Klink had two other titles along this theme: *Why I am not an Atheist* (1931) and *Why I am not a Modernist* (1938). Bertrand Russell's infamous lecture "Why I am not a Christian" was delivered in March 1927 and was likely the source for Klink's titles.

advanced physically, intellectually, or morally from ancient civilizations despite technological inventiveness. "We do not speak more poetically than Homer or Ovid or Virgil," he observed, "not more philosophically than Plato or Socrates, not more dramatically than Sophocles, or shorter and more to the point than the Spartans, or sweeter than David or Job. . . . Kindly explain that, Mr. Evolutionist."[66] Klink dismissed the antiquity of man like Piltdown and Java as either hoaxes or fabrications.[67] Klink represents this transition from evolution as a curiosity to evolution as a serious challenge to Pentecostal belief and the increasing alignment of Pentecostals to fundamentalist positions.

In his writings Charles Elmo Robinson championed "design intelligence" without assailing the specific points of evolution. *The Adventures of Blacky the Wasp* (1936), which chronicled the history of a fictional insect from birth to motherhood, aimed at instructing children in God's providence in nature.[68] Robinson did not fret over the moral implications of Blacky's children eating the innards of a juicy, living katydid but did stress the innate sense which God gave such creatures to know how to build nests and gather food without having to be told. "Haven't we a wonderful God who makes Blacky know just how to do all of that hard work?"[69] Robinson continued the argument from design in *God and His Bible* (1939), an antimodernist volume geared towards adults. Reminiscent of William Paley's natural theology, Robinson regarded the construction of the watch and the arrangement of bricks to form a wall as evidences of intelligence in nature.[70] He focused both here and in other stories for children on the properties of water and the instincts of animals in order to disparage any notion that our world had been formed by chance.[71]

66. Klink, *Evolutionist*, 35.

67. See Klink, *Evolutionist*, 40–44, for his treatment of pre-historic man.

68. C. E. Robinson, *The Adventures of Blacky the Wasp* (Springfield, MO: Gospel Publishing House, 1936); "Attention—Parent and Teachers—A New Book," *Pentecostal Evangel* 1139 (7 March 1936) 13.

69. Robinson, *Adventures*, 87.

70. C. E. Robinson, *God and His Bible* (Springfield, MO: Gospel Publishing House, 1939) 53 [watch], 112–13 [bricks]. Chapter 14 was written "to confute" "Evolutionist Teaching." Robinson quotes from Paley's *Horæ Paulinæ* on 124—proving St. Paul wrote the thirteen epistles traditionally attributed to him.

71. Robinson, *God and His Bible*, 118–20, on water; see also Robinson's *The Gnat's Lifeboat and Other Stories* (Springfield, MO: Gospel Publishing House, 1936).

Myer Pearlman gave little thought to the subject of evolution, addressing the topic in just three paragraphs. In one place he viewed it as "a plausible and fascinating theory" except that it wasn't true.[72] In another he rejected evolution because of the gulf between man and the kingdom of animals.[73] Yet again, examining the supposed improvement of civilization, he viewed nations to be ruled by devolution (which Frodsham would label "Devil-ution") and not evolution.[74] You can train a monkey to act like a human, but you cannot teach it anything about God, he concluded.

In the early thirties several short articles attempted to prove the "scientific" reliability of Scripture, a fundamentalist theme seldom used before then. Early Pentecostals had defended Holy Writ on its theological claims but rarely on its material claims. Now, quoting from the evangelical periodical *Revelation*, "[The Bible] tells us many things which are above science, but it tells us nothing which is against science."[75] Frodsham commented, "While the words of scientists are are [sic] ever changing, the Word of God abideth certain and sure forever."[76] Titles like "The Uncertainty of Science" and "The Bible and Science" suggested an awareness of fundamentalist issues which would have seemed out of place in the early years of the movement.[77]

Nobody typified this alignment towards fundamentalism more than the evangelist J. N. Hoover, former pastor of First Baptist Church in Santa Cruz, California. Hoover's tracts on Communism, the National Recovery Administration and atheism could have sold as steadily through "Scripture Truth Depot" as "Gospel Publishing House." Hoover

72. Myer Pearlman, "Some Modern Definitions," *Pentecostal Evangel* 971 (29 October 1932) 10.

73. Myer Pearlman, *The Heavenly Gift* (Springfield, MO: Gospel Publishing House, 1935) 39.

74. Myer Pearlman, *Daniel Speaks Today* (Springfield, MO: Gospel Publishing House, 1943) 64; Stanley Frodsham, "A Bloody Century," *Pentecostal Evangel* 1314 (15 July 1939) 8. Frodsham made a similar pronouncement on the 'devolution' of civilization from Daniel 2; see his "Sudden Destruction," *Pentecostal Evangel* 847 (10 May 1930) 4.

75. [Stanley H. Frodsham], "Is the Bible Unscientific?" *Pentecostal Evangel* 986 (18 February 1933) 7. *Revelation* was edited by Donald Grey Barnhouse, pastor of Tenth Presbyterian Church in Philadelphia.

76. [Stanley H. Frodsham], "The Uncertainty of Science," *Pentecostal Evangel* 1004 (24 June 1933) 14.

77. See [Frodsham], " Uncertainty of Science," and [Stanley H. Frodsham], "The Bible and Science," *Pentecostal Evangel* 1087 (23 February 1935) 8.

told audiences over a Kansas City radio station (KWKC), "Evolution is the chair of religion in the school of modern theology, and you are taking atheism in small doses when you accept the theories of evolution," and he accused liberal theologians of inflicting more harm on the church "than all the motion pictures combined."[78] By discrediting divine creation, he preached to another group, "[Man] drifts into the fog of egotism, and dies on the rocks of atheism."[79] Hoover's basic thesis throughout was that evolution could not account for the origin of life, and his primary fear was that it undermined faith in Scripture. Not to worry, however, for agnosticism could only raise a "feeble" hand against the Almighty.[80]

Fresno minister John Elsom gave a series of lectures on the origins of man in 1934. Elsom saw in "sand, mud and rocks" confirmation for Moses' account of creation.[81] Elsom tried to reconcile the days of Genesis with the geological ages, just as Riley or Bryan might have done. The order of creation matched that known to science, with marine preceding land animals in appearance. The earth had been covered in vapor in its earliest stages and lifted later to reveal the sun and stars, thus accounting for the appearance of the sun on the fourth day. "Absolute science is always in agreement with truth and truth with science," he postulated tautologically.[82] God was certainly capable of arranging the chemicals of the earth to form living creatures as we know them today in as many varieties as He chose, but no new species was known to have evolved from another. The story of evolution was less credulous than the story of Genesis, for a hungry fish seeking food on land would certainly have died there and not passed on his "desire" to the next generation—unless we are to believe that man will soon sprout a third arm, for myriads of humans have professed a "desire" for an extra hand.[83] Today's fish were too self-satisfied to leave their aquatic existence, which was to Elsom

---

78. J. N. Hoover, "The Origin of Man," *Word & Work* 57:3 (March 1935) 8.

79. J. N. Hoover, "The Origin of Life," *Latter Rain Evangel* 27:8 (May 1936) 20. Parts of this sermon were rearranged from "The Origin of Man."

80. J. N. Hoover, "Origin of Life," 22.

81. John R. Elsom, "Man Created or Evolved?" *Word & Work* 56:1 (January 1934) 7. Unfortunately, the gap in issues from March through May give us an incomplete record of Elsom's thought.

82. John R. Elsom, "Man Created or Evolved?" *Word & Work* 56:2 (February 1934) 8.

83. Elsom, "Man Created or Evolved?" 9.

the only plausible explanation why we did not see evolution now in action (if it were true).[84]

The area, however, where evolution was most critically thwarted was in the Sunday School literature. Most references were slipped into a lesson tangentially, such as where one commentator found a proven case for evolution in the resurrection of Christ and the transformation of our earthly bodies into heavenly ones.[85] "Evolution" was yet future and sudden. Other times an entire lesson would counteract evolution, such as in the CG lesson for October 1931. A Miss Jackson's proof against the doctrine of evolution consisted of four points establishing the authority of Scripture: the changed character of saints, the unity of the Bible, its claim to inspiration, and the fulfillment of prophecy.[86] That was reason sufficient enough for her and the adolescent students.

Concern erupted at AG headquarters when they discovered that evolution had infiltrated the lower grades of the local schools.[87] As the sapling needed more care than the fully developed tree, so children needed godly guidance before error could whisk their hearts away, they reckoned.[88] To offset the "awful tide of evil," the editors at *The Pentecostal Evangel* decided to launch a new periodical in 1936 for the consumption of the youngsters at home, the *Primary Story Paper*. "The first issues contain the story of creation, told in a simple way, emphasizing the truth that God created man in His own image," they informed.[89] The publication was intended as a supplement to Sunday School instruction.

Gospel Gleaners, an AG organ for older children, targeted evolution on several occasions after its 1928 inception. In one story by Robinson, "Tom and Betty" argue the merits of evolution after Betty received her Pentecostal baptism and urged Tom to get saved—otherwise she would not marry him.[90] "You have an unproven theory," she tells him, "while I

---

84. John R. Elsom, "Man Created or Evolved?" *Word & Work* 56:6 (June 1934) 12.

85. Anonymous, "Jesus Rises from the Dead (Easter Lesson)," *The Pentecostal Teachers' Quarterly* 6:2 (1932) 104.

86. E. Jackson, "Topic: Evolution," *The Lighted Pathway* 3:4 (October 1931) 14–15.

87. Anonymous, "Does Your Heart Respond to this?" *Pentecostal Evangel* 1123 (9 November 1935) 5.

88. Anonymous, "To Help the Little Ones," *Pentecostal Evangel* 1140 (14 March 1936) 3.

89. Anonymous, "Does Your Heart Respond to this?" 5.

90. Rajoma, "Tom and Betty," *Gospel Gleaners* 5:3.1 (6 March 1932) 3.

have an experience."[91] Tom drifted into atheism, hoping to be as famous as Bob Ingersoll, but was imprisoned for forgery and forced in his cell to consider Betty's argument pertaining to the harmony of the beehive, which could not have simply "evolved."[92] The outcome resulting in Tom's conversion seemed predestined under Robinson's hand. Later articles became more direct, appealing to young scholars minds rather than their emotions. "The Bee's Knees," "The Story of the Apis," "Whence? How about Evolution?" (a five part series), "Is the Bible Unscientific?" by Methodist fundamentalist leader L. W. Munhall, and "Present Day Science" by Price, all dared evolutionists to account for their theory.[93]

The AG became increasingly disturbed over the "Modernistic" bent of the International Sunday School Lessons, developed by the Religious Education Council and used by most denominations of the day. Moody professor Clarence Benson had estimated that two-thirds of the Bible had not been covered by the latest seven-year lesson plan, but the AG thought the fraction was closer to three-fourths.[94] In the midst of preparing a new lesson plan, headquarters was approached by Standard Publishing Company, a fundamentalist curriculum provider in Cincinnati.[95] The editor at Standard was equally alarmed with the modernist leanings and hesitated at printing the next cycle. He had discovered a previous three-year curriculum "by very godly men," likely "The Whole Bible Course" of the World's Christian Fundamentals Association, published in 1923.[96] Naturally, the new lesson, likewise called "The Whole Bible Course," began at "the beginning"—Genesis. The AG supplemented this material in its teacher's quarterly and in its children's literature.[97]

---

91. Rajoma, "Tom and Betty," *Gospel Gleaners* 5:3.2 (13 March 1932) 1.

92. Rajoma, "Tom and Betty," *Gospel Gleaners* 5:4.1 (3 April 1932) 2.

93. Munhall supported Aimee Semple McPherson's Philadelphia campaign in 1921 and offered to ordain her in ministry, which she turned down. She did accept a license, though.

94. Anonymous, "The 'Whole Bible' Course for our Sunday School," *Pentecostal Evangel* 1144 (11 April 1936) 8.

95. Standard had printed the first "uniform lesson" when it originated in 1873.

96. Anonymous, "The Whole Bible Sunday School Lesson Series," *The Searchlight* 6:43 (7 September 1923) 1; Anonymous, "'Christian Fundamentals' Sunday-School Lessons," *Sunday School Times* 65:33 (18 August 1923) 485. The WCFA only ran the series once and discontinued its use.

97. Myer Pearlman, "Creation," *The Adult and Young People's Teachers' Quarterly* 10:1 (January-March 1937) 3–7. The January issue of the youth magazine *The Christ's*

Conclusion

Pentecostals did not start out as fundamentalists. Their churches were not ravaged by modernism, evolutionists did not ply their trade under their cloak, and higher critics did not disparage miracles from their pulpits. They were however attuned to the issues facing conservatives in the mainline denominations where such things occurred. They heartily ascribed to the "five points of fundamentalism" but were too busy promoting their distinctive faith and combating their own internal struggles to do much about it. The fundamentalist-modernist controversy was not their fight, and thus they largely stayed clear of the battles except to remind their own flock on occasion of the dangers of modernism and the Holy Spirit's protection from its unsound doctrine.

At the beginning, Pentecostals shared with fundamentalists a passion for lost souls and the anticipated soon-return of the Lord Jesus Christ. By degrees they adopted the dispensationalist view of the world with its doomsday predictions of a gloomy end. Evolution was just one piece that figured into this dispensational puzzle. Bryan's antievolutionary crusade exposed Pentecostals to these perils more than any other event. It is here that they began to speak up about the issues waylaying fundamentalists. To be sure, most of their rhetoric was reserved for the faithful with the noteworthy exception of McPherson. And most of what they did say was gleaned from fundamentalist authors to whom they often turned.

Ronald Numbers speculates that the lack of Pentecostal participation in the antievolutionary statutes "may have reflected their general indifference to formal education and, hence, to what American youth were learning in school, or it may have resulted from their intense focus on receiving the gifts of the Spirit rather than decoding the Word."[98] In fact, it was the first point which spurred them into action at all. As Robinson exhorted parents above, "Don't think it doesn't matter much." Insulated in their own religious ceremonies, adults had little cause to fret over the "evil" of evolution, but when it came to the education of

---

Ambassadors Herald is non-extant and evolution only gets brief mention in February and March. E. Yngve Olson, "'God's Foolishness,'" *The Christ's Ambassadors Herald* 10:2 (February 1937) 7, and Glenn M. Horst, "The Church on Fire," *The Christ's Ambassadors Herald* 10:3 (March 1937) 8; "The Wasp Surgeon," *Gospel Gleaners* 10:1 (January 1937) 8 (likely written by Charles Robinson).

98. Numbers, *Darwin*, 119.

their children in the public schools, all bets were off. Early Pentecostals, those who came into the experience as adults, had relatively little training above a rudimentary education. Evolution in their day was presented most often at the universities which they did not attend.

By the 1920s however evolution had been introduced into an expanding high school system, and, as the AG noticed, even down to the tykes below. Further, their growing numbers in the 1920s and their rising fortunes—Pentecostals were snapping up abandoned denominational churches in the inner cities or constructing their own edifices in the more rural areas during the early 1920s—inevitably meant exposure to the wider culture and the institutions which ruled it. Unable any longer to avoid the menace of evolutionism, they joined the battle. And because they lacked the formal education of fundamentalists and the larger audiences they commanded, Pentecostals turned to their literature for help.

By the 1930s Pentecostals were adopting fundamentalist arguments as their own. Literary spokesmen like Frodsham, Robinson, and Klink put evolution towards the forefront of the movement, and an ex-fundamentalist like Hoover could extol the doctrines with Pentecostal zeal. The AG, with its history of connections to more fundamentalist-minded organizations like the Christian and Missionary Alliance and the Baptists, had more exposure to these currents than did the CG, which stuck more closely to its Wesleyan-holiness roots. There were also regional differences—fundamentalism and the AG grew more in urban areas in the north and west while fundamentalism came later to the CG's stronghold in the south. The shifting alignment towards fundamentalism which had begun in the 1920s in the AG lagged by a decade in the CG—evidenced by S. W. Latimer's dispensational teaching in 1937.[99]

By the late 1930s fundamentalists and Pentecostals were finding themselves in even closer alliance as illustrated by the teaming up of the resources of the AG and Standard Publishing. The *Pentecostal Evangel* also assailed modernism more directly while Klink wrote *Why I am not a Modernist* in 1938 and journalist-turned-Baptist-turned-Pentecostal evangelist Mae Eleanor Frey an antimodernist novel *The Minister* in

---

99. Latimer penned six articles on the dispensational ages in *Church of God Evangel* in March and April.

1939.[100] Pentecostals had grown sufficiently in numbers to generate the notice and perhaps reluctant respect of fundamentalists. On their side, many of the "old-guard" fundamentalists like R. A. Torrey, C. I. Scofield, and James Gray had died, paving the way for a younger generation of evangelicals who were less threatened and less critical of Pentecostal enthusiasm. Fundamentalists had clout and Pentecostals had followers. They needed each other—and ultimately found each other in the National Association of Evangelicals. The foray against evolution helped forge this alliance both philosophically and emotionally.

100. Otto J. Klink, *Why I am not a Modernist* (Minneapolis, MN: Northern Gospel Publishing House, 1938); Mae Eleanor Edick Frey, *The Minister* (Springfield, MO: Gospel, 1939). *The Minister* features a romantic relationship between a modernist pastor and a pentecostal transplant into his fold.

PART THREE

Theological Explications

7

Preaching the "Full Gospel" in the Context of Global Environmental Crises

Shane Clifton

Introduction

It is the case, sadly, that environmental concern has rarely if ever been an important element of the Pentecostal message. By way of illustration, a review of the nine decades of the *Australian Evangel*, published monthly by the Assemblies of God in Australia, could not locate a single article that focused attention on ecological concerns and environmental ethics, except the occasional reference to environmental destruction as proof of end-times prophecy.[1] The situation in the global Pentecostal academy is not much better,[2] a fact that is noteworthy given that there

1. See the complete collection of the Australian Evangel (in all its manifestations) available at the Pentecostal Heritage Centre, Southern Cross College. Part of this collection has been digitalized, and is available at http://aps.webjournals.org/.

2. This is, however, changing, as is apparent in this present conference. See also Augustinus Dermawan, "The Spirit in Creation and Environmental Stewardship: A Preliminary Pentecostal Response Toward Ecological Theology," *Asian Journal of Pentecostal Studies* 6:2 (2003) 199–217; Amos Yong, *The Spirit Poured Out on All Flesh: Pentecostalism and the Possibility of Global Theology* (Grand Rapids, MI: Baker, 2005) ch. 7.

has been a proliferation of academic publications by the wider church in the field of ecotheology in recent decades, as well as the criticisms (and encouragements) given by influential scholars of the movement such as Walter Hollenweger.[3] Our purpose in this essay is to ask why this might be so; what is it about Pentecostal culture and praxis that has, at least to date, prevented the development of an ecological dimension to its understanding of the gospel? Thereafter, our concern is to attempt to locate symbolic dimensions of Pentecostal identity, which might be used to facilitate such development, with the goal of helping twenty first century Pentecostals to continue to claim, along with their forebears, that they are proponents of a "full gospel."

It is important to begin with the observation that Pentecostals are not alone in their failure to prioritise environmental issues and develop an ecological ethos. The Christian tradition as a whole and, in particular, fundamentalist movements and denominations, have been widely criticised for their "otherworldly" orientation, and their concomitant dogmatic rejection of "this worldly" concerns, including concern for the contemporary global environmental crises. It can be argued that it is the appropriation of fundamentalist categories of faith that is largely responsible for the more socially restrictive, and environmentally ignorant, aspects of Pentecostal culture. Harvey Cox (along with other commentators such as Margaret Poloma[4]) suggests that there exists in Pentecostalism a "contest between the fundamentalist and the experientialist impulse."[5] This leaves Cox wondering whether the substantial influence of the over 400 million Pentecostal Christians worldwide will be a force that "opens people to new outpourings of the divine Spirit," and thereby builds harmonious, open (and earthkeeping) communities,

---

3. Walter Hollenweger, as early as the late 1978, challenged Pentecostals to develop a pneumatology capable of motivating Christian responsibility now, in this present life (rather than focus primarily on the future). This challenge included the need to develop a pneumatology that was not subordinated to ecclesiology but that understood the Spirit as the "Spirit of Life" which links and values all creation; see Hollenweger's articles such as "Creator Spiritus: The Challenge of Pentecostal Experience to Pentecostal Theology," *Theology* 81 (1978) 32–40, and "All Creatures Great and Small: Towards a Pneumatology of Life," in David Martin and Peter Mullen, eds., *Strange Gifts? A Guide to Charismatic Renewal* (Oxford: Blackwell, 1984) 41–53.

4. Margaret Poloma, *The Assemblies of God at the Crossroads: Charisma and Institutional Dilemmas* (Knoxville, TN: University of Tennessee Press, 1989).

5. Harvey Cox, *Fire from Heaven: The Rise of Pentecostal Spirituality and the Reshaping of Religion in the Twenty-first Century* (Reading, MA: Addison-Wesley, 1995) 310.

or otherwise a force that rejects new colours and stokes "the fires of xenophobia and hostility"[6] and, we might add, remains unconcerned about environmental issues.

This essay follows a similar assumption. In the first place, we shall consider the inadequate and undeveloped theology of creation, borrowed from fundamentalist Christian theologies, that have led to a narrow Pentecostal proclamation of the gospel and restricted the development of an ecological ethos. We shall then ask whether those same elements of Pentecostal self-understanding, oriented away from fundamentalism and toward the experience of the creative and liberative power of the Spirit, might actually be capable of sustaining a thoroughgoing ecological revisioning.

A Critical Ecological Analysis of Pentecostalism's Theology of Creation

The place to begin in seeking to understand a Pentecostal theology of creation is the recognition that the movement's outlook is coloured by its eschatological orientation. Commenting on the situation in early Pentecostalism, various commentators have observed that the most popular theme of preaching and teaching was the second coming of Christ.[7] Taking the premillennialist position, Pentecostals read world events through literalistic interpretations of biblical apocalyptic literature, looking forward to the immanent return of Jesus which was to be accompanied by the rapture of the saints and subsequent global devastation. While acting as a motivating force for missionary activity, premillennial pessimism has been blamed for the tendency of twentieth century Pentecostalism to ignore the social responsibility of the church. As Dwight Wilson observes, "since the end is near, [classical] Pentecostals are indifferent to social change and have rejected the reformist methods of the optimistic postmillennialists and have concentrated on 'snatching brands from the fire' and letting social reforms

---

6. Cox, *Fire from Heaven*, 310.

7. See, for example, D. William Faupel, *The Everlasting Gospel: The Significance of Eschatology in the Development of Pentecostal Thought* (Sheffield: Sheffield, 1996). In respect to the Australian context from which I write, see Barry Chant, "The Spirit of Pentecost: Origins and Development of the Pentecostal movement in Australia, 1870–1939" (PhD diss., Macquarie University, 1999) 476.

result from humankind being born again."[8] This indifference extends to the movement's concern for environmental matters, since there is little point in focusing attention on a doomed environment, made even less significant by the shadow of eternal life in heaven (or death in hell).

Of course Pentecostals are not alone in conceiving of the future of creation in apocalyptic terms. Also, the eschatological fervour that categorized early Pentecostalism is, in the twenty first century, not as entrenched as it once was.[9] While this has given rise to some concern about the motivation for Pentecostal missionary activity,[10] it does pave the way for a more positive attitude toward the future of the earth. What is noteworthy, however, is that the changing eschatological outlook has not yet resulted in substantial developments in the movement's ecological ethos. Eschatology is only one aspect of Pentecostalism's theology of creation, which is often framed at the other end of history with six day, young earth creationism. This fundamentalist outlook finds its theological impetus in literalistic readings of the Scripture and in the affirmation of the uniqueness of humankind; the complete distinction between intelligent humanity and the "dumb" ape.

Apart from the hermeneutical and scientific issues surrounding this fundamentalist understanding of the beginnings of the universe, the ecological problem relates to the explicit setting of humankind above nature. Douglas Hall, in critiquing the Western church's conception and application of the doctrine of the *imago dei*, argues that Christian theology has too readily created a hierarchical evaluation of creation which "bequeaths to all subsequent Christian anthropology a view of the human as being incapable of solidarity with other creatures and, in fact, hardly a creature at all."[11] While Hall's critique is of the entire Western Christian tradition, particularly its establishment of oppositions between body and soul, his analysis is relevant to movements which hold to six day

---

8. Dwight J. Wilson, "Pentecostal Perspectives on Eschatology," in Stanley M. Burgess and Eduard Van Der Maas, eds., *The New International Dictionary of Pentecostal and Charismatic Movements* (Grand Rapids, MI: Zondervan, 2002) 601–5, 605.

9. See Shane Clifton, "An Analysis of the Developing Ecclesiology of the Assemblies of God in Australia" (PhD diss., Australian Catholic University, 2005) 262–64.

10. Mark Hutchinson, "The New Thing God is Doing: The Charismatic Renewal and Classical Pentecostalism," *Australasian Pentecostal Studies* 1 (1998) 5–21, 17.

11. Douglas John Hall, *Professing the Faith: Christian Theology in a North American Context* (Minneapolis, MN: Fortress, 1993) 267.

creationism precisely because this view entrenches humanity's separation from creation by refusing any association between humankind and other species (specifically apes). This is significant not only because it reinforces the premillennialist tendency to focus on salvation of the human soul and make everything else relatively unimportant, but because it sets up an explicit rejection of the inter-connectedness of all of the earth—its climate, its geography, its vegetation and its creatures—that has become the cornerstone of almost all theologies and philosophies grounding environmental movements. It is generally the case, therefore, that fundamentalist groups (including Pentecostals) advocating strict views of six day creation combine their vehement criticism of evolutionary science with an equally aggressive criticism of "greenies." This leads, for example, to the now common tendency of people holding such views to align themselves with climate change sceptics.[12] In fact, the larger issue is that the establishment of a Bible/science opposition (which reflects the soul/body distinction) results in an overriding suspicion of the various scientific disciplines that are essential not only to the identification of environmental problems, but that are necessarily part of any workable solutions.

Once again, it should be noted that neither young earth creationism, nor the effective separation of humanity from the creation, are essential to Pentecostalism.[13] While, for example, the Assemblies of God in Australia includes a doctrinal statement affirming literalistic views of creation, this was not added to the movement's constitution until 1992, and it is not a common component of Pentecostal doctrinal statements in other places. Yet it cannot be denied that the tendency toward a truncated view of creation (i.e., as only six thousand years old, and at the rapture to be rendered obsolete), the consequent anthropological focus, and the establishment of a Bible/science and Christian/greenie divide has coloured the movement's proclamation of the gospel as a whole.

12. See, for example, the numerous skeptical references to climate change on the influential Answers in Genesis website, www.answersingenesis.org.

13. As argued by Yong, *Spirit Poured Out*, 269–71.

A Critical Ecological Analysis of Pentecostalism's "Full Gospel"

Traditionally, Pentecostals have proclaimed what is variously labelled the "fourfold" or "full gospel," which announced Jesus as saviour, baptizer in the Spirit, healer, and soon coming king.[14] What is readily apparent is the way in which these various elements of the Pentecostal proclamation have been framed in a manner that excludes an ecological focus. In the first place, salvation is understood to be solely, or at least primarily, about salvation of the human soul. From this perspective, even social action takes second place to evangelism (understood in the narrow sense of term). In early Australian Pentecostalism, for example, the Pentecostal matriarch Sarah Jane Lancaster was roundly criticized for establishing a soup kitchen in the church, being told that "the money spent in feeding the unemployed would be better spent in evangelizing Victoria, thus building up the Apostolic Faith Mission."[15] If social action is thus considered irrelevant or unimportant, environmental issues fall even lower on the list of priorities. While subsequent decades have seen the broadening of this stance, Pentecostals still tend to assume that the purpose of social action lies in its service to the task of evangelism. Social action is affirmed as a means of pre-evangelism, a method of selling the ministry of the church to individuals and society as a whole, rather than something intimately connected to the gospel. While giving food to the poor might lead to their listening to the gospel, Pentecostals struggle to see how environmental action can similarly lead people to salvation.

In respect to the other elements of the Pentecostal fourfold gospel, a similarly restricted focus is apparent. The distinctive motif of baptism in the Spirit, which contains a wealth of meaning for Pentecostal culture and social structure,[16] has at a minimum been associated with empowerment—both for missionary service and for sanctification.[17]

14. See Donald Dayton, *Theological Roots of Pentecostalism* (Metuchen, NJ: Scarecrow, 1987).

15. See Shane Clifton, "Analysis of the Developing Ecclesiology," 136, and Sarah Jane Lancaster, "Amongst the Unemployed," *Good News* 23:2 (February 1932) 10–11.

16. See Frank Macchia, *Baptized in the Spirit: A Global Pentecostal Theology* (Grand Rapids, MI: Zondervan, 2006). Also Shane Clifton, "The Spirit and Doctrinal Development: A Functional Analysis of the Traditional Pentecostal Doctrine of Baptism in the Spirit," *PNEUMA: The Journal of the Society for Pentecostal Studies* 29:1 (2007) 5–23.

17. Dayton, *Theological Roots*, 65.

The former has tended to link baptism in the Spirit to the movement's restricted proclamation of salvation of the soul, and the latter has focused on individual sanctification, often understood in a world-denying fashion. The fact that baptism in the Spirit facilitates the separation of the empowered believer from the world again does little to encourage an earth affirming ecological ethos. Likewise, the Pentecostal emphasis on divine healing has been focused almost exclusively on the individual person, rarely toward social concerns and almost never related to the environmental crisis. In fact, the tendency of Pentecostals to thereby be oriented to "the miraculous," and away from "the natural," might be seen to have contributed to the failure to appropriate the various theologies of nature that have generally grounded ecotheological developments in ecumenical contexts.[18] As we have already noted, in relation to the final eschatological element of the fourfold gospel, the usual association of Jesus' return with the rapture of the saints and apocalyptic destruction of the world, actively discourages concern for the earth.

While the fourfold gospel constitutes the focus of early Pentecostalism, there are other elements of the Pentecostal proclamation that can also be shown to have contributed to the failure to develop an environmental ethos. It is beyond the scope of this essay to address them all, although it is perhaps worth concluding this critical section of analysis by discussing the implications of the contemporary trend in Pentecostal contexts to adopt various forms of prosperity theology.[19] In Australia, as in other western contexts, many Pentecostals have

18. I am using the phrase "theologies of nature" as distinct from the technical (and loaded) phrase, "natural theology." It is not my purpose to enter the debate between so-called revealed and natural theology, except to note that the tendency in contemporary theology is to hold these two ideas together. It is also generally accepted that a re-appropriation of natural theology (understood within the frame of God's revelation) helps to ground an ecological theology. See, for example, Jürgen Moltmann, *God in Creation: An Ecological Doctrine of Creation,* trans. Margaret Kohl (London: SCM, 1985) 57–60.

19. Dr Yonggi Cho, for example, has taught what he calls the "fivefold gospel," which added "the gospel of blessing" to the traditional fourfold gospel, and which assumes that material blessing, including financial prosperity, is part of the liberation from the curse. Cho's preaching of the gospel of blessing has come under substantial international critique, although it is now widely recognised that he has been unjustly associated with the American word of faith movement, and that critics of his theology have failed to account for the contextual nature of his message. See Allan Anderson, "The Contribution of David Yonggi Cho to a Contextual Theology in Korea," *Journal of Pentecostal Theology* 12:1 (2003) 85–105.

appropriated a theology of blessing, which locates its starting point in the assertion that God desires His people to prosper and, further, that Jesus became poor that we might become affluent, through faith, positively confessed and made real in the act of giving.[20] As stated on the website of the Assemblies of God in Australia, "Prosperity is not an option but a mandate and responsibility given to all who believe in the authority of the name of Jesus. We are called to show forth the wonders of His increasing Kingdom, and this clearly requires an increasing measure of affluence so that we can have an increasing measure of influence."[21] It is not our current purpose to debate the validity of the prosperity gospel, but it is noteworthy that prosperity emphases, associated as they are with the tendency to prioritise (at the cost of all else) affluence and wealth creation, share a particular resonance with the capitalist and materialist ideologies of Western society. Consequently, whether explicitly identified or not, the prosperity message draws its impetus from the consumerist culture that is largely responsible for the current environmental crisis. As Jürgen Moltmann observes:

> As technological civilisation expands and spreads, the ecological crisis grows with it: the increasing destruction of the natural environment, the increasing annihilation of vegetable and animal species, the increasing exploitation of the earth's irreplaceable resources of energy, and the pollution of earth, water and air through poisonous waste and fumes. Human technological science subjugates and exploits nature for human purposes . . . The fundamental values of society which give birth to these sciences provide the dominating knowledge for nature's subjection. The fundamental values of society which give birth to these sciences and technologies, and also govern them, are: the acquisition of power, the consolidation of power, and the pursuit of profit.[22]

The challenge for Pentecostals who have appropriated prosperity thinking is that, generally, they fail to contemplate the extent to which the economic system around which they frame their theology (including the pursuit of power and profit, as well as the means through which

20. This is my summary of Brian Houston, *You Need More Money: Discovering God's Amazing Financial Plan for Your Life* (Sydney: Maximised Leadership, 1999).

21. Steve Penny, "Assemblies of God in Australia, Core Values," (2004) Available online: http://www.aogaustralia.com.au/default.asp?ContentID=1002228.

22. Jürgen Moltmann, *The Way of Jesus Christ*, trans. Margaret Kohl (London: SCM, 1990) 67.

they are able to attain financial prosperity) is responsible for the global environmental crisis (as it is for the poverty of the exploited third world). The result is a too easy acceptance of Western society's "ingrained faith in progress and continual material prosperity and the ability of science and technology to satisfy the insatiable wants of humanity."[23] Of course the solution is not necessarily rejection of capitalism *per se*. While capitalism sustains and frames the attitudes that have created global environmental crises, it might also provide the financial resources necessary to generate solutions (note the fact that environmental pollution is worse in poorer nations), in the same way that technology, although the cause of the problems in the first place, might well provide the platform for creative ways to sustain and even help revitalize the earth. What is required is not a return to pre-industrialisation or an alternate economic system but, rather, a critical attitude toward the underlying values within capitalist societies which ignore environmental issues. As we shall suggest below, reframing prosperity teaching in this light might well be possible.

The analysis above has focused primarily on theological and cultural dimensions which can be seen to contribute to the lack of priority given by Pentecostals to environmental concerns. There are, of course, a myriad of other explanations, not the least of which relate to the social structures that frame Pentecostal communities. These would include, for example, the alienation in many Pentecostal fellowships of an academic community capable of the sort of critical and constructive thinking that gives rise to ecotheology;[24] the almost exclusive focus on the growth of the local church (which restricts a broader outlook such as is required in an ecotheology); the simple busyness of church life in the modern age and the consequent passivity relating to new ideas and programs which are seen to be tangential to church ministry. While social factors such as these are beyond the scope of this essay, unless they are also accounted for, ecological theologies will be incapable of translation into the praxis of Pentecostal church life.

---

23. Ernst M. Conradie, "Towards an Agenda for Ecological Theology: An Intercontinental Dialogue," *Ecotheology* 10:3 (2005) 281–343, quotation from 299.

24. See, for example, my analysis of the anti-intellectualism of the Assemblies of God in Australia, Shane Clifton, "Pragmatic Ecclesiology: The Apostolic Revolution and the Ecclesiology of the Assemblies of God in Australia," *Australasian Pentecostal Studies* 9 (June 2005) 23–47, 38–40.

Toward a Pentecostal Ecological Ethos

In the light of the critical analysis thus far, the question arises as to whether or not global Pentecostalism is capable of developing and sustaining an ecological ethos, or even if it should do so? In respect to the latter question, the assumption throughout this essay is that in the face of the contemporary global ecological crisis, the failure to incorporate an environmental theology essentially entails the rejection of the claim that Pentecostals preach a "full gospel."[25] In response to the former question, it can be argued that those aspects of the Pentecostal proclamation that resist environmental concerns are not central to Pentecostal identity but are, rather, appropriated unnecessarily, either from fundamentalism or Western materialism. In fact, it can be shown that core Pentecostal symbols are capable of generating and sustaining strong earthkeeping praxis. Before outlining these symbols, it is worth observing that the solution to the problem is not the simple addition of a sixth element to the (current) fourfold/fivefold gospel (the gospel of environmental empowerment?), or the addition of another "program" to the overcrowded life and ministry of the local church.[26] Rather, what is necessary is a thorough revisioning of Pentecostal worldview, one that encompasses an earth affirming theology of creation, and that thereby touches on all dimensions of the church's theology and proclamation, finding its way into the very ethos of the movement. Obviously, the constraints of this essay allow us to only begin an exploration of such revisioning.

A Pneumatological Theology of Creation[27]

Beginning (this time) at the beginning, it is important to note that the development of a Pentecostal theology of creation involves a critical evaluation of literalist six day young earth positions. As suggested earlier, appropriation of theistic evolutionary theories would have the advantage of drawing out the inter-relationships between humanity and the created order, and overcoming the unhelpful and unnecessary

25. A point that is clarified below in the attempt to set the parameters for a Pentecostal understanding of the gospel that includes an ecological dimension.

26. See a similar comment by Conradie, "Ecological Theology," 282.

27. I have borrowed this phrase from Yong, *Spirit Poured Out*, and note my debt to his "pneumatological imagination," which has stimulated many of my own thoughts.

disjunction that results in the rejection of science by theologians[28] (and vice versa), instead, facilitating the sort of theology and science dialogue that is the necessary foundation to an environmental theology. That is to say, the same science that has given us the theory of evolution is informing us of the nature and extent of the various environmental crises, and provides insight into potential solutions.[29] The difficulty, no doubt, is that an anti-evolutionary stance is so entrenched in the psyche of many Pentecostals that the linking of ecotheology to an evolutionary position may actually entrench the bias against an ecological priority, reinforcing the view that environmental Christians are "liberal." It is also no solution to simply equate humanity with creation, as though *homo-sapien* is merely another animal. Instead, it will be necessary to revision the Pentecostal understanding of creation such that our anthropology continues to affirm humanity's unique status and role, while at the same time recognizing its creatureliness.

For Pentecostals in particular, the revisioning of a theology of creation starts with the Spirit, leading to the development of what Amos Yong describes as a "pneumatological theology of creation."[30] Central to Pentecostal self-understanding is the priority afforded to the experience of the Spirit (or, rather, the experience of the triune God through the power of the Spirit[31]). At a minimum, Pentecostals describe their experience of the Spirit in terms of the empowering of the flesh (e.g., tongues as the "initial physical evidence"), and understand the power of the Spirit of the incarnate Jesus in healing the physical body. This orientation provides an experiential basis for Pentecostals to challenge their appropriation of traditional (gnostic) oppositions between the

28. While it is outside the scope of this essay, it can also be argued that six day creationism arises as a result of poor exegesis. As Gordon Wenham notes, "the bible-verses-science debate has, most regrettably, sidetracked readers of Gen 1"; Gordon J. Wenham, *Word Biblical Commentary: Genesis 1–15* (Waco, TX: Word, 1987) 40.

29. As per Yong, *Spirit Poured Out*, the simple rejection (or subordination) of science to religious revelation is fideism, and what is instead needed is dialogue that preserves the integrity of both theology and science. He goes on to suggest that many Pentecostals are becoming upon to such dialogue, and are thus coming to place where discussion of theistic evolution is possible.

30. Yong, *Spirit Poured Out*, 267.

31. In speaking of the Spirit, it is important to recognise the fact that the Spirit is the Spirit of the Father (and the Son) so that when we speak of the Spirit's role in creation—as the source and sustainer of life—we recognize that we are actually speaking of the work of triune God in creation (following Augustine's doctrine of appropriations).

Spirit and the flesh (or matter). It also provides a point of agreement that will enable Pentecostals to engage with the ecumenical discussions surrounding ecological pneumatology, which have generally included a critique of the Spirit/flesh antithesis.[32] In contrast to the Greek definition of Spirit, as the opposite of matter, the biblical portrayal of *ruach* and *pneuma* as the giver of life specifically rejects such antithesis, since the Spirit itself is discovered as the life force of God, the gift of grace that empowers and is at work within the material universe. This insight has led to wide-ranging ecumenical developments which frame the Spirit's role in creation.

A pneumatological theology of creation recognizes the Spirit's work from "the perspective of the beginning of time."[33] Lyle Dabney, for example, notes that while an understanding of God as creator reveals the autonomy and distinction of the creature from the creator, the affirmation of the presence of the Spirit, hovering even in the darkness of the pre-populated world (Gen 1:2), helps us to affirm that the transcendent God is, in fact, never absent from creation. Even in the most remote location and desolate situation, the Spirit's creative presence pervades the world as the certain reality that the wholly Other God is nonetheless completely present, serving as "the premonition of God's creative possibility."[34] The creation that is infused with the Spirit is also declared to be inherently valuable (i.e., "good"), and intimately connected to the purposes of giving glory to God. In this light the unique function of the human creature made in God's image is to exercise "dominion," not in terms of domination, but in terms of participation with the Spirit in God's stewardship of the world.

From the perspective of historical and future time, the Spirit that in the beginning breathed life "to the void" continues, in the face of the

32. See, for example, Veli-Matti Kärkkäinen, *Pneumatology: The Holy Spirit in Ecumenical, International, and Contextual Perspective* (Grand Rapids, MI: Baker, 2002) 160–61; Jürgen Moltmann, *The Source of Life: The Holy Spirit and the Theology of Life*, trans. Margaret Kohl (London: SCM, 1997) 40.

33. See Moltmann's description of the three perspectives of the time of creation; the perspective the perspective of the beginning of time (God's having created); the perspective of historical time (God's continuing creative activity) and; the perspective of eschatological time (the new heaven and new earth) (*God in Creation*, 55).

34. Lyle Dabney, "The Nature of the Spirit: Creation as a Premonition of God," in Gordon Preece and Stephen Pickard, eds., *Starting with the Spirit: Task of Theology Today* 2 (Adelaide: Australia Theological Forum and Openbook, 2001) 83–110.

myriad "voids" generated by human sin (which have created devastation not only for humankind, but in the whole earth), to infuse creation with the premonition of God's possibility, an idea which challenges both passivity and pessimism when it comes to social and environmental problems. This understanding of the Spirit gives rise to the affirmation, often neglected in fundamentalist theologies, that creation continues.[35] As Clark Pinnock observes, "A power of creativity is a work in the universe, which can be viewed as a creaturely perichoresis of dynamic systems echoing the Trinitarian mystery."[36] It thereby reinforces the unity of Christian conceptions of creation and redemption. The Spirit of life is the messianic Spirit of creation and new creation, overcoming corruption and transforming the world into its consummate status as "the Kingdom of God." The Spirit of creation is also the Spirit who raised Jesus from dead (Rom 8:11), both as the first fruits of humanity's resurrection and as the promise for the renewal of the heavens and the earth. This has substantial implications for the way in which the gospel is understood, including the "full gospel" of Pentecostalism.

Reframing the "Full Gospel"

It is immediately apparent that the affirmation, "Jesus saves," is misunderstood if applied only to salvation of the soul. The messianic Spirit who raised Jesus from the dead is the Spirit of human transformation and resurrection, body and soul. It[37] is also the Spirit in whom creation itself groans for liberation, and through whom creation will be renewed

---

35. Moltmann, *God in Creation*, 55.

36. Clark Pinnock, *The Flame of Love: A Theology of the Holy Spirit* (Downers Grove, IL: InterVarsity, 1996) 67.

37. The use of the impersonal pronoun for the Spirit here is deliberate. I have attempted to avoid the use of the masculine pronoun, but I am not really happy with the alternative, suggested by Clark Pinnock and others, of referring to the Spirit using the female pronoun (see Clark Pinnock, "The Role of Spirit in Creation," *McMaster Journal of Theology & Ministry* 1 [1998] Online: http://www.mcmaster.ca/mjtm/volume1.htm. The difficulty, as noted by feminist scholars such as Elizabeth Johnson, is that such uses, in the context of the filioque, can reinforce patriarchy (Elizabeth Johnson, *She Who Is: The Mystery of God in Feminist Theological Discourse* [New York: Crossroad, 1992] 50). So, the use of the impersonal pronoun (it, itself) as an alternative is not to deny the personhood of the Spirit, but to avoid gender language and, further, since it captures something of the unfathomable/uncontainable identity of the Spirit (as blowing where it wishes—as fire, wind, etc.).

and perfected. The gospel thereby encompasses the good news that Jesus Christ, through the power of the Spirit of life, has (and will) overcome the impact of human evil, alienation and bondage, for the sake of humanity and the whole created order. If this is the case, then the way in which Pentecostals narrate and embody the declaration that "Jesus saves" needs to be expanded. Following the basic logic of the gospel and drawing on a pneumatological theology of creation, the story of salvation should begin with the observation that the heavens and earth are created, and infused with the Spirit, for the sake of God's glory (Psalm 148). The specific task of humankind made in God's image is to exercise dominion over the earth; dominion understood in terms of social and ecological stewardship—our delegated responsibility for the way in which we interact with one-another and together care for God's earth. This story will go on to describe the problem, which is the self-evident fact that human sin has undermined this purpose, and that the effect of this sin extends not only to the individual soul (and its future destiny), not only to the corruption of local, national and global human communities, but to the destruction of the vegetation and creatures of the earth itself, whose "gardens" (through human sin) have become weed filled desserts (Gen 3:17-19) mourning their inability to fulfil their created purpose (Jer 9:10). But, as foreshadowed in the Old Testament in the shared Noahanic salvation of humanity with creatures of every kind and in the Messianic longings of Israel which incorporated a renewed creation (Isa 55:12-13), the gospel story concludes with the good news of Jesus; that his death and resurrection and his sending of the Spirit extends to the salvation of humanity, and through this liberation, to the renewal of the whole "groaning" creation (Rom 8:18-25).[38]

This summation of the narrative of salvation in Christ (which invites further biblical and theological reflection at every point), is not the proclamation of many Pentecostal movements, but nor would it require a major departure from current emphases. It is noteworthy that recent decades have, in fact, seen a broadening in the way in which Pentecostals are proclaiming, in word and deed, the gospel. As Murray Dempster observes, social involvement "born out of concern for the disadvantaged and marginalized of society seems to have multiplied

---

38. This is merely a summary of the gospel story. The Scriptures cited are illustrative only, as it is not my intention to "proof text" a biblical defense of ecotheology.

among Pentecostals."[39] This sets the stage, when accompanied by a pneumatological theology of creation, to extend this message to include earthkeeping praxis.

Such praxis could be seen to arise from the implications of an ecological pneumatology for the distinctive Pentecostal doctrine of baptism in the Spirit. If Spirit baptism is understood as empowering by the Spirit, for the work of the Spirit, then it should incorporate participation with the Spirit in breathing life to the earth. Baptism in the Spirit functions in Pentecostal communities, first to frame Pentecostal identity and culture, and second to empower mission. With respect to the former, the connection between the Pentecostal affirmation that Christians can be "filled with the Spirit" and the biblical declaration that the earth is likewise "Spirit filled" (Ps 139:7–9) provides a ready means for overcoming the fundamentalist separation between humanity and the remainder of creation, and paves the way for the inclusion of an ecological ethos in the movement's identity and culture. Regarding the latter, Pentecostals can understand themselves as empowered by the possibilities of the always present creative Spirit for earth transforming mission.

As indicated by the third component of the fourfold gospel, this mission is a ministry of healing. Pentecostals have generally linked healing to salvation, arguing that "healing is in the atonement."[40] Obviously, narrow understandings of salvation led to narrow conceptions of healing ministry (focusing on supernatural personal physical healing), but a broader soteriology implies that the healing ministry of the church should be extended to include healing of the sick and dying environment. The ministry of healing, drawing on a pneumatological theology of creation, should affirm by faith the Spirit's presence as the premonition of God's miraculous possibility in the face of the hopelessness and despair confronting sick people and the sick environment. In the same way that the message of healing has led Pentecostals to pray for the sick and establish practical ministries of healing, so too should this message

39. Murray Dempster, "Christian Social Concern in Pentecostal Perspective: Reformulating Pentecostal Eschatology," *Journal of Pentecostal Theology* 2 (1993) 53. For a specific example in the Australian situation, see Clifton, "Analysis of the Developing Ecclesiology," 226–27.

40. See, for example, William Menzies and Robert Menzies, *Spirit and Power: Foundations of Pentecostal Experience* (Grand Rapids, MI: Zondervan, 2000) 160.

lead to prayer "for God's sick creation,"[41] and active participation in earth-healing ministry. It should also inspire the motivating forces of faith and hope, which refuse to accept that the earth's sickness is beyond the miraculous power of the Spirit.

Of all the traditional elements of the fourfold Pentecostal proclamation, it is the movement's eschatology that, in the face of the global environmental crisis, is perhaps most in need of reformation. This topic (largely beyond our scope) has been the subject of ongoing discussion in the global Pentecostal academy.[42] In respect to ecological concerns, what is needed is to find a mediating point between the apocalyptic pessimism that tends to lead to the complete rejection of any ecological priority, and its opposite, the reactive neglect of eschatology which has arisen in many contemporary Western Pentecostal churches,[43] and which leads to passive acceptance (or even active affirmation) of the status quo. If eschatology is understood, not in terms of the end-times cessation of creation but, in the light of a pneumatological theology, in terms of transformation and fulfilment, then it is capable of standing as a motivating force for change. This hope for the future is grounded on the resurrection of Christ, achieved in the power of the Spirit (Rom 8:11), and understood as the first fruits of the new creation.[44] In Christ, we do not hope for the destruction of our bodies and the earth, but for resurrected bodies—"the body that is sown perishable is raised in imperishable" (1 Cor 15:42). This does not mean that the future is nothing more than a continuation of the present. Rather, what we hope for entails both continuity and discontinuity.[45] For this reason, apocalypticism need not be rejected altogether, but reframed and understood in terms of the divine judgment upon sin that is necessary for evil to be

41. Harold D. Hunter, "Pentecostal Healing for God's Sick Creation?" *The Spirit and the Church* 2:2 (2002) 145–67.

42. Dempster, "Social Concern in Pentecostal Perspective"; Faupel, *Everlasting Gospel*; Wilson, "Pentecostal Perspectives on Eschatology."

43. As Hutchinson, "The New Thing God is Doing," 17, notes, "Bigger congregations meant bigger churches meant, quite often, that we stopped looking for the millennium and started building for it."

44. Bruce Stevens, commenting on "Pentecostals and Ecology," *Pentecostal Discussions blog*, http://scc.typepad.com/scc_faculty_pentecostal_d/2006/05/eschatology_is_ .html#comments.

45. See, for example, the argument set out by Macchia, *Baptized in the Spirit*, 91–107.

overcome and for God to reign. That is to say, premillennialism might be able to be reconceived in such a way that its purpose is to identify the corrupt nature of our sin ravaged society—a society that has generated injustice, poverty and ecological devastation—and the need for judgement that necessarily accompanies renewal of the cosmos through the power of the Spirit of Christ. As Macchia notes, this gives rise to an eschatology of both the future and the here and now, in which the "Kingdom of God comes through the divine presence in the transformation of all things by the Spirit into the image of Christ."[46] Understood in this way, our participation with the Spirit in earthkeeping praxis, judging sin (including sins inflicted upon the earth), and ministering salvation and healing will have eternal value as we participate in the earth's renewal.

The final element of Pentecostal proclamation discussed in the critical section above is the recent trend toward an appropriation of the prosperity gospel. A thoroughgoing critique of this doctrine is a task for another time, but for now it is worth observing that, at its best, prosperity theology can be an affirmation of the "this-worldly" implications of the gospel. One of the proponents of prosperity in Australia, Brian Houston, has begun to describe prosperity in terms of "flourishing," as evident in his book *How to Flourish in Life: Principles for Building a Thriving, Productive Life*.[47] Neil Ormerod suggests that the kingdom of God can be understood as "a symbol of total human flourishing, a symbol of life as God originally intended, freed from the distortions of evil."[48] When such an anthropology is brought within a pneumatological theology of creation, this message of flourishing can be easily applied to the earth. The result might be a prosperity gospel that includes the affirmation of environmental flourishing, and the active involvement of the church toward that purpose.

46. Macchia, *Baptized in the Spirit*, 104.

47. Brian Houston, *How To Flourish In Life: Principles for Building a Thriving, Productive Life* (Sydney: Maximised Leadership, 2003).

48. Neil Ormerod, "Church: Mission, Dimensions, Structures, Ministry," unpublished draft of a book chapter on the topic of Ecclesiology, Catholic Institute of Sydney, 7–8.

Conclusion

I have sought to understand the reasons for the tendency of Pentecostals to be indifferent to environmental concerns. We have concluded that, in appropriating fundamentalist conceptions of creation, salvation, and eschatology, and materialist understandings of prosperity, Pentecostals have proclaimed a message that in the face of the contemporary global environmental crisis can no longer be called a "full gospel." We have also suggested that the Pentecostal orientation to the Spirit is capable of facilitating a holistic pneumatological theology of creation, and thereby establishing an ecological ethos that can redirect its Spirit empowered mission to include concern for the earth.

We should note, in conclusion, that this essay represents only a small component of a full-blown Pentecostal ecotheology. Beyond the transformation of the movement's theology and culture is the task of infusing its social structures with an ecological ethos. There is also the need to address the very practical questions relating to the identification of environmental issues (what actually are the global and glocal problems facing the earth) and deciding how the church can participate in their healing. Answers to these questions entail much more than theological reflection, but require broad dialogue with scientists, politicians, environmentalists etc. (a challenge if fundamentalism prevails). It will also be necessary to work out how to translate global ecological concerns into the practical mission of the local church. The task is potentially overwhelming, but a church empowered by the Spirit sees not impossibility but the "premonition of God's possibility."[49]

49. Dabney, "Nature of the Spirit," 4.

8

Pentecostal Ecology

A Theological Paradigm for Pentecostal Environmentalism

Matthew Tallman

Introduction

My introduction to postmodernism's concern for ecology came at a meeting I had organized at the University of Oregon on the subject of "Jesus the Ecologist." I was disappointed by the attendance but shockingly surprised by the diversity of the audience as several international students, an agnostic, a Buddhist monk, a neo-Nazi skinhead, a self-proclaimed Wiccan warlock, and an albino transvestite gathered, apparently intrigued by the subject matter. However, while it may have been the subject matter that captured their attention, it was my conclusion that captured their hearts as I suggested that God is in the "recycling business." Through the Spirit, God takes old things and makes them new. It was the possibility of new creation through the Holy Spirit that drew them to Christ.

The subject of pneumatology has also begun to capture the hearts and minds of scholars in the Pentecostal/Charismatic movement as a way of responding to the growing ecological crisis in the world today. Unfortunately, in past decades, participants in this pneumatological revival have all too often reduced their understanding of the work of the Holy Spirit to their own spiritual experiences or charismatic praxis thus impeding the Spirit "from becoming a transforming force in the relations between human beings and between us and the whole of creation. As a result, the most dynamic expression of Christianity shows itself to be almost indifferent to the most crucial questions of today's world."[1] In addition, by "stressing the Spirit as the eschatological Spirit of the kingdom to come, Pentecostals have tended to neglect the full breadth and depth of the Spirit's work in all of creation today."[2] So, by accepting a theology of dominion or domination combined with anthropocentric thought, much of Pentecostal Christianity has not only succeeded in ignoring a looming ecological crisis, but even participating in its demise.

Sadly, the concept of dominion theology, as most succinctly expressed in an improper exegesis of Gen 1:28, combined with uncontrolled greed and materialism, have led to the degradation of the environment and the possibility of ecocide. While one side accuses the other of being Chicken Little and certain elements of the other side blow up animal laboratories, landfills continue to seep toxic waste, factories and automobiles continue to pollute the air, cruise ships continue to dump raw sewage into the oceans, and numerous species teeter on the brink of extinction. With perhaps only a few scholars in the Pentecostal/ Charismatic community who have written articles on environmental or ecological issues, Jean-Jacques Suurmond and Harold Hunter may seem like lone voices crying in the wilderness when a chorus of voices in this movement should be crying for the wilderness.[3] In contrast, the Ameri-

---

1. Juan Sepùveda, "The Perspective of Chilean Pentecostalism," *Journal of Pentecostal Theology* 4 (1994) 49.

2. Frank Macchia, "Tradition and the *Novum* of the Spirit: A Review of Clark Pinnock's *Flame of Love*," *Journal of Pentecostal Theology* 13 (1998) 38.

3. While other renewal theologians such as Clark Pinnock, Juan Sepùveda and Michael Harper have mentioned this topic in other articles, until recently Harold Hunter's article "Pentecostal Healing for God's Sick Creation," *The Spirit and Church* 2:2 (November 2000) 145–67, and Jean-Jacques Suurmond's article "Christ King: A Charismatic Appeal for an Ecological Lifestyle" *PNEUMA: The Journal of the Society for Pentecostal Studies* 10:1 (Spring 1988) 26–35, were perhaps the only two articles exclusively devoted to en-

can Theological Library Association database contains 3077 articles on the subject of ecology and faith from a variety of ecclesiological and religious perspectives.

Nevertheless, the modern renewal movement can help provide a helpful, productive paradigm for pneumatological ecology in the Church, and contribute a relevant pneumatological and ecological witness and praxis to a postmodern world. The challenge lies in becoming so christocentric or anthropocentric that we no longer remain ecological, or becoming so pneumatocentric or terracentric that we no longer remain Christian. One of the more popular approaches to an ecological theology has involved a pneumatological approach,[4] and this would seem naturally appealing and promising in developing a Pentecostal ecology.

Such a Pentecostal ecology could utilize Donald Dayton's summary of the theological roots of Pentecostalism by integrating motifs of salvation, healing, Spirit baptism, and the parousia—alternatively known as the Four-fold Gospel of Jesus as savior, healer, baptizer, and coming king.[5] While Dayton does not suggest or even discuss a proposal for eco-

---

vironmental concerns from a Pentecostal/Charismatic perspective. Fortunately, others have begun to write on this topic: Augustinus Dermawan, "The Spirit in Creation and Environmental Stewardship: A Preliminary Pentecostal Response Toward Ecological Theology," *Asian Journal for Pentecostal Studies* 6:2 (July, 2003) 199–217; Marthinus Daneel on African Independent Churches and their role in the environmental movement titled, "Earthkeeping Churches at the African Grass Roots," in Dieter T. Hessel and Rosemary Radford Ruether, eds., *Christianity and Ecology: Seeking the Well-Being of Earth and Healing* (Cambridge, MA: Harvard University Press, 2000) 533–48; a helpful chapter in Ogbu Kalu, *Power, Poverty and Prayer: The Challenges of Poverty and Pluralism in African Christianity, 1960–1996* (Trenton, NJ: Africa World Press, 2006); and a chapter in Amos Yong's *The Spirit Poured Out on All Flesh: Pentecostalism and the Possibility of Global Theology* (Grand Rapids, MI: Baker, 2005). However, no book has been devoted to the subject of Pentecostal/Charismatic or renewal ecology while many such volumes have been written by evangelical publishers and authors, and hundreds of volumes have been written from other Christian perspectives. Nevertheless, it was encouraging to see three articles on environmentalism from a renewal perspective, including a slightly modified version of this essay, presented at the 2008 meeting of the Society for Pentecostal Studies. In addition, it is also encouraging to see that same emphasis reflected in this book. However, it is hoped that this emphasis will continue with further dialogue, essays, and books written on Pentecostal environmentalism for the purpose of developing Pentecostal ecological pedagogy and allowing the Pentecostal and Charismatic communities to respond to the growing environmental crisis with informed action and a relevant witness.

4. For example, see Mark I. Wallace's *Fragments of the Spirit: Nature, Violence, and the Renewal of Creation* (Harrisburg, PA: Trinity, 2002).

5. Donald Dayton, *Theological Roots of Pentecostalism* (Peabody, MA: Hendrickson, 1987) 21.

logical theology, his historical analysis offers a helpful matrix through which a Pentecostal ecological theology can be constructed.[6] I suggest that Dayton's framework invites us to develop a Pentecostal ecotheology in soteriological, healing, pneumatological, and eschatological perspective, while incorporating some of the theological and historical roots of Pentecostalism. The remainder of this essay will attempt to construct just such a theology using these four categories.

Soteriological Ecology

Early Pentecostals, in spite of their factions, universally agreed that Jesus is the Savior. Pentecostal soteriology, in addition to almost all of Christianity, includes the idea that Christ died for sinful humanity. As such, both christological and anthropological possibilities and problems should be considered in the construction of this aspect of a Pentecostal ecology. In addition, much of the discussion regarding soteriological ecology has also included the range of Christ's salvific effect upon all creation. Isaiah's messianic soteriology includes a vivid description of creation far beyond humanity (Isa 11:1–9).

This messianic vision implies the restoration of something that was lost. The account of the Fall in Genesis and the devastating effects of this one act of sinful humanity extended far beyond human beings

6. It is sometimes difficult to decide where to start when tackling such a seemingly insurmountable challenge as environmental degradation to a large segment of Christianity that sometimes chooses to ignore or dismiss it. In my dialogue with other colleagues and members of the Society for Pentecostal Studies, some have suggested that the four-fold gospel that Dayton discusses may not be the appropriate starting point for constructing a Pentecostal ecological theology. The challenges and hindrances a four-fold approach faces cannot be ignored, including the historic anthropocentrism and the contorted eschatologies of Pentecostalism that continue to exacerbate any attempts at constructive dialogue regarding environmentalism for renewal communities. However, some attempts at constructing an ecological theology for Pentecostal and Charismatic traditions have been dismissed or rejected by these communities simply because they do not honor the ethos of most renewal theologies. In addition, while a four-fold approach may have problems, these problems are not insurmountable with a fresh examination and reinterpretation of historic renewal theology, precisely what I propose here. I am hoping that my four-fold approach may offer some fresh insight to the larger Christian community regarding environmental theology and constructive dialogue and action, especially in terms of the renewal community's emphasis upon pneumatological experience and healing praxis. A theology of healing, in particular, is one topic the renewal thought can offer environmental theology that no one in the broader Christian community is writing about.

(Gen 3:14–19). As such, humanity's sin affected more than a relationship with God. However, as Paul suggests, the effects of sin were negated through the work of Christ (Rom 5:12–21). Such work goes beyond any human capability and beyond the anthropological elements of Jesus to issues of divine power and cosmic Christology, "because Christology is not just about a prophet . . . but about *God* . . . It means salvation is not just for me or for humans, but for all of creation; it gives hope for the well-being of all."[7]

Typically, Pentecostal Christianity has little difficulty accepting the Divine aspects of Christology. However, because pneumatic groups throughout church history, including Pentecostalism, have dualistic tendencies, they often have difficulty considering the broader implications and the extent of a cosmic Christology for all of creation. Perhaps one helpful paradigm to bridge this gap would be to consider the Moltmannian concept of a crucified God, the *pneumatologia crucis* that Lyle Dabney proposes, or the Catholic concept of the suffering Christ.[8] But Pentecostal triumphalism often ignores these aspects of Christology in favor of a *Christus Victor* who triumphed over death, hell, and the grave. Yet while historical Pentecostals sometimes wonder why Roman Catholics wear a cross with a suffering Christ, they often forget that Christians do not celebrate an empty cross—they celebrate an empty tomb and worship a Christ who suffered and died for a world full of sin. As such, both the cosmic dimensions and the cruciform dimensions of Christology need to be incorporated to assist in the development of a Pentecostal soteriological ecology.

While realizing the cosmic christological implications of soteriological ecology, at the same time, the human admission of guilt must be considered. The human complicity in the degradation of the environment was something initiated from the very beginning of the biblical

7. Sallie McFague, "An Ecological Christology: Does Christianity Have It?" in Dieter T. Hessel and Rosemary Radford Ruether, eds., *Christianity and Ecology: Seeking the Well-Being of Earth and Humans* (Cambridge, MA: Harvard University Press, 2000) 37.

8. See Jürgen Moltmann, *The Crucified God: The Cross of Christ as the Foundation and Criticism of Christian Theology*, trans. R. A. Wilson and John Bowden (New York: Harper and Row, 1974) and D. Lyle Dabney, "Naming the Spirit: Towards a Pneumatology of the Cross," in Stephen Pickard and Gordon Preece, eds., *Starting with the Spirit* (Hindmarsh: Australian Theological Forum, 2001) 28–59, for further discussion.

story, and it has continued throughout the history of humanity, and accelerated at the advent of the industrial age. This human complicity leads to further discussion on the relationship between theological ecology and theological anthropology. Sally McFague speaks of the interconnectedness or the relatedness between humanity and all living things, and she demonstrates how this relationship is part of the biblical story.[9] Yet somehow this relationship has become either bifurcated through the influence of dualistic philosophies or developed into a hierarchal anthropocentrism with humanity as the measure of all things.[10]

Anthropocentrism has often been mentioned as one of the primary Christian ideologies or perhaps the primary Christian perspective that has led to the modern condition of ecological degradation. Many ecological theologians have often considered anthropocentrism "false thinking,"[11] a form of Greek humanism,[12] even a form of idolatry.[13] There is almost irrefutable evidence that dualistic and anthropocentric forms of thinking have led to a hierarchical or dominion form of creation theology and to environmental degradation and destruction.[14] This has most commonly been developed from a reading of Genesis 2 that places humanity at the center or climax of the creation story having "dominion" over nature (Gen 1:28). Interestingly, Jürgen Moltmann

9. Sallie McFague, *The Body of God: An Ecological Theology* (Minneapolis, MN: Fortress, 1993) 104.

10. For a helpful discussion of these dualistic philosophies and types of dualism see Donald L. Gelpi's *The Gracing of Human Experience: Rethinking the Relationship between Nature and Grace* (Collegeville, MN: Liturgical, 2001) 28. For a helpful discussion concerning the development of anthropocentrism and further discussion on the influence of dualism see Steven Bouma-Prediger's *The Greening of Theology: The Ecological Models of Rosemary Radford Reuther, Joseph Sittler, and Jürgen Moltmann* (Atlanta: Scholars, 1995) 136–38.

11. Rosemary Radford Reuther, *Gaia and God: An Ecofeminist Theology of Earth Healing* (San Francisco: HarperCollins, 1992) 147.

12. Thomas Berry, "Christianity's Role in the Earth Project," in Dieter T. Hessel and Rosemary Radford Ruether, eds., *Christianity and Ecology: Seeking the Well-Being of Earth and Humans* (Cambridge, MA: Harvard University Press, 2000) 128.

13. Fred Van Dyke, David C. Mahan, Joseph K. Sheldon, and Raymond H. Brand, *Redeeming Creation: The Biblical Basis for Environmental Stewardship* (Downers Grove, IL: Intervarsity, 1996) 51.

14. See Theodore Hiebert, "The Human Vocation: Origins and Transformations in Christian Traditions," in Dieter T. Hessel and Rosemary Radford Ruether, eds., *Christianity and Ecology: Seeking the Well-Being of Earth and Humans* (Cambridge, MA: Harvard University Press, 2000) 135–54.

has suggested an alternative reading to the creation story in which the Sabbath, not humanity, is the apex of the Genesis account.[15] While this has been helpful in displacing some of the harmful or destructive aspects of this philosophy, some have advocated the complete deconstructionism of anthropocentrism to be replaced by biocentrism,[16] but others have suggested a reorientation towards the *imago Dei*[17] or towards Divine intimacy that recognizes an inherent value with all of creation.[18]

Anthropocentrism has not only placed a hierarchical relationship between humanity and nature, but often created dissonance or disconnection in our human relationships with one another. James Cone writes in typical prophetic fashion against racial oppression as well as ecological oppression by fighting "for life in all its forms," while pointing out fairly convincingly how people of color are disproportionately affected by environmental degradation.[19] Harold Hunter vividly recounts a blatant example of environmental racism and its devastating effects upon a pastor and his household delivered at the Pentecostal and Charismatic Churches of North America conference on October 2, 1997 in Washington D.C.[20] Ecofeminists such as Rosemary Reuther have also suggested the connection between patriarchal dominance and the destruction of the environment.[21] The connection between

15. Jürgen Moltmann, *God in Creation: New Theology of Creation and the Spirit of God*, trans. Margaret Kohl (San Francisco: Harper & Row, 1985) 31.

16. Paul F. Knitter, "Deep Ecumenicity versus Incommensurability," in Dieter T. Hessel and Rosemary Radford Ruether, eds., *Christianity and Ecology: Seeking the Well-Being of Earth and Humans* (Cambridge, MA: Harvard University Press, 2000) 377.

17. Vassilios Giultsis, "Creation and the Ecological Problem," in Gennadios Limouris, ed., *Come Holy Spirit: Renew the Whole Creation* (Brookline, MA: Holy Cross, 1990) 231.

18. Van Dyke, et al., *Redeeming Creation*, 51.

19. James H. Cone, "Whose Earth is it Anyway?" *Cross Currents* 50 (Spring/Summer 2000) 36, 40–42.

20. Harold Hunter, "Pentecostal Healing," 148–49. In this example, a Church of God in Christ minister and his family lived in an urban area where a landfill had been established by the city near a low income area. Several family members experienced cancer, in addition to unusual and abnormally high incidents of disease common in cases of toxic waste poisoning among other family members. For further examples of environmental poisoning, degradation, and pollution among the urban poor see Cone, "Whose Earth is it Anyway?" 36–46.

21. See, for example, Reuther, *Gaia and God*, 144–47.

dominance and economic destruction is woven into the aftermath of anthropocentristic ecological degradation. However, a renewal movement that often prides itself in its racial diversity and temporary racial reconciliation that occurred at Azusa Street and the involvement of significant female participation in the early history of Pentecostalism remains strangely silent about environmental reconciliation.

In spite of our poor ecological track record, Pentecostals cannot deny what was lost because of sin, and Pentecostals typically never underemphasize the need for a savior, Christ the Lord, who restored what was lost in the beginning. Many Pentecostals may not accept or recognize all of the theological ramifications of anthropocentrism or throw off the patriarchal chains of dominance that ecofeminists propose, but they cannot deny their complicit guilt in the destruction of the environment and their need for a savior, Jesus Christ, who extends the hope of reconciliation, not only to themselves, but also to others, and ultimately to all of creation.

Ecological Healing

One other primary tenet and practice of global Pentecostalism is the doctrine and practice of healing. Pentecostals typically have included healing as part of salvation and also as evidence of God's divine presence in their midst.[22] Much like Pentecostal soteriology, the question remains as to how far beyond humanity, if at all, does the possibility of God's healing power extend.

While early Pentecostals may not have spent much time constructing a theology of nature, those in agricultural communities would not hesitate to pray for a sick cow or horse. Perhaps some of these broader healing practices could be traced back to John Wesley's prayer for his lame horse,[23] but beyond any genetic explanations for Pentecostal healing praxis, early Pentecostals were biblical realists who expected God to not only forgive their sins, but also heal them, and meet their practical everyday needs. Pre-Pentecostal healing innovators such as Johann Christoph Blumhardt not only developed a significant healing ministry in the nineteenth century, but he also developed a more holistic approach

---

22. Dayton, *Theological Roots of Pentecostalism*, 115.

23. John Wesley's Journal Entry, March 17, 1746.

to healing with the development of his spa in Württemburg, Germany.[24] Other leaders in the pre-Pentecostal healing movement such as Charles Cullis followed his example. Even early Pentecostal leaders such as John G. Lake continued this holistic approach to healing with his healing homes and F. F. Bosworth developed a practical theology of healing that incorporated the body's natural ability to heal, natural medicines, and the use of doctors, in addition to Divine supernatural intervention as part of God's healing provision.[25] However, one wonders if John G. Lake would have developed a healing home for injured raptors or if John Wesley would have been willing to pray for the recovery of depleted salmon runs in today's society as readily as he prayed for the recovery of his horse. Of course there are a few notable exceptions that broadened the scope of their healing prayers beyond domesticated creation such as William Branham when he prayed for a sick opossum.[26]

Considering some of these holistic and healing approaches adapted by Pentecostal and pre-Pentecostal leaders, Harold Hunter suggests, ironically that "Pentecostals who prohibit cigarette smoking and drinking of alcohol find themselves passively taking in as many of the same chemicals and seem little concerned about keeping enough air for future generations to breathe."[27] His point is well taken considering the irony of Pentecostals who promote holy living along with their lists of specific taboos but ignore the reality of an unhealthy lifestyle and specific ecological sins that have led to disease and death. However, while asthma and even more serious pulmonary conditions are on the rise (likely as a direct result of air pollution) and various carcinomas and gastrological diseases continue to increase as a result of water pollution, Pentecostals continue to ignore calls for reduction or recycling either out of ignorance or as a blatant form of arrogance concerning their own position in the world and in the Church.

Nevertheless, the doctrine of divine healing has always been a preeminent part of Pentecostal praxis and theology. What is needed, as in Pentecostal soteriology, is an expansion of healing theology and praxis

24. Dayton, *Theological Roots of Pentecostalism*, 120–21.

25. See Douglas Jacobsen, *Thinking in the Spirit: Theologies of the Early Pentecostal Movement* (Indianapolis, IN: Indiana University Press, 2003) 296–305.

26. William Branham, "God's Cure for an Opossum," *Voice* 3:6 (September, 1955) 3–11.

27. Hunter, "Pentecostal Healing for God's Sick Creation," 153.

from all of humanity to all of creation. Some Pentecostal groups have already offered promising expressions of this broader healing praxis. One example is the Association of African Earthkeeping Churches (AAEC) an ecumenical consortium of African Independent Churches, classified as Neo-Charismatics, who have joined together in response to the environmental degradation and deforestation caused primarily by the Zimbabwean civil war in the 1960s and 1970s.[28] What is most significant is the liturgical and sacred nature of the tree-planting ceremony in which members of this organization confess ecological sins, the recognition of Christ as savior of the world (including the environment) and the planting of a new tree, representing the restoration or healing of nature and the beginning of new life. In this *maporesanyika* ceremony, the significance of Christ's healing ministry is proclaimed and incorporated so that participants understand "the fact that Christ had come to heal the sickness of the entire world."[29]

Nevertheless, most of the Pentecostal/Charismatic movement has remained strangely silent on this issue while liberal, process, and World Council of Churches theologians have written extensively on their concern for the environment for over thirty years.[30] While other ecclesiologies have spoken extensively about environmental praxis and ecological theology, renewal groups run the risk of either being ignored or marginalized in a postmodern world increasingly concerned about the global environment. But even if Pentecostal denial of ecological destruction hampers progress in restoring the environment, a Pentecostal praxis and theology of healing extended to all of creation can extend hope to a hopeless and nihilistic generation of postmoderns. However, "the twin habits of denial that refuses to groan in acknowledgment of a failed creation and despair that groans but entertains no prospect of newness"[31] leave little or no genuine hope of ecological recovery. Nevertheless, given time and the proper conditions, salmon runs can recover, migrating gray whales can repopulate, bald eagles can flourish, the Chesapeake Bay can be cleaned up, global warming can be reversed, and the earth can be healed. Just as F. F. Bosworth suggested the pos-

28. Yong, *Spirit Poured Out on All Flesh*, 61–63.

29. Daneel, "Earthkeeping Churches," 543–44.

30. Hunter, "Pentecostal Healing," 150.

31. Walter Brueggemann, "The Matrix of Groan," *Journal for Preachers* 24:3 (Easter 2001) 46.

sibility of natural healing in early Pentecostalism, modern Pentecostals can and should suggest the healing of nature for a postmodern world and begin preaching and living out the lifestyle necessary to begin the process of global ecological healing.

Pneumatological Ecology

Along with renewal healing and praxis, the pneumatological emphasis of Pentecostal and charismatic communities share the most pronounced and promising area for the development of a Pentecostal ecology. Pentecostal pneumatological theology has lagged behind Pentecostal pneumatological experience, but that is changing as more Pentecostal theologians are exploring and emphasizing various aspects of pneumatology. Led by Lyle Dabney and his call for an emphasis upon "the third article of the Trinity,"[32] this generation of Pentecostal pneumatologists is beginning to go beyond the initial theological speculations of glossolalia towards new avenues or new vistas of what Amos Yong would call the "pneumatological imagination."[33] Of course much of this pneumatological reflection started much earlier with Charismatic theologians such as Yves Congar and Heribert Mühlen.[34] However, much of this pneumatological reflection has also come from feminist and liberation theologians who seem to reflect a pneumatological preference for the suffering and the disenfranchised first expressed in Pauline thinking (1 Cor 1:26–29).[35]

32. See Lyle Dabney, "Starting with the Spirit: Why the Last Should Now be the First," in Stephen Pickard and Gordon Preece, eds., *Starting with the Spirit* (Hindmarsh, Australia: Australian Theological Forum, 2001) 3–27.

33. Yong, *Spirit Poured Out on All Flesh*, 28.

34. See Yves Congar, *I Believe in the Holy Spirit*, trans. David Smith, 3 vols. (New York: Geoffrey Chapman, 1983) and Heribert Mühlen, *Der Heilige Geist als Person: In der Trinität bei der Inkarnation und im Gnadenbund*, 4. Aufl. (Münster: Aschendorff, 1963); for an excellent English summary of Mühlen's work, see Wolfgang Vondey's, *Heribert Mühlen: His Theology and Praxis; A New Profile of the Church* (Lanham, MD: University Press of America, 2004).

35. For example, see Elizabeth A. Johnson, *She Who Is: The Mystery of God in Feminist Theological Discourse* (New York: Crossroad, 1992) esp. ch. 7, and Juan Sepúlveda, "Pentecostalism and Liberation Theology: Two Manifestations of the Work of the Holy Spirit for the Renewal of the Church," in Harold D. Hunter and Peter D. Hocken, eds., *All Together in One Place: Theological Papers from the Brighton Conference on World Evangelization* (Sheffield: Sheffield, 1993) 51–64; Sepúlveda himself is a Pentecostal in dialogue with liberation theologians.

For many of these theologians, a pneumatological gestalt occurred in February, 1991 at the seventh World Council of Churches (WCC) convocation in Canberra, Australia, with its theme of "Come Holy Spirit, Renew the Whole Creation." Many of the participants also reflected upon a pneumatological ecology and praxis at this conference with sessions such as "Giver of Life—Sustain Your Creation!" However, in spite of the size of the Pentecostal/Charismatic movement at the time, it was grossly underrepresented at this conference. Perhaps some of this under-representation was due to the historic suspicion of some Pentecostal groups towards the WCC.[36] Some of this theological suspicion, however, may not be unfounded. Ecofeminists and process theologians, among others, have developed a pneumatology that is helpful for an ecological praxis, but in the process, may have sacrificed any semblance of Christianity by teetering between pantheism, panentheism, and Wicca.[37] Paul Santmire offers a more helpful revisionistic and christocentric emphasis for a Christian ecological paradigm, but he seems to ignore a pneumatological role in his proposal when he suggests that a revisionist theology of nature must be biblical, christological, ecological, and ecclesiological.[38] Through the retrieval of Gregory of Nazianzus' Trinitarian pneumatology, Sigurd Bergmann has offered one of the most helpful recent pneumatological ecologies that are also thoroughly biblical, historically orthodox, christological, and ecclesiological.[39]

---

36. See for example, Cecil M. Robeck, "Pentecostals and the Apostolic Faith: Implications for Ecumenism," *PNEUMA: The Journal of the Society for Pentecostal Studies* 9:1 (Spring 1987) 61–84. However, Robeck points out clearly that in its early history, the Assemblies of God maintained a relationship with the National Council of Churches in North America to assist their foreign missionaries who were in difficult political or ecclesiological situations.

37. See, for example, feminist philosophers, Mary Daly or Carol Christ, or process theologians as discussed in Reuter's *Gaia and God*, 146–49, and C. Robert Mesle's, *Process Theology: A Basic Introduction* (St. Louis, MO: Chalice, 1993). For a helpful discussion of these views, read Mark Wallace's *Fragments of the Spirit*. Wallace does a better job of synthesizing his ecological pneumatology with orthodox theology into a form of panentheism, but Ruether seems to veer away from orthodox theology towards a reconstructive pantheistic pneumatology.

38. H. Paul Santmire, "In God's Ecology: A Revisionist Theology of Nature," *Christian Century* 117:35 (2000) 1302.

39. Sigurd Bergmann, *Creation Set Free: The Spirit as Liberator of Nature*, trans. Douglas Stott (Grand Rapids, MI: Eerdmans, 2005) see especially 92–97.

Two of the most helpful dialogues that could help provide a more comprehensive treatment of an ecological pneumatology among Pentecostals and Charismatics have involved Jürgen Moltmann and Clark Pinnock.[40] Moltmann as a Reformed theologian and Pinnock as a Baptist touched by Charismatic renewal have both provided renewal theologians fodder for a broader pneumatology that includes both a holistic view of the work of the Spirit in humanity and the work of the Spirit in creation. Interestingly, it was the spirituality of the African independent churches, such as the previously mentioned AAEC, that attracted Moltmann to develop his pneumatological ecology.[41] Clark Pinnock's own passion for pneumatology was drawn from his own charismatic experiences and as "an attempt to recover the cosmic range of activities of the Spirit under the conviction that the Spirit is much more than an ornament of personal piety."[42]

Jürgen Moltmann's search for a holistic pneumatology has offered a helpful paradigm for Pentecostals who are often "hindered by a one-sided emphasis on the miraculous nature of the Spirit's work."[43] His pneumatology has also helped "broaden the horizons of those readers whose Pentecostal or evangelical perspective may be too Platonistic, otherworldly and overly individualistic."[44] The advantage of his "pan-entheistic conception of God is that it enables the development of a doctrine of the Spirit which assumes cosmic proportion."[45] While many

40. Moltmann's *The Church in the Power of the Spirit: A Contribution to Messianic Ecclesiology*, trans. Margaret Kohl (New York: Harper & Row, 1977) and *The Spirit of Life: A Universal Affirmation*, trans. Margaret Kohl (New York: Harper & Row, 1977) 89, and Clark Pinnock's *Flame of Love: A Theology of the Holy Spirit* (Downers Grove, IL: Intervarsity, 1996) are most helpful in developing a broad pneumatology. Moltmann's dialogue with various Pentecostal/Charismatic scholars occurred in the *Journal of Pentecostal Theology* in 1994, and Pinnock's dialogue occurred in 1998. While both expressed concern for ecological praxis, Moltmann provided a more thorough ecological treatment in *God in Creation*.

41. Jürgen Moltmann, "A Response to my Pentecostal Dialogue Partners," *Journal of Pentecostal Theology* 4 (1994) 61.

42. Clark Pinnock, "A Bridge and Some Points of Growth: A Reply to Cross and Macchia," *Journal of Pentecostal Theology* 13 (1998) 51.

43. Frank Macchia, "The Spirit and Life: A Further Response to Jürgen Moltmann," *Journal of Pentecostal Theology* 5 (1994) 121.

44. Peter Kuzmic, "A Croatian War-Time Reading," *Journal of Pentecostal Theology* 4 (1994) 24.

45. Simon Chan, "An Asian Review," *Journal of Pentecostal Theology* 4 (1994) 38.

Pentecostals and Charismatics may disagree with a panentheistic theology, Moltmann avoids a nihilistic view of reality and does not ignore the human condition, but rather places the cross of Christ and a crucified God at the foundation of any panentheistic understanding of God.[46] In direct response to accusations of pantheism, Moltmann responds by saying that a cosmic doctrine of the Holy Spirit cannot "become animistic or pay homage to New Age pantheism or Buddhism: Jesus makes the difference."[47]

Pinnock's pneumatology came about through his own charismatic experience and through the writings of Moltmann and Pannenberg.[48] However, in *Flame of Love*, Pinnock manages to go further by developing pneumatology into a marvelous synthesis of his own experience and a retrieval of Cappadocian pneumatological and trinitarian perichoresis that invites the reader, through prayer, to join "an already occurring conversation. The Spirit calls us to participate in the relationship of intimacy between Father and Son and to be caught up in the dance already begun."[49]

Another theologian who has recently done an excellent job of retrieving Cappadocian pneumatological thought is Sigurd Bergmann. Bergmann mines the soteriological, christological, and pneumatological elements of Gregory of Nazianzus cosmology in his development of an ecological theology: "the key soteriological feature of Gregory's theology is his conscious and rigorous incorporation of the *entirety* of creation into salvation history, which the Spirit itself perfects."[50] He even suggests how the context of Gregory's environment, including the possibility of ecological devastation, contributed significantly to his holistic pneumatology.[51] His analysis of Gregory's anthropology helps replace an anthropocentric or hierarchical view of creation with a more trans-spatial view of anthropology in which human beings uniquely live above and below.[52] Reflecting a modern theological ecology of

---

46. Moltmann, *Spirit of Life*, 213.

47. Moltmann, "A Response," *Journal of Pentecostal Theology* 4 (1994) 67.

48. Pinnock, "A Bridge," 51.

49. Pinnock, *Flame of Love*, 46.

50. Bergmann, *Creation Set Free*, 53.

51. Bergmann, *Creation Set Free*, 61.

52. Bergmann, *Creation Set Free*, 97.

stewardship, as such, Bergmann suggests that because human beings "are capable of moving toward God, they are entrusted with considerable responsibility in the redemptive process of material creation."[53] He also offers some helpful insight into how terms such as "Gaia" and "Mother Earth" can be incorporated into theological dialogue with the environmental community without abandoning God's uniqueness or transcendence when he states "The body of Mother Earth, rather than actually *being* God, *reveals* God economically. That is, Gaia is a functional *instrument* of God's activity and is not to be identified with God's essence."[54] Bergmann's analysis will hopefully entice more scholars in renewal circles to reexamine and retrieve patristic material in the development of a thorough pneumatological and ecological theology.

The pneumatological experience and praxis of Pentecostals and Charismatics prevent them from ignoring pneumatology, and their christological piety most often prevent them from deviating too far from orthodox Christianity in developing an ecological pneumatology. Amos Yong reflects this pneumatological and christological tension by suggesting that Pentecostal theology is "pneumatologically driven and christologically centered."[55] Clark Pinnock describes this synthesis with a memorable metaphor when he suggests that "Calvary is something like a black hole into which is sucked all the power of death and law, wrath and alienation, to be annihilated. In its wake, the Spirit summons us to enter reconciliation and actualize by faith what is anticipated."[56] Even Dabney, with his clarion call for a pneumatological emphasis, synthesizes Christology and pneumatology in his construction of a "*pneumatologia crucis.*"[57] However, Pentecostals must continue to develop a broader pneumatology that incorporates all of creation if they are to offer a prophetic voice and a relevant message to a modern world desperate for solutions to environmental degradation. In order to do this, much like Paul sometimes incorporated the terminology of Greek philosophy and Greek poetry in his witness, Pentecostals, in dialogue

53. Bergmann, *Creation Set Free*, 97. Bergmann points out succinctly how Gregory's concepts of movement, sociality, and relationality distinguish themselves from the contemporary Plotinian influence of emanations.

54. Bergmann, *Creation Set Free*, 195 (italics in original).

55. Yong, *Spirit Poured Out on All Flesh*, 28.

56. Pinnock, *Flame of Love*, 109.

57. Dabney, "Naming the Spirit," 30.

with the rest of the world, may need to consider using terminology like "Gaia" in the creation of a pneumatological ecology that can be communicated in terms the rest of the environmental community can understand, appreciate, and appropriate. As Pentecostals begin this dialogue they may gain unexpected dialogue partners—perhaps a few agnostics, certainly some Buddhists, and maybe even an albino transvestite—but is not that part of our witness and our mission?

Eschatological Ecology

For many readers, this last segment might seem a bit oxymoronic. After all, has not an eschatological emphasis upon an imminent parousia caused all Pentecostals to completely disregard any future hope for the rest of creation by suggesting that "it's all going to burn anyway"? However, if the soteriology, healing praxis, and pneumatology of Pentecostals begin to expand beyond humanity to all of creation, can they truly believe in such a tortuous demise for the rest of the earth? After all, no Pentecostal would ever stop witnessing to other human beings and suggest that it does not matter because "they're all going to burn anyway." Then why would they treat the rest of creation any differently?

The belief in the imminent return of Christ and his millennial reign has been at the core of most Pentecostal belief and practice. The sense of urgency involved in preparing for the parousia facilitated much of Pentecostal growth, focusing on spiritual salvation rather than ecological or social concerns, and even viewing ecological destruction as a prophetic fulfillment of scripture and a sign that Christ was coming soon.[58] This "perceived inadequacy in Christian eschatology"[59] has created an ecological ignorance, denial, or pessimism among many, if not most, Pentecostals. While some aspects of extreme eschatology have occasionally led to tragic results in church history, an expectation upon the imminent return of Christ has almost universally been a part of renewal history. What is needed is a reorientation or reinterpretation of cosmological eschatology.

Miroslav Volf has aptly pointed to two alternative perspectives regarding historic Christian eschatology.[60] One position stressed the

---

58. Dermawan, "The Spirit in Creation," 206–7.

59. Bouma-Prediger, *Greening of Theology*, 3.

60. Miroslav Volf, *Work in the Spirit* (Oxford: Oxford University Press, 1991) 89–91.

complete destruction of the earth and the creation of a new earth while the other position stressed a transformation of the present universe into a new heaven and earth. Both of these positions have radically different implications for ecological theology and even more import for ecological praxis. If the end of the age results in complete destruction then ecological preservation seems almost futile, but if the eschaton brings transformation, ecological praxis can be seen as something holy, and even something that contributes to ultimate transformation in a glorified future.[61]

Jürgen Moltmann's "theology of hope" has also offered some helpful insight for an eschatological contribution to an ecological theology.[62] His eschatological tension between the "yet" of the crucified God on the cross and the "not yet" of an eschatological future of transformation offers hope to a nihilistic world of ecological despair and to an atheistic future of ecocidal degradation.

> Without the cross of Christ this vision of "the world in God" would be pure illusion . . . . Without perception of the suffering of God's inexhaustible love, no pantheism and no panentheism can endure in this world of death. They would very soon end up in pan-nihilism. It is only knowledge of the crucified God which gives this vision of the world in God its foundation and endurance.[63]

At the same time, Moltmann's eschatology avoids the dualism or Gnosticism reflected in many popular Pentecostal and Evangelical eschatologies by suggesting "that we shall be redeemed with the world, not from it."[64]

Not all popular Pentecostal eschatologists promote a dualistic eschatological demise of destruction upon the earth. Jack van Impe regularly promotes a "world without end" in his television programs in which the earth will not be destroyed but transformed. One helpful addition to his eschatological vision for Pentecostal pedagogy might be an

61. Hunter, "Pentecostal Healing," 161–62.

62. See Jürgen Moltmann, *The Coming of God: Christian Eschatology*, trans. Margaret Kohl (Minneapolis, MN: Fortress, 1996) and *Theology of Hope: On the Ground and the Implications of a Christian Eschatology*, trans. James Leitch (New York: Harper and Row, 1967).

63. Moltmann, *Spirit of Life*, 213.

64. Moltmann, *The Church in the Power of the Spirit*, 89.

ecological theology of glory in which "the glorification of the Creator is not yet completed, the future of creation lies in its contribution to that glorification."[65] In the midst of Isaiah's messianic eschatological vision he declares that "the mountains and the hills will burst into song before you, and all the trees of the field will clap their hands" (Isa 55:12), and in the midst of the multitude praising Christ the King, the Messiah warns the Pharisees that "if they keep quiet, the stones will cry out (Luke 19:40). If Pentecostals' limited view of eschatology prevents them from even accepting the need for environmental healing, ecological theology, and environmental praxis, they will have an incomplete doxology and an inaccurate perception of what God is ultimately drawing all of creation towards. Even more importantly, if Pentecostals choose to ignore this issue because of their eschatological dualism and anthropocentric orientation, the ecologically apocalyptic warnings found in Revelation may soon become a "realized eschatology."

Conclusion

Based on their current size and growth, Pentecostals have offered an extremely effective Christian witness in the twentieth century. For the development of an ecological theology and praxis, they need to consider expanding that witness beyond humanity to all of creation. Based on the theological roots of the Pentecostal movement, the foundation for an ecological theology has already been laid; it just needs some re-orientation, re-examination, and re-interpretation. Perhaps Pentecostals have already been ecologists, they just did not know it. However, if they expect to be an effective global witness to a postmodern world in the twenty-first century, they will need to expand their witness and their praxis to all of creation.

This expansion should include a broad soteriology exemplified by a cosmic Christology that includes all of creation and a sober anthropology that admits fallen humankind's complicity in the destruction of fallen creation. It should also include an ecological theology of healing which offers not only the hope of healing to all of creation, but also living examples of ecological healing and praxis. The case of the

65. Peter Scott, "The Future of Creation," in David Fergusson and Marcel Sarot, eds., *The Future as God's Gift: Explorations in Christian Eschatology* (Edinburgh: T. & T. Clark, 2000) 92.

African Earthkeeping Churches certainly may be one of many models that offer ecological healing. In addition, Pentecostals are beginning to move beyond initial reflection upon glossolalia, charismata, and Spirit baptism to a much broader pneumatology that can and should include the ecological implications. After all, the same Spirit who descended at Pentecost is the same Spirit who hovered over the waters at the creation of the universe. Finally, Pentecostals should develop a broader eschatology that can help provide praxis and healing for the "yet" of the new creation, and hope for the "not yet."

New metaphors, new dialogue partners and the retrieval of old ones will also prove helpful in the process of refining Pentecostal ecological theology and praxis. Jürgen Moltmann, Clark Pinnock, and Sigurd Bergmann have been helpful in the development of a robust pneumatology. New metaphors that speak powerfully to inform a Christian perspective and create new venues of healing and transformation for all of creation may also prove essential for a comprehensive ecological praxis.[66]

However, the task of developing a thorough ecological theology that honors the basic tenets of Pentecostalism's past, prophetically speaks to the present state of Pentecostalism's denial and complicity, and steers this movement towards the future hope of salvation, healing, and transformation of all creation—all may require dialogue partners we don't always agree with, or even expect, and metaphors we do not normally consider. Unfortunately, some of the most powerful metaphors that can inform our ecological theology are disappearing at an alarming rate.[67] Passenger pigeons are extinct, the Smoky Mountains are filled with smog, and the Gulf of Mexico is filled with pollution and is uninhabitable in many areas due to hypoxia; yet these and billions of other organisms and materials on this planet were created for the glory of God.

As a result of their silence, our doxology is diminished and our Pentecostal witness has become more irrelevant in a postmodern world that groans and cries out for the healing of God's sick creation. However, as the hope of a healing praxis for all of creation becomes more preeminent in Pentecostal theology, and as the hope of transformation for

66. See Dermawan, "Spirit in Creation," 213–16, for further discussion on his proposal for new metaphors.

67. Berry, "Christianity's Role in the Earth Project," 127. Consider that global extinction of this magnitude has not occurred in over sixty five million years.

all creation becomes more prominent in Pentecostal eschatology, the Pentecostal witness for the twenty-first century may far exceed the past century as "we plumb the depths of the Spirit, in love we explore its breadth, and in hope its open horizons. God's Spirit is our space for living."[68]

68. Moltmann, *Spirit of Life*, 161.

9

Implications of the Kenosis of the Spirit for a Creational Eschatology

A Pentecostal Engagement with Jürgen Moltmann

Peter Althouse

Introduction

Jürgen Moltmann proposes a theology of divine kenosis in which the descent of the Spirit as the presence of God in creation becomes vulnerable in the suffering of the world. Kenosis of Spirit starts in a triune creative act, in that the space for creation involves a divine self-limitation in which omnipotence is restricted in the outflow of love. Spirit kenosis coincides with the kenosis of the Word, in that the Spirit, who dwells in the incarnate Christ, becomes vulnerable in the weakness of Jesus' flesh. The kenotic Spirit is the authority by which Jesus is energized, through whom he heals and charismatically empowers, but simultaneously the Spirit participates in the suffering and death of the cross. Through the kenosis of the indwelling Spirit, the sacrifice of Christ is made vicarious. As the Spirit of Christ sent forth on the day of Pentecost, the Spirit who empowers and sustains Christ in his sufferings is also the Spirit who empowers and sustains us in identity with Christ and is present with the suffering of all creation groaning for its redemption. Moltmann therefore speaks of a descent of the Spirit in which the power of God in the world is possible through the Spirit's kenotic self-emptying.

The implications of a kenotic pneumatology for creation can be seen in the double movement of descent and ascent of the Spirit, in which the presence of God's Shekinah is both continuous and discontinuous with creation. The Spirit is immanent in creation in identity with cosmic sufferings, but discontinuous in creating the possibilities of the novuum as the in-breaking of the eschaton. The continuity/discontinuity of the Spirit's presence coincides with a creational eschatology, in which kenosis is evident in creation, the event of the cross, and Pentecostal outpouring, but also in terms of the eschatological dawning in which the Spirit who suffers with the sufferings of creation draws humanity and the whole cosmos into the new creation as it groans for its redemption (Rom 8:22).

The Pentecostal understanding of the Spirit in Spirit baptism, tongues, giftings, and healing would be nourished by an awareness of the Spirit's kenotic self-emptying. The Spirit's presence in all its charismatic dimensions is not merely for ecstatic self-gratification or ecclesial triumphalism, in which the eschaton is already present among the people of God, but for ecclesial self-giving to the community and world that experiences pain and suffering, hoping for the day when the Spirit brings forth the consummated reign of Christ. Yet the charismatic dimensions of the Spirit as understood by Pentecostals offer a dimension to kenotic self-emptying. The charismatic presence of the Spirit helps people in the midst of their sufferings and concerns, giving them hope for the coming of God. It supports a missional focus in that the presence of the self-giving Spirit shifts the church's internal maintenance to an ecclesial giving to the world and all of creation.

I propose to outline a kenotic pneumatology in dialogue with Jürgen Moltmann, strengthened by a Pentecostal doctrine of the Spirit. Within the context of a creational eschatology, the kenosis of the Spirit has implications for understanding God's presence as continuous with creation, but also in discontinuity with the coming eschaton. In kenosis, charismatic giftings are not simply for personal gratification in the divine encounter, but the extension of the mission of the self-giving Spirit through the church to others for the sake of the world.

Kenosis of the Spirit in Creation

Typically, discussion of divine kenosis focuses on the Christ event. Drawing upon Phil 2:6–9, theologians wrestle with the language of what it means to take on the "form of a servant," to have been "made in the likeness of men," and to have "humbled himself, and became obedient unto death, even the death of the cross" (KJV). However, Moltmann starts by exploring a Trinitarian understanding of divine kenosis in which self-emptying is a divine act affecting the whole Trinitarian being. According to Moltmann, "The *outward incarnation* presupposes *inward self-humiliation*" and as such the incarnation is taken up into the intra-trinitarian relations.[1]

Divine kenosis is not, strictly speaking, solely an extra-trinitarian act, but flows out of an intra-Trinitarian movement. Moltmann argues that the theology of kenosis has focused predominantly on the outward trinitarian act of self-limitation and self-emptying, but has overlooked God's immanent limitation. "God is nowhere greater than in his humiliation. God is nowhere more glorious than in his impotence. God is nowhere more divine than when he becomes man."[2] In Trinitarian "self-limitation" which is in reality a "self-realization," God limits himself and determines to withdraw his omnipotence in order to "concede space" for a finite creation.[3] The "primordial kenosis" in the inner trinitarian relations of God, the self-surrender of the triune persons to one another in perichoretic penetration, is the expression of boundless love flowing outward in creation, reconciliation, and eschatological transformation.[4] Divine self-limitation likewise involves a restriction of omniscience, not that God does not know all things, but in the sense that "God doesn't know everything in advance because he doesn't will to know everything in advance. He waits for the response of those he has created, and lets their future come."[5] In Moltmann's theology, then, omnipresence is maintained in that the Spirit is immanent in creation

1. Jürgen Moltmann, *The Trinity and the Kingdom: The Doctrine of God*, trans. Margaret Kohl (Minneapolis, MN: Fortress, 1993) 119. Italics here and elsewhere in Moltmann quotations are original to Moltmann, unless otherwise noted.

2. Moltmann, *Trinity and the Kingdom*, 119.

3. Jürgen Moltmann, *Science and Wisdom*, trans. Margaret Kohl (Minneapolis, MN: Fortress, 2003) 62.

4. Moltmann, *Science and Wisdom*, 57.

5. Moltmann, *Science and Wisdom*, 64.

as the source that undergirds all life, but omnipotence and omniscience have been limited through an intra-trinitarian and extra-trinitarian act of kenosis.

For Moltmann creation is enacted out of trinitarian self-limitation, in which God withdraws himself into himself, in order to make "space" for the cosmos. This is a tripartite act that includes creation-in-the-beginning, the ongoing process of creation, and the eschatological new creation.[6] Creation is then a trinitarian "process." The Spirit makes the creative act efficacious. "Everything that is, exists and lives in the unceasing inflow of the energies and potentialities of the cosmic Spirit" in which the Creator, by virtue of the Spirit's energies and potentialities of the novuum, is present in creation.[7] God creates "out of the powers and energies of his own Spirit. It is the powers and energies of the Holy Spirit that bridge the difference between Creator and creature, the actor and the act, the master and the work—a difference which otherwise seems to be unabridged by any relation at all. This certainly does not make creation divine, but it nevertheless brought into the sphere of the Spirit's power, and acquires a share in the inner life of the Trinity itself."[8] In Moltmann's panentheistic theology, God opens himself up to creation, but not to the extent that divine Spirit infuses the created order in a pantheistic sense, but as the divine energies that under gird and sustain created life.

The key to understanding Moltmann's view of Spirit kenosis in creation is through the concept of Shekinah. Shekinah is a Hebrew expression for the indwelling presence of God. Shekinah is "the descent and indwelling of God in space and time, a particular place and a particular era of earthly beings and in their history,"[9] and therefore an inverse expression of kenosis. In a sense, the Spirit is only present in creation and in God's people who form the messianic community through a prior act of self-emptying. The Spirit's kenosis sustains creation and its creatures, mediates the infinite God to the finite, and is the blessed hope of the perfected world for this world of sin and sorrow. Nevertheless, the

6. Jürgen Moltmann, *God in Creation: An Ecological Doctrine of Creation*, trans. Margaret Kohl (London: SCM, 1985) 88.

7. Moltmann, *God in Creation*, 9.

8. Moltmann, *Trinity and the Kingdom*, 113.

9. Jürgen Moltmann, *The Spirit of Life: A Universal Affirmation*, trans. Margaret Kohl (Minneapolis, MN: Fortress, 1992) 47.

panentheistic withdrawal of the infinite God into himself in order to create is an act of self-limitation, which Moltmann defines in dialogue with Isaac Luria as *zimsum*. In ancient Judaism, God's presence was through the Shekinah of the Temple, a concentration of divine presence in a specific time and place. However, Luria transformed the concept to argue that *zimsum* represents God's withdrawal to make space for the universe.[10] Moltmann takes the concept further, to argue that *zimsum* corresponds to Shekinah. Creation-in-the-beginning is the inauguration of the Spirit's kenotic presence, in that the Spirit is immanent in all creation, supporting created life with divine life. Without the Spirit's presence as the life-giving sustainer of life, all created life would cease to exist (cf. Ps 104:9ff).[11] The Spirit therefore sustains creation by indwelling it, drawing it to its completion and transfiguration in the ongoing process of creation, in anticipation for the coming of the divine novuum. The new creation is the time when God will indwell creation, and creation in God, the time when God will be "all in all" (1Cor 15:8).[12]

Yet kenosis for Moltmann is not simply in the event of creation, but multi-dimensional. The Spirit kenotically dwells in the individual, in the community of faith and in creation as a whole. Thus David Beck claims that, "These various levels mean that the kenosis of the Spirit is ever new with each fresh situation and has many different levels (in creation, in Israel, in the church, in Jesus, in believers). Thus, when speaking about the kenosis of the Spirit Moltmann would be better off speaking of a particular instance or type out of the many *kenosi* of the Spirit."[13] Be that as it may, the supreme instance of divine kenosis is in the sacrifice of the cross.

Kenosis of Spirit in the Christ Event

In the incarnation of Jesus Christ, we witness a kenosis of Spirit in trinitarian dimensions. In *The Crucified God*, Moltmann explores the meaning of the death of Jesus on the cross in terms of the trinitarian relationship between the Father and the Son, but absent is the affect

10. Moltmann, *Trinity and the Kingdom*, 104.

11. Moltmann, *Trinity and the Kingdom*, 111.

12. Moltmann, *Trinity and the Kingdom*, 110.

13. T. David Beck, *The Holy Spirit and the Renewal of All Things: Pneumatology in Paul and Jürgen Moltmann* (Eugene, OR: Pickwick, 2007) 160.

that the death of the Son has on the Spirit. In the crucifixion, Jesus is forsaken by God, abandoned to the torment of godforsakenness. Jesus' death cry, "My God, My God, Why hast thou forsaken me," is understood as a separation between the Father and the Son, which changes the history of the Triune God. According to Moltmann:

> The abandonment on the cross which separates the Son from the Father is something that takes place within God himself; it is *stasis* within God—"God against God"—particularly if we are to maintain that Jesus bore witness to and lived out the truth of God. We must not allow ourselves to overlook this "enmity" between God and by failing to take seriously either the rejection of Jesus by God, the gospel of God which he lived out, or his last cry to God upon the cross.[14]

It is not a "death of God" as proclaimed by the protest atheists. Rather, "death *in* God,"[15] presents a theology of the cross that hears the claims of protest atheism and responds with the possibility of God, that God too suffers with us and all creation: "God's being is in suffering and the suffering is in God's being itself, because God is love."[16]

The abandonment on the cross is co-mutual—Jesus is abandoned by the Father and becomes godforsaken for the sake of the world, and

14. Jürgen Moltmann, *The Crucified God: The Cross of Christ as the Foundation and Criticism of Christian Theology*, trans. R. A. Wilson and John Bowden (London: SCM, 1974) 151–52.

15. Moltmann, *Crucified God*, 207.

16. Moltmann, *Crucified God*, 227. Alister McGrath traces the reasons for the renewed concern regarding divine passibility. One was the rise of protest atheism which started in the late-nineteenth century with Nietzsche, Dostoyevsky and later Camus, as well as the early-twentieth century reaction to the optimism of liberal Protestantism following World War I; protest atheism was a specific protest against an invulnerable God. The second was a rediscovery of Luther's "theology of the cross," as a God who is "hidden in suffering." The third was the impact of the "history of doctrine" movement, which revealed that numerous Greek ideas had made their way into Christian theology. Impassibility was a Greek philosophical concept, not a Jewish-Christian one. See Alister E. McGrath, *Christian Theology: An Introduction*, 4th ed. (Oxford: Blackwell, 1993) 211–16.

Moltmann also speaks about the development of the idea of a suffering God in the Christian-Marxist dialogue of the mid 1960s, which critically addressed Feuerbach and Marx's critiques of God as a specific conceptualization of an invulnerable God, by proclaiming Jesus' "passion for the poor." A suffering God seeks the liberation of a world in pain. Cf. Jürgen Moltmann, *God for a Secular Society: The Public Relevance of Theology*, trans. Margaret Kohl (London: SCM, 1999) 50.

the Father abandons his Son to the cross, creating enmity between God and God. Mutual surrender affects the trinitarian being in different ways, however: "in the surrender of the Son the Father surrenders himself too—but not in the same way. The Son suffers his dying in this forsakenness. The Father suffers the death of the Son. He suffers it in the infinite pain of his love for the Son. The death of the Son therefore corresponds to pain of the Father."[17] The pain of separation in the god-forsakenness of the cross is not merely temporal, however, but infinite in that out of love the crucified and forsaken One is forever marked by the indelible pain of forsakenness by the Father, and the Father forever experiences the infinite pain of having forsaken his only begotten. The beatific vision of our Lord will be of the one marked by nail scarred hands and feet, but more crucially as the one rejected by God. "The Father has become 'another' through the Son's self-giving, and the Son too has become 'another' through his experience of suffering in the world."[18] Yet the death of the cross affects Trinitarian life. This is not an ontological separation of the divine, otherwise the triune collapses into tritheism; rather it is an existential separation. The "relationship" between the Father and the Son is changed in the paschal sacrifice.

But what of the Spirit? Little is said in the early stages of Moltmann's theology on what the cross means for the Spirit. If there is enmity between God and God in the Father's abandonment of the Son, and the Son's abandonment by the Father, then what role does the Spirit play in this kenotic event? We glimpse hints of a Spirit kenosis in *The Church in the Power of the Spirit*, but only in terms of the Spirit's sending in relation to the messianic history of Christ: "This history of Christ in the Spirit is also interpreted in the light of its origin, so that it is understood as the history of God's dealings with the world. The experiences of the Holy Spirit are comprehended in the light of the sending of the Spirit."[19] By implication, the Trinity is not static but open from eternity, and makes itself open in the sending of the Spirit.[20] "In the sending of the Son and the Spirit the Trinity does not only manifest what it is in itself; it also

17. Jürgen Moltmann, *The Way of Jesus Christ: Christology in Messianic Dimensions*, trans. Margaret Kohl (London: SCM, 1990) 173.

18. Jürgen Moltmann, *The Church in the Power of the Spirit: A Contribution to Messianic Ecclesiology*, trans. Margaret Kohl (London: SCM, 1977) 62.

19. Moltmann, *Church in the Power of the Spirit*, 54.

20. Moltmann, *Church in the Power of the Spirit*, 55.

opens itself for history and experience in history . . . the history of the self-communicating livingness of God which overcomes death."[21] Is the Spirit, though, who kenotically binds himself to the messianic history of Jesus, even to the death of the cross, also somehow abandoned and godforsaken? If one follows Augustine, for instance, to argue that the Spirit is the "bond of love" between Father and Son, then what does it mean to say that the Spirit emptied himself on the cross? Can we even claim this? Is there a relational separation of some sort in the trinitarian life of God? Yet if there is a trinitarian renting, then does God become something other than God?

In *The Way of Jesus Christ*, Moltmann fleshes out the relationship between Jesus and the Spirit as mutual kenosis in terms of the life of Jesus, but less so in terms of the crucifixion. The condescension of Jesus coincides with the condescension of the Spirit. Like Christ, the Spirit descends from eternity to indwell the weak and vulnerable flesh of Jesus. The Spirit authorizes and empowers Jesus, but also "participates in his weakness, his suffering, and his death on the cross."[22] The Spirit binds himself to Jesus' mission as the godforsaken one. The life, death and resurrection of Jesus are made possible by the Spirit. Jesus' life is nourished by the "life-giving Spirit" (1 Cor 15:45); he travels the way of the cross and offers up his life through the Spirit (Heb 9:14). By the Spirit Jesus endures the suffering of death, and more importantly the experience of abandonment, and is vindicated in his raising to new life.[23] At this point in Moltmann's thinking, we see that Christ and the Spirit are intimately related to one another, faithfully fulfilling the tri-une mission of sending. The Spirit anoints Jesus; the Spirit reveals to Jesus that he is the Son of the Father, enabling Jesus to call him Abba. The Spirit leads Jesus into the desert to be tempted. The Spirit sustains Jesus in his sufferings and death. The Spirit raises Christ from the dead to eternal life.[24] The Spirit of God is the one who empowers Jesus in ministry and proclamation, vindicating who and what he was, is, and will be. The resurrection of Jesus is not merely a synchronic event oc-curring at his death, but a diachronic exoneration of the life of Jesus in

---

21. Moltmann, *Church in the Power of the Spirit*, 56.

22. Moltmann, *Way of Jesus Christ*, 93–94.

23. Moltmann, *Way of Jesus Christ*, 248.

24. Moltmann, *Way of Jesus Christ*, 73.

its entirety, from birth, through baptism, to death and resurrection,[25] and a guarantee for the coming of God in resurrection hope, when the Spirit empowered kingdom of Christ is manifested in this world.

In the resurrection, then, the Spirit of God who kenotically binds himself to the life and death of Christ, in which he is identified as the Christ of the Spirit, becomes the Spirit of Christ. "The Spirit proceeds from the Father and rests on Jesus, so that it goes forth from Jesus and comes upon men and women. In this way God's Spirit becomes *the Spirit of Christ*. It surrenders itself wholly to the person of Jesus in order to communicate itself through Jesus to other men and women."[26]

It is not until *The Spirit of Life*, however, that we see in Moltmann a full-fledged understanding of the meaning of Spirit kenosis in the death of Christ. In *The Way of Jesus Christ*, Moltmann simply says that the activity of the Spirit is transformed from an "active power" to a "suffering power." "By virtue of this mutual indwelling (perichoresis) of the Father and the Son," insists Moltmann, "Jesus' sufferings are divine sufferings, and God's love is love that is able to suffer and is prepared to suffer. The power of the divine Spirit *in* Jesus is transformed from an active power that works wonders to a suffering power that endures wounds."[27] The Spirit mediates the suffering of the godforsaken one to the Father, in order to overcome all suffering. In *The Spirit of Life*, however, Moltmann argues that "The path the Son takes in his passion is then at the same time the path taken by the Spirit, whose strength will be proven in Jesus' weakness. The Spirit is the transcendent side of Jesus' immanent way of suffering. So the '*condescendence*' of the Spirit leads to a progressive *kenosis* of the Spirit, together with Jesus."[28]

The Spirit gives Jesus the strength to endure the sufferings of the cross. The suffering of the messianic Christ is also the suffering of the Spirit. In the moment of abandonment, though, "the Spirit suffers the suffering and death of the Son, without dying with him. So what the Spirit 'experiences' . . . is surely that the dying Jesus 'breathes him out' and 'yields him up' . . . [A]s his [Jesus'] senses left him and he went down to death, the Holy Spirit interceded for him, with inexpressible

25. Moltmann, *Way of Jesus Christ*, 76.

26. Moltmann, *Way of Jesus Christ*, 93–94.

27. Moltmann, *Way of Jesus Christ*, 177.

28. Moltmann, *Spirit of Life*, 62.

groanings, helping his weakness also."[29] Through the indwelling Spirit, Jesus offers himself up as the vicarious atonement, enduring the forsakenness of God on our behalf, so that the Spirit may now reconcile the world to God.[30] In the abandonment of Jesus, a moment when the Spirit sustains Christ in his death cry, we are deemed acceptable before God by the mediation of the Spirit.

Moltmann then comments that a theology of the power of the Spirit without the corresponding suffering of the Spirit would make the Spirit superfluous to Christ's paschal sacrifice. The cross would therefore not be a trinitarian event. The extra-trinitarian enactment of redemption would not touch the intra-trinitarian relations, if not for the Spirit's mediation, and would therefore suggest a modalistic view of divine nature. "We have assumed a kenosis of the Spirit," argues Moltmann, "which is to be seen in his Shekinah in the suffering, assailed and dying Jesus. But if we take a different starting point, looking only at the power of the Spirit and not at this weakness too, then we are ascribing to the Spirit a merely external influence on the sacrifice which Christ brings the Father through his self-surrender."[31] A fuller understanding of vicarious atonement is one in which the Spirit acts in perichoretic unity with the Father and the Son. However, for Moltmann, vicarious atonement is one in which the Spirit is actively participating in the event of abandonment and mediating the suffering of life to the Father in order to overcome all suffering. Moltmann insists:

> If God himself was *in* Christ, then according to Pauline language (in which God always means the Father of Jesus Christ) the Father suffered *with* and *in* the Son; and he did so by virtue of his indwelling in the Son through the Holy Spirit, as we may interpretatively add. If the Spirit is God's empathy, this means that the eternal Spirit is also involved, in profoundest and identifying suffering. It is precisely his suffering with the Son to the point of death on the cross which makes the rebirth of Christ from the Spirit inwardly possible. The Spirit participates in the dying of the Son in order to give him new "life from the dead."

29. Moltmann, *Spirit of Life*, 64.
30. Moltmann, *Spirit of Life*, 65.
31. Moltmann, *Spirit of Life*, 67.

Because he accompanies Christ to his end, he can make his end a new beginning.[32]

D. Lyle Dabney argues that Moltmann's theology of kenosis creates possibilities for constructing a pneumatology of the cross. The history of the messianic Christ is integrally related to the history of the Spirit, in that suffering and sacrifice of Jesus Christ is possible in and by the Spirit of God. In the life of Christ, both words and wonder *and* suffering and sacrifice are signs of the Spirit's presence.[33] The Spirit, who is eschatological life, is at work on both sides of the cross. The Spirit of the cross, who is the life-giving Spirit, enters into death in order to raise Jesus to new life. "The Spirit of God is, thus, the *Spirit of the cross, the Spirit of self sacrifice and resurrection of Jesus Christ.*"[34] Dabney asks, what then does the cry of abandonment on the cross mean for the Spirit? The point of abandonment represents the complete nullification of the Spirit's work, an abnegation of the Spirit that coincides with the negation of the Son. In the cross, the Father abandons and loses the Son and the Son is abandoned by the Father. "But the Spirit suffers neither such a 'loss' nor such an 'abandonment'. Rather, what the Spirit experiences is a function not of *absence* but of *presence*. For the Spirit of the Cross is the *presence of God with the Son in the absence of the Father.*"[35] The kenotic experience of the Spirit, then, is one in which the Spirit binds himself so intimately to the Son that with the Son he descends into death and hell, and so abnegates the totality of his life-giving work and love, in order to bring resurrection life. The Spirit brings about the novuum, and is therefore the possibility of God. Dabney emphatically writes:

> *The Holy Spirit is the Spirit of the self-sacrifice and resurrection of Jesus Christ made manifest in the Trinitarian kenosis of God on the cross, the possibility of God even in the midst of every impossibility that God could be present and active, the divine possibility that the living God might be found even in the midst of chaos and death, indeed, precisely in the midst of chaos and death, the possibility that God might yet be for us and we might yet be for God,*

32. Moltmann, *Spirit of Life*, 68.

33. D. Lyle Dabney, "Naming the Spirit: Towards a Pneumatology of the Cross," in Gordon Preece and Stephen Pickard, eds., *Starting with the Spirit* (Australia: Australian Theological Forum, 2001) 45.

34. Dabney, "Naming the Spirit," 53 (author's emphasis).

35. Dabney, "Naming the Spirit," 56 (author's emphasis).

and thus the possibility that even those who suffer that deadly estrangement might beyond death be raised to new life, transformed life, a life in which the crushed and broken and incoherent bits and pieces of life are taken up anew and made whole. The Spirit of God, therefore, is not to be identified simply as "power" or as "life" or as "relationship" or as "gendered," male or female—as is so often the case. For in brief, *the Spirit of God is the possibility of God.*[36]

The power of the Spirit of God is the power of suffering sacrifice, opening the universe up to the possibilities of eschatological transformation.

If we return to the question of the role of the Spirit in the event of the cross, the kenosis of Spirit is the realization of divine love. Contra impassibility, God is a God who chooses to love, and in doing so opens himself up to the vulnerabilities of love. In love, God sovereignly chooses to commit himself to his covenant, even if it brings about pain and suffering in the rejection of his loved ones.[37] "God is love; love makes a person capable of suffering; and love's capacity for suffering is fulfilled in the self-giving and the self-sacrifice of the lover. Self-sacrifice is God's very nature and essence."[38] In his love for the world (John 3.16), God opens himself up to vulnerability, to pain and suffering. In opening himself to vulnerability, God makes a way for the future of creation and its creatures. The Spirit's kenosis in Jesus on the cross is therefore embedded in the logic of possibility, in that the Spirit mediates the pain of love between the Father and the Son, and as the Spirit of Christ mediates the love of God to us, as God identifies with, and seeks to overcome all suffering in, creation, creatures, and ultimately the entire cosmos.

Kenosis and the Charismatic Spirit

Creation and the Christ event are two integrated "modes" of divine kenosis. The third is the charismatic dimensions of indwelling Spirit. Charismatic presence is the outcome of the Spirit's sending. Divine kenosis, I will argue, corresponds to divine mission. Moltmann implies this in his doctrine of kenosis, but I want to make it more explicit.

---

36. Dabney, "Naming the Spirit," 58 (author's emphasis).

37. Moltmann, *Trinity and the Kingdom*, 27.

38. Moltmann, *Trinity and the Kingdom*, 32.

Divine kenosis and the missio dei are mutually coherent acts of the triune God.

Moltmann links the experience of the Spirit to the missio dei.[39] "The experiences of the Holy Spirit are comprehended in the light of the sending of the Spirit."[40] Stated stronger, "It is not the church that has a mission of salvation to fulfil to the world; it is the mission of the Son and the Spirit though the Father that includes the church."[41] At the primordial "moment" in the triune life, when God willed to send his Son into the world and the Son willed to empty himself and come into the world for its sake, the Spirit too was sent. Divine sending embraces creation and redemption as integral components in divine mission. "God's mission is nothing less than the sending of the Holy Spirit from the Father through the Son into the world, so that this world should not perish but live."[42] In sending the Spirit, God affirms life and protests against its destruction.[43] The mission of the Spirit is tied to the messianic mission of Christ, and as we have seen, the Spirit is the energy that provides the strength for Christ to fulfill and complete his messianic mission.[44] Because both Christ and the Spirit are sent together by the Father, Moltmann eschews the *filioque* addition to the Western creed, preferring an Eastern orientation, in which "the Spirit proceeds from the Father," and "is 'now' sent by the Son" who is poured out in

39. David Bosch was instrumental in developing a theology of mission, which expands beyond missions as functions of the church, to mission as the activity of the triune God:

> The primary purpose of the *missiones ecclesiae* can therefore not simply be the planting of churches or the saving of souls; rather, it has to be service to the *missio Dei*, representing God in and over against the world, pointing to God, holding up the God-child before the eyes of the world in a ceaseless celebration of the Feast of Epiphany. In its mission, the church witnesses to the fullness of the promise of God's reign and participates in the ongoing struggle between that reign and the powers of darkness and evil.

See David Bosch, *Transforming Mission: Paradigm Shifts in Theology of Mission* (Maryknoll, NY: Orbis, 1991) 391.

40. Moltmann, *Church in the Power of the Spirit*, 54.

41. Moltmann, *Church in the Power of the Spirit*, 64.

42. Jürgen Moltmann, *The Source of Life: The Holy Spirit and the Theology of Life*, trans. Margaret Kohl (London: SCM, 1997) 19.

43. Moltmann, *Source of Life*, 19.

44. See Moltmann, *Way of Jesus Christ*, 73ff.

order to make "all things new," because the Spirit of God has become
the Spirit of Christ.[45] "The Father begets the Son in the power of the
eternal Spirit. The Father breathes out the eternal Spirit in the presence of the Son. The Son and the Spirit—if we keep the image of Word
and Breath—proceed simultaneously from the Father. The one does not
precede the other."[46] Divine kenosis and divine mission are implicitly
connected, in Moltmann, as a prior determination in God to open up
the trinitarian life to the possibilities of creation, redemption, and the
novuum of the new creation.

The outworking of the mission of God, in sending his only begotten Son, and breathing out the Spirit in the affirmation of life, is the
incorporation of the people of God, all life and its environment, and
indeed all of the cosmos, in the charismatic dimensions of the Spirit.
The Shekinah presence of God as a kenotic act is key in understanding
the charismatic manifestation of God. Just as God's Shekinah was and is
present in creation, so too is it in the redemptive and charismatic presence of the Spirit, who draws the community of faith and the universe
itself into the eschaton. Shekinah is understood as: 1) the efficacious
presence of the Spirit, not as an attribute of God, nor even as gift, but as
God in person. Through his Shekinah the Spirit empathizes with God's
creatures, who are the loved of God. 2) Shekinah points to a "sensibility,"
in that the Spirit indwells, is grieved, is quenched. The Spirit rejoices with
its creation and grieves in the suffering of the weak. The presence of the
Spirit "in us" fills us with longing for unity with God, drawing us along
in the journey. The Spirit groans for the new creation, the transformed
universe, when it will be at blissful rest in the transfigured cosmos.
3) Shekinah coincides with kenosis in that divine love is a passible and
suffering love. Theophanies of the Spirit are then not anthropomor-
phisms, but the presence of the indwelling Spirit.[47] Images of the Spirit,
such as "outpouring," "flowing," "birth," "washing," etc., are indicators of
the Spirit's kenotic activity. "The charismatic, the gift and energies of the
Spirit in the new fellowship will not be 'created'; as fruits of *charis*, the
gift of the Spirit itself, they will be 'effect' (1 Corinthians 12). These are

---

45. Moltmann, *Trinity and the Kingdom*, 89.

46. Moltmann, *Spirit of Life*, 71–72.

47. Moltmann, *Spirit of Life*, 51.

divine energies which already quicken life now, in the present, because they are the energies of the new creation of all things."[48]

The cosmic implications of the kenosis of the Spirit are profound. Moltmann's concern for the care of the environment can be seen in the subtitle of *God in Creation: An Ecological Doctrine of Creation.* He explicitly states, "The divine secret of creation is the Shekinah, God's indwelling; and the purpose of the Shekinah is to make the whole creation the house of God."[49] Creation has an anthropological side as the world of human beings, but also an ecological side as the dwelling place of the Spirit in the bio-ecological and cosmic systems of creation, systems that are dependent on the enlivening efficacy of the Spirit.[50] Creation is not limited to the constituent components of human life, the realm of animals, or micro-organisms, but necessarily includes non-living components: minerals, molecules, atoms, and subatomic particles and forces.[51] Yet creation has an eschatological side in that all life and non-life in the universe will be transfigured and transformed in the new creation, in that creation groans in suffering for its redemption (Rom 8:22–23).

How does this relate to Spirit kenosis? Creation is the whole cosmos, which is currently sustained by the life-giving presence of the Spirit, but also the eschatological dwelling place of God, when it will be in God, and God in it. On a human level, this means that we as God's creatures must care for God's creation. The world is not ours to use as we please, but we are servants to creation because God has entrusted us with it. On a biological level, kenosis of Spirit means that life is constituted in self-giving. The galaxies in which we live were formed from the death of older stars. Life is supported by the death of previous life, and death will further support new life, physically uniting the structures of life with creation on an atomic level. Cosmically, the self-giving of life to support new life means that resurrected life is a commingling with all other life, in that all the structures of the cosmos are intrinsically interrelated. The eschatological resurrection is an interpenetration of all life in a way analogous with the perichoretic life of the persons of the

---

48. Moltmann, *Trinity and the Kingdom,* 104.

49. Moltmann, *God in Creation,* xii–xiii.

50. Moltmann, *God in Creation,* xiii.

51. Moltmann, *God in Creation,* 203.

triune God.[52] The self-giving Spirit, who experiences the death throes of Christ Jesus, and descends into death to raise him to new life, is the Spirit who enables Christ to transform death into the outpouring of new life. The Spirit of the crucified Christ likewise transforms the destruction of death in creation into life giving presence.

Yet the Shekinah presence of God as the outworking of divine mission is to draw the community of faith into God's mission, which is the growing of the kingdom and celebration of the divine life. God's Shekinah, which was once restricted to the Temple, now fills the people of God personally, and corporately, fills the universe as its seeks its transfiguration, and looks to the glorifying presence of God in new creation. Moltmann asserts:

> A *new divine presence* is experienced in the experience of the Spirit . . . . In the Spirit God dwells in man himself. The experience of the Spirit is therefore the experience of the Shekinah, the divine indwelling. The Shekinah is a divine presence which was otherwise only experienced in the Temple, in worship on the Lord's day. But now men and women themselves, even in their own bodies, already become the temple of the Holy Spirit (I Cor. 6.13–20). In the end, however, the new heaven and new earth will become the "temple" of God's indwelling. The whole world will become God's home. Through the indwelling of the Spirit, people and churches are already glorified *in* body, now, in the present. But then the whole creation will be transfigured through the indwelling of God's glory.[53]

In God's Shekinah, the charismatic presence of the Spirit endows God's people to participate in God's mission, which includes the whole cosmos.

Moltmann's theology also makes room for the charismatic presence of the Spirit in which gifts are distributed throughout the church. The charismatic energies of the Spirit liberate the world from violence and oppression, giving hope in despair. The Spirit raises Christ from the dead, overcoming sin and death, and is the guarantee for the coming of the new reign. The energies of the Spirit draw this world into the community of the new creation. The gifts of the Spirit are not merely for

---

52. Nonn Verna Harrison, "Theosis as Salvation: An Orthodox Perspective," *Pro Ecclesia* 6:4 (1997) 439.

53. Moltmann, *Trinity and the Kingdom*, 104–5.

the community of the saved, but oriented toward the suffering, the lost, and the downtrodden in the world, freeing the world from the powers of death, and liberating creation as it groans for its redemption.[54] The Spirit mediates the coming reign of Christ to this world, a reign that is both already inaugurated in the resurrection of Jesus (and therefore creating anticipatory hope for the new heavens and the new earth), and an indictment of the dark powers that try to destroy God's creation, the people of God, and indeed all people everywhere. The Spirit mediates the kingdom in the creative energies of the life-giver, and is therefore continuous with a creation that God has deemed good, but also stands in judgment over sin, death, and destruction, demonstrating a stark discontinuity between the eschatological vision and the godforsakenness of this world.

A kenosis of Spirit that is present with us in this world in charismatic dimensions must demonstrate not only the distinct reality of anticipatory hope in the promise of God's presence, but also that the real crisis in this world is that it is still ruled by the powers of death and destruction. The Spirit is the power by which we overcome this darkness. The self-emptying Spirit fulfills his sent mission in unity with Christ, through a condescension which brings about the Spirit's presence in the world and draws the people of God into the mission of God. It is also by that Spirit—who empowered Jesus to endure the suffering of the cross, but raised him to new life—that we are empowered and "sent out" to be a light, salt, leavening yeast, and city on a hill, to shine forth the hope of the world. The charismatic presence of the Spirit, who calls us and empowers us with diverse giftings, mediating to us the hope of Jesus' reign, also urges us to empty ourselves, to give ourselves to the world for the sake of the Father's creation. The Spirit empowers us to become servants to others. Yet the charismatic presence of the Spirit already presupposes a kenosis of Spirit, a sacrifice for the other; and likewise the Spirit empowers us to be servants for the kingdom, participating with God in his mission to reconcile the whole world. The charismatic gifts—whether they are healings, dreams and visions, tongues, prophecy, or such like—are not for personal gratification, but for the other, for the lost, the heartless, the poor and the weak, to raise them up and show them their inherent dignity before God. We participate in God's

---

54. Moltmann, *Church in the Power of the Spirit*, 293–94.

self-emptying in becoming servants to God and others, looking to the messianic coming of God's new creation.

Concluding Remarks

Moltmann has offered the world a creative theology of the Spirit in kenosis. The self-emptying of the Spirit is an inward and outward trinitarian event, primordial in its enactment, inaugurated in creation, vicarious in the enduring pain of the Father's abandonment of the Son on the cross and of the Son's abandonment to the powers of darkness, and "poured out" into the world for the sake of the world to come. The charismatic presence of the Spirit is a kenotic experience that enables the people of the crucified One to celebrate in anticipation of God's eschatological presence, inviting those who are weak and impoverished to participate in grace and be reconciled to God and with one another. Understanding the Spirit's presence as a kenotic occurrence would make it possible for Pentecostals to construct a theology of Spirit as missional service: service to God, service to others, and service to the creation itself as the outworking of God's love.

PART FOUR

Contextual and Disciplinary Applications

10

"God's Laws of Productivity"

Creation in African Pentecostal Hermeneutics

J. Kwabena Asamoah-Gyadu

Introduction

Questions relating to the origin of creation—its wonder, mystery, and purpose—matter to Pentecostals in Africa, although like their compatriots elsewhere around the world, the discussion has mainly been in "polemical and defensive ways."[1] Yet as one Ghanaian Pentecostal averred in a conversation on "creation and science," "for us God created the world and the discoveries of science underscore that fact; after all it is God who created the brains of the scientist too." Thus African Pentecostals do not share separatist worldviews that dichotomize creation and science as belonging to different realms of reality. God is

---

1. Amos Yong, *The Spirit Poured Out on All Flesh: Pentecostalism and the Possibility of Global Theology* (Grand Rapids, MI: Baker, 2005) 267.

present in the work of science. This chapter looks at these various understandings of creation from the viewpoint of African Pentecostals.[2]

African Indigenous Churches

Pentecostalism has blossomed in many directions since the emergence of the African Independent Churches (AICs) at the turn of the twentieth century. Although Harvey Cox described the AICs as "the African expression of the worldwide Pentecostal movement,"[3] we must be careful in casting them as "Pentecostal" without qualification particularly because of the close proximity of their healing rituals to traditional African religious practices. Nevertheless these AICs blazed the trail in incorporating charismatic renewal phenomena into African church life. They are important for our work because they were the precursors of modern African Pentecostalism and their emphasis on the supremacy of God could be taken as the premise upon which the African Pentecostal understanding of creation is generally based. In the hermeneutic of the AICs God is supreme because he created the world and has absolute control over what happens in it.

Within such a religiously pluralistic context as that of traditional Africa with its pantheon of gods and deities, the message of indigenous charismatic prophets whose fiery preaching brought the AICs into being upheld the supremacy of God as the source of creation. They challenged their followers to repent, throw away their smaller deities—invariably consisting of items of nature-like stones enchanted with spirits—and come to this God of the Bible in whom alone there was fullness of life. One of these prophets who operated around the Niger Delta in the early years of the twentieth century, Garrick S. Braide, sought to prove the supremacy of God by calling upon him to deliver rain in the midst of drought, a feat originally associated with the "gods of rain" that traditional religious cultures recognized. Quoting Lamin Sanneh:

2. Readers should note that most of my generalizations in the first part of this chapter about African Christianity and African Pentecostalism are derived primarily from West African sources. While I do not think that West African views are exhaustively representative of the wider continent in every respect, I have decided not to clutter the chapter with endless qualifications that in the end will not mean much to western readers (where this book is being published). Readers more familiar with other African perspectives will know when to make the necessary adjustments.

3. Harvey Cox, *Fire from Heaven: The Rise of Pentecostal Spirituality and the Reshaping of Religion in the Twenty-First Century* (Reading, MA: Addison-Wesley, 1995) 246.

In his duel with traditional rainmakers, for example, he settled the dispute by calling on what he regarded as a higher power to achieve precisely what his opponents had previously achieved by calling on intermediary powers. It is clear that Braide had merely asserted the power of a Christian God over a territory of long familiarity, rather than shifting the religious contest to totally new ground.[4]

Following the AICs, Western mission-related classical Pentecostals evangelized sub-Saharan Africa from the 1920s, but through the 1950s and 60s the region produced its own version of such denominations, notably the Church of Pentecost and various apostolic churches in Ghana.

Contemporary Charismatic Christianity, Creation, and Science

The growth in Pentecostalism has continued apace with the fresh stream of Pentecostal churches popularly referred to as "charismatic ministries" burgeoning in sub-Saharan Africa since the late 1970s. It is this latest wave of Pentecostal churches, especially in West Africa that constitute the focus of this chapter. The new Pentecostal/Carismatic churches (PCCs) are noted for their mega-sized congregations, gifted and highly articulate leadership, the large numbers of upwardly mobile youth they attract, their extensive appropriations of modern media technologies, exuberant worship, and the innovative ways in which the Bible is interpreted to contemporary African audiences. Emory University educated Ghanaian pastoral theologian, Emmanuel Y. Lartey, writes of their influence in Africa:

> The success of charismatic Christianity in Africa has lain largely in its ability to propagate itself as "powerful and efficacious" in enabling people to be set free from the dangers and troubles of life. The worship and teaching of these churches have by and large been geared towards the experiencing of the effective presence of the Holy Spirit. Christians have been urged and have experienced "God in their midst" in demonstrable, even tangible ways. . . . Charismatic churches in Africa have managed to develop a crisp, clear and direct message which speaks to many

4. Lamin O. Sanneh, *West African Christianity: The Religious Impact* (Maryknoll, NY: Orbis, 1983) 182.

concerns of the average person in terms that are both appealing and interesting.[5]

The "crisp, clear and direct message" spoken of by Lartey includes the hermeneutics of creation. This chapter examines African Pentecostal understandings of creation and the role of science in explaining its dynamic primarily by looking at the sermons and publications of selected charismatic personalities like Pastor Matthew Ashimolowo and Pastor Mensa Otabil. In relation to creation in particular, the emphasis of Pentecostal/charismatic preaching is usually on "dominion" and "empowerment." On that score science itself, with its ability to unravel and explain that which is incomprehensible, simply bears testimony to the greatness and supremacy of God who has given men and women such abilities to explain what is otherwise inexplicable. Thus science is one proof of the dominant role that God has given the human person within the created order.

We should note that the books from Pentecostal/charismatic stables, written by some of the most popular charismatic church pastors from Africa, are not academic publications. They tend to be published versions of sermons preached both from church pulpits and television and radio ministries. I will also refer to *Jesus of the Deep Forest,* a collection of "prayers and praises" from the late Afua Kuma, an illiterate Ghanaian member of the Church of Pentecost. In keeping with these recent developments in African theology, then, I rely almost entirely on the oral theological discourses of African Pentecostals in forming my conclusions.

In this essay, I will seek to show that the questions of science and creation and the contentious debates that they have generated in the West do not arise as far as the African Pentecostal hermeneutic of creation is concerned. Rather, contemporary African Pentecostals admire creation as God's handiwork and seek to understand and work out their own purposes within it, that is, to "dominate" creation by working it for the advancement of humankind. Indeed unlike the AICs and the African classical Pentecostals in their earlier years in the 1930s and 40s, the new Pentecostal or charismatic churches have attracted significant numbers of highly educated persons with many of them being founders

5. Emmanuel Y. Lartey, "Of Formulae, Faith and Fear," *Trinity Journal of Church and Theology* 11:1–2 (January/June 2001) 8–9.

of such churches. Thus there are churches such as Lighthouse Chapel International founded by Bishop Dag Heward-Mills, a trained medical doctor, and Deeper Life Bible Church founded and led by Dr. William F. Kumuyi, who taught mathematics at the university level in Nigeria before becoming a pastor. The leaders and members of these churches therefore have a sense of the debates relating to the role of science in creation but the core of their messages on the subject relate more to the supremacy of God in bringing creation into being and granting the human person dominion over it than to how science disproves the African understanding of the biblical position that creation took place within six days.

God: Source of Creation

One way to understand how Pentecostals/charismatic churches view creation is to look at their corporate worship. As a movement that does not articulate its theology in very formal ways, worship is an important medium for the expression Pentecostal beliefs. God is worshipped precisely because he is the source of creation. Enlightenment mentality and sophisticated advances in science and technology have brought much of Western Christianity to the point where transcendence seems to have been crowded out of public space through rationalization and secularization. However, the growth of Pentecostalism, a highly experiential movement, reverses these trends among its faithful. To that end, as far as the rise of Pentecostalism in the twenty-first century is concerned, to use the words of Harvey Cox, "it is secularity, not spirituality that is headed for extinction."[6] African Pentecostals in particular have chosen a path different from that of the Enlightenment by functioning theologically within a worldview in which the "transcendent God, Jesus Christ crucified, risen and exalted, the Holy Spirit and all other spiritual presences are perceived as actively impinging upon human life."[7] That God created the world and literally did so in six days is a non-negotiable theological fact in African Pentecostal/charismatic hermeneutics.

But God as Creator, Provider, and Sustainer of the universe is also central to African traditional religious belief. Here there is no dichot-

---

6. Cox, *Fire from Heaven*, xv.

7. Kwame Bediako, "Worship as Vital Participation: Some Personal Reflections on Ministry in the African Church," *Journal of African Thought* 2:2 (December 2005) 4.

omy between sacred and secular realities; the two are fused and undifferentiated at all levels and in most cases, the physical becomes a vehicle for the spiritual. In this primal worldview the earth is sacred because it originates from the Supreme Being himself. The Earth is not worshipped as such but its sanctity is expected to be maintained through the observation of taboos. Like the "ground" of the days of Cain and Abel, the Earth abhors the shedding of innocent blood and must not be defiled (for example, by having sexual intercourse directly on it). Thus in the creation narratives in Genesis African Pentecostals encounter an idea of God that resonates with traditional ideas. The Earth is the Lord's and all that is in it. Based on the work of Inus Daneel among the Shona of Zimbabwe for instance, Cox illustrates the interface between traditional religious ideas on the sanctity of the Earth and the environmental theology of the AICs:

> Wizardry has come to have a larger meaning. It now includes offenses against the "Earthkeeping Spirit," which is itself an African understanding of the Christian Holy Spirit. Violations of the Earthkeeping Spirit encompasses any activities that lead to soil erosion, fouling the water supply, or chopping down trees without replacing them. . . . More specifically, this ethic is based on a spirituality that mixes ancient African religious sensibilities with modern environmental awareness, and it is taking place within a movement that has arisen as Christian Pentecostal impulses have interacted with the throbbing universe of African primal religion.[8]

Pentecostal/charismatic preaching, singing, and writing on the creation narratives serve to underscore God's position as an omnipotent being capable of all things. The creation is thus interpreted in terms of a "dominion theology" that underlies religious discourses in African Pentecostal/charismatic Christianity.

The key expression in this understanding of how the world came to be is the "power of the spoken word." In contemporary African Pentecostal/charismatic Christianity, words have lives of their own, so that God spoke creation into existence becomes a noteworthy fact.

8. Cox, *Fire from Heaven*, 245; cf. M. L. Daneel, "African Independent Church Pneumatology and the Salvation of all Creation," in Harold D. Hunter and Peter D. Hocken, eds., *All Together in One Place: Theological Papers from the Brighton Conference on World Evangelization* (Sheffield: Sheffield Academic, 1993) 96–126.

Pentecostal/charismatic preachers thus enable their audiences not to discount science as such, but to see God himself as the "master scientist" with specific purposes within creation for his children. This message is encapsulated in the work of his hands, especially, in the grandeur of the created order.

In the African cosmology, then, creation speaks and its unfathomable mystical nature demonstrates God's glory and majesty. Thus, as is often heard in African Pentecostal preaching, those who question the divine architectural source of the created order are like the fool who "says in his heart that there is no God." Indeed, in African traditional religious thought, creation is sacred precisely because its origin is divine. It is the Supreme Being who created the world. Thus among Africans nature in itself, as with the Earth, is enchanted with the supernatural and mountains, rocks, rivers, lakes and trees—anything that is super-size and whose presence overwhelms human understanding—is considered to be divine in some way. The natural environment is the abode of different kinds of spirits with many of them considered messengers or agents of the one Supreme Being who created them all. Much of this worldview explains why Africa has often been presented as "animistic" worshippers of nature. Although Pentecostals do not share this belief in a "sacramental environment," the divine origin of creation is taken for granted and worship is then viewed as an opportunity to acknowledge God's majesty and power as revealed in his creation.

Creation as "Confession of Faith"

In an important essay that takes off from the encounter between Jesus and Nicodemus, D. Lyle Dabney makes the point that the creation narratives in the opening chapters of Genesis should be recognized as "confession of faith" concerning the relationship existing between the God of the Patriarchs and the world and how that relationship with God determines the nature of the world:

> The creation narrative in Genesis, therefore, is not primarily about "*how* the world came to be," but rather about "*who* is the world's Creator and what does that mean for creation." By speaking of creation in this way, Genesis demonstrates the connection between the story of Israel and that of all the world: the God of all creation is the One who has called and thereby created Israel

so that God's good purposes of blessing all creation might be achieved.[9]

If the story of the "God and Israel" is to be understood within the larger story of "God and the world," as Dabney suggests, then African Pentecostals can place themselves within that story too. The reference to the creation narratives as "confession of faith" is particularly important. For worship is usually driven by faith. We worship that which we have come to believe in as "Ultimately Real" to us. Fundamental to all authentic Christian worship therefore, African theologian Kwame Bediako notes, "is the self-revelation of God, given in and through the Scriptures and supremely in Jesus Christ, and imparted to the body of Christ, namely the Church, by the Holy Spirit."[10] The Creator-Spirit is the one who hovered over the waters in order to bring "order" out of the primordial "chaos" we encounter in the opening verses of Genesis 1.

Against this background we can see the importance, in Pentecostal corporate worship, of the special segment that is always reserved for extolling the virtues of God as the power behind the universe. This is articulated in the lyrics of one African Pentecostal worship song:

> When I look up the mountain
> When I look down the valley
> When I look at the sea
> O My Lord, you are God!

In Africa this type of Pentecostal oral theological discourse mediated through preaching, singing, and praying is deliberately crafted to recall the beauty of creation, God's relationship to it, and humankind's place within it. Invariably these ways of appreciating the divine source of creation are seen to concur with the words of the Psalmist:

> The heavens declare the glory of God; And the firmament shows His handiwork. Day unto day utters speech; and night unto night reveals knowledge. There is no speech nor language where their voice is not heard. Their line has gone out through all the earth; and their words to the end of the world. In them He has set a tabernacle for the sun, which is like a bridegroom coming

9. D. Lyle Dabney, "The Nature of the Spirit: Creation as a Premonition of God," in Michael Welker, ed., *The Work of the Spirit: Pneumatology and Pentecostalism* (Grand Rapids, MI: Eerdmans, 2006) 74; emphases Dabney's.

10. Bediako, "Worship as Vital Participation," 3.

> out of his chamber, and rejoices like a strong man to run its race.
> Its rising is from one end of heaven and its circuit to the other
> end; And there is nothing hidden from its heat. (Ps 19:1–6)

Here, the created order is presented as bearing witness to the existence of God and acknowledging him as the source of its own being.

Through African Pentecostal confessions of faith—prayers, songs, and messages—creation have both pneumatological and christological significance. The ultimate aim of Pentecostal theology is to remain true to the Bible and to recover for present experience what is demystified and demythologized in liberal academic theology and Christianity. Science remains relevant in the scheme of things because through it, God has given men and women the means to help unravel the mysteries of creation. To that extent, it is thought that science affirms the existence of God rather than edges him out of the universe he has created.

Creation and Dominion Theology

In the Pentecostal/charismatic churches under consideration here, therefore, creation is discussed not in terms of the debates between "evolution" and "intelligent design" but in terms of the dominant role that humankind was supposed to play in creation. The black race and what it has done with the "power of dominion" granted by God is a matter of great concern for Africa's new charismatic leaders.[11] Pastor Matthew Ashimolowo of the Kingsway International Christian Center in London and Pastor Mensa Otabil of the International Central Gospel Church in Ghana are two of the leading and most articulate voices within this new stream of African Pentecostalism. Ashimolowo has written *What is Wrong with Being Black?* and Otabil wrote *Beyond the Rivers of Ethiopia.*[12] The basic arguments of these two publications and several others from African charismatic leaders are that first, God

11. Although I do not generally subscribe to the view that African PCCs are a North American import, there is no doubting the fact that its "dominion theology" is one area in which the American influence is very evident. The leadership of PCCs consciously access North American televangelistic media resources through which such theological ideas are received and reappropriated for local contexts.

12. Matthew Ashimolowo, *What is Wrong with Being Black: Celebrating our Heritage, Confronting our Challenges* (Shippensburg, PA: Destiny Image, 2007), and Mensa Otabil, *Beyond the Rivers of Ethiopia* (Accra: Altar International, 1992, and Bakersfield, CA: Pneuma Life, 1993).

has given the human person dominion over creation, and that second, contrary to what some believe, the black race has never been cursed and definitely it is not meant to be subservient to whites.

With regard to the first theme, Mensa Otabil writes of creation in the opening pages of his other book, *Four Laws of Productivity*, as follows:

> *Genesis* is "the book of beginnings," and in the beginning, God had a purpose and a plan. That purpose and plan for creation is summed up in Genesis 1 . . . . Special attention is given to the details of His purpose for Man—to have *dominion*. But the big question is: "How was that dominion to be exercised[?]" The answer is in Genesis 1:28, "And God blessed them and said to them, be fruitful, and multiply, and replenish the earth, and subdue it: and have dominion over the fish of the sea, and over the fowl of the air, and over every living thing that moveth upon the earth."[13]

Pastor Mensa Otabil explains that God "looked at this creation of his, and the first words he muttered to Adam were, 'be fruitful, multiply, replenish the earth, subdue the earth.'"[14] The four laws Pastor Otabil derives are fruitfulness, multiplication, replenishment, and subjugation of the earth. These laws, he continues, "became principles, or instincts, on which the whole of human life would operate. After declaring these four laws to Adam, God then continued with his first expressed purpose: 'and have dominion.'"[15] Part of the process of exercising dominion, Otabil notes, involves being fruitful by using the raw materials of the earth to bring forth the ideas God puts in our minds. God has provided each of us with a seed, he explains, and our responsibility within creation is to work on it so that our full potential would be realized to his glory. "Every person on earth has a seed inside that God can reproduce to bring a harvest. Everything we have is a product of fruitfulness. Everything God wants us to be is found in Gen 1:28, the four laws of productivity."[16]

13. Mensa Otabil, *Four Laws of Productivity: God's Foundation for Living* (Tulsa, OK: Vincom, 1991) 11.

14. Otabil, *Four Laws of Productivity*, 13.

15. Otabil, *Four Laws of Productivity*, 13.

16. Otabil, *Four Laws of Productivity*, 3–4.

The question of "dominion" in relation to creation is thus critical to the charismatic understanding regarding why God created heaven and earth in the first place. Otabil then draws a connection between scientific inventions and the theology of dominion, and his words are worth quoting at some length:

> You see, God's main expressed purpose for making man was for mankind to have dominion. Part of the process of exercising dominion involves being fruitful by using the raw materials of the earth to bring forth ideas God puts in our minds. Every invention of man that has been produced in the world has been developed out of the raw material of the earth. When God impregnates our minds with his seed-ideas, they remain invisible and immaterial until we are able to fashion a body for them out of the resources of the earth. The iron, steel, platinum, gold and other precious metals that have given substance to the inventive ideas of men all were derived from the earth. . . . The same is true of vaccines, books and computer chips . . . [17]

In the foreword to Pastor Otabil's *Four Laws of Productivity*, Myles Munroe, himself a popular Caribbean charismatic preacher, refers to the relationship between creation and human purpose in it in terms of the dominion theology:

> Our Creator purposely placed within the earth everything necessary for life, health and happiness, and then provided us with the mental and intellectual ability and capacity to maximize and efficiently utilize these resources. However, he also established laws and principles by which the relationship between creation and the Creator should function. When these laws our violated, the result is lack, poverty, depression and recession.

These thoughts sustain the thrust of Pastor Otabil's understanding of creation and its purposes in God's economy.

Pastor Ashimolowo continues the theme, writing that Genesis 1 "is the beginning of God's purpose for our lives" and that "the manifestation of that purpose or the lack of it is what makes people's lives fulfilled or frustrated."[18] This purpose of God in creation is considered synonymous with "the dominion we have" and the reason for this dominion "is

17. Otabil, *Four Laws of Productivity*, 19.
18. Ashimolowo, *What is Wrong with Being Black*, 18.

in order to dominate the earth and to continue the process God himself began"; "God rested," he continues, "so we can continue."[19]

Publications and sermons that engage with questions relating to the different interpretations of the origins of creation are not considered important in the Pentecostal/charismatic discourses that I am familiar with. The world was created by God and humankind's role in it is to take dominion and rise to the heights that God has purposed for them.

The second major theme of African Charismatic leaders' writings on creation concerns the role of the black race in taking dominion over and subduing the earth. That the black race has constantly under-achieved and ceded her dominion to the Caucasian provides an impor-tant context for the emphasis on "dominion theology" in the African Pentecostal/Charismatic worldview. It also explains why the story of Jacob and Esau is very important for African Pentecostal/Charismatic preachers. It is as if like Esau, representing the black race generally and Africans in particular, have sold their birthrights and now constantly looking to the western world for help when we should instead seize our divinely given opportunities and forge ahead in life. In these un-derstanding Jacob is an icon and not a cheat who swindled members of his family out of their customary heritage. Pastor Ashimolowo quotes several authors in order to make the point that actually ancient Africa was more developed than Europe but our acquiescence in the evils of slavery and mental laziness over the centuries have ensured that the continent has remained underdeveloped and its peoples consigned to lives of poverty and deprivation.[20] He then writes, "the wealth of Africa was the chief attraction for many people from ancient times . . . . [T]he continent of Africa still stands as possibly the wealthiest on earth, but the oxymoron of it is that the wealthiest continent has the poorest oc-cupants. The wealthiest continent has the occupants who seek for gifts and aid from around the world."[21] The moral of the story drawn is that our new life in Jesus Christ must not only point to eschatological hope, but must be translated into existential relevance because where God wants us to make our impact on this earth.

19. Ashimolowo, *What is Wrong with Being Black*, 19.

20. Ashimolowo, *What is Wrong with Being Black*, 24–25.

21. Ashimolowo, *What is Wrong with Being Black*, 51–52.

Creation, Christology and African Pentecostal Hermeneutics

Part of the Christological import of African Pentecostal creation hermeneutics may be seen in Afua Kuma's little book *Jesus of the Deep Forest*.[22] In Jesus Christ the God of Genesis 1 became part of his own created order. The "Prayers and Praises" of Afua Kuma, an illiterate African Pentecostal woman, not only extol the place of Jesus Christ as Savior and Lord but also provides some poignant perspectives on creation. These have in turn become a source of serious of academic theology in her native Ghana. For example, Kwame Bediako points out that "Jesus of the Deep Forest" is also the "Jesus of the Gospels . . . . He is the miracle worker who does the impossible, who triumphs over the obstacles of nature, who provides food for the hungry and water for the thirsty, who delivers from all manner of ailments and who bestows the wholeness of salvation."[23]

As the "owner" of the created order, Jesus could assume the roles of phenomena like stones, rocks, and mountains as he intervenes in the lives of his people:

> The great Rock we hide behind; the great forest canopy that gives cool shade:
> The Big Tree which lifts its vines to peep at the heavens
> The magnificent Tree whose dripping leaves
> Encourage the luxuriant growth below.[24]

Jesus can also use things in the created order to serve his salvific purposes:

> O great and powerful Jesus, Incomparable Diviner
> The sun and the moon are your *batakari* [apparel of war]
> It sparkles like the morning star.
> *Sekyere Buruku*, the tall mountain
> All the nations see your glory.[25]

---

22. Afua Kuma, *Jesus of the Deep Forest: Prayers and Prayers of Afua*, trans. Jon Kirby (Accra: Asempa, 1981).

23. Kwame Bediako, *Jesus in Africa: The Christian Gospel in African History and Experience* (Yaoundé and Akropong-Akwapim, Ghana: Editions Clé and Regnum Africa, 2000) 11.

24. Kuma, *Jesus of the Deep Forest*, 5.

25. Kuma, *Jesus of the Deep Forest*, 6 (italics in original translation).

> You weave the streams like plaited hair;
> With fountains you tie a knot
> Magician who walks on the sea:
> He arrives at the middle
> Plunges his hand into the deep and takes out a whale![26]

In other words, Jesus has such control over creation that he can turn it around the way he wants to serve his own purposes. The thought that God has creation under his control is also present in the Psalms. God is omnipresent. His presence so animates the created order that as creatures it is fruitless to make any attempt to hide from God. Adam and Eve had attempted to "hide from the Lord God among the trees of the garden" (Gen 3:8). It did not work then and so such an attempt to hide from the omnipresent God within his own creation is considered impossible, as we read from the Psalms:

> Where can I go from your Spirit? Where can I flee from your Presence? If I go up to the heavens, you are there; if I make my bed in the depths, you are there. If I rise on the wings of the dawn, if I settle on the far side of the sea, even there your hand will guide me, your right hand will hold me fast. If I say, "surely the darkness will hide me and the light become night around me, even the darkness will not be dark to you; the night will shine like the day for darkness is as light to you" (Ps 139:7–12).

The reference to the inability of darkness or night to incapacitate and restrict God's actions as outlined in Psalm 139 is a theme that is also present in the "praises and prayers" of Afua Kuma. But she draws out its Christological significance by applying those qualities to Jesus Christ:

> When he walks in darkness he carries no lamp.
> He is led by the sun and followed by lightening
> As he goes his way.[27]

Jesus simply does the impossible not only by breaking through the barriers of darkness but also by catching whales with his bare hands. Further, he can also use weak items such as the spider's web as fishing net, and he can retrieve things from unlikely places such as catching fish in the forest:

---

26. Kuma, *Jesus of the Deep Forest*, 6.

27. Kuma, *Jesus of the Deep Forest*, 11.

The spider's web is his fishing line.
He casts it forth and catches a crocodile.
He casts his fishing net, and catches beds.
He sets a trap in the forest and catches fish.
Holy One![28]

These "prayers and praises" recall New Testament narratives that place the creation firmly under the control of Jesus. One of the most loved of such stories among African Pentecostals is the Jesus who walks on the sea and commands the waves to hold their peace. He even brings the dead back to life in Lazarus and these powers culminate in his own resurrection. In an indigenous religious context in which deities are relied upon to intervene in crisis, a hermeneutic perspective that affirm the ability of Jesus to reverse the normal processes of the created order appeals very strongly to people. Thus African Pentecostal theologians do not speak amiss when they affirm the Christological import of the creation and its control because John already establishes that the Word who "became flesh and dwelt among us" was involved in creating the world: "Through him all things were made; without him nothing was made that has been made" (John 1:3–4).

Conclusion

Much of the resistance to critical thinking and scientific explanations of creation by African Pentecostals has stemmed from the fear that such approaches to faith leads to theological liberalism. They tend to weaken faith, African Pentecostals generally believe, and eventually edge God out of human life. Higher biblical criticism associated with theological education in particular has challenged the assumptions of African Pentecostal biblical literalism. The fear of losing one's faith and becoming liberal like a Western trained mainline church cleric has kept African Pentecostals away from the Western-style seminary educational institutions established by the historic mission denominations in Africa. Anecdotally, Pastor Mensa Otabil of the Central Gospel Church has even described Ghana's premier ecumenical seminary, the Trinity Theological Seminary where pastors of the mainline churches are trained, as a "cemetery" from where only "dead bones" could come.

---

28. Kuma, *Jesus of the Deep Forest*, 6.

While the suspicion has not gone away, the situation has improved tremendously. Over the years hostility has turned to collaboration with pastors of Pentecostal churches now actively pursuing theological training in institutions they initially accused of compromising biblical infallibility through critical theological reflection. The changes have come partly through the increasing numbers of Pentecostal pastors and leaders who are themselves highly trained professionals, including engineers and medical doctors as we saw in the case of Bishop Heward-Mills of the Lighthouse Chapel in Ghana. It is unlikely in this context that the ardent belief in a literal six-day creation of the world will persist among the emerging crop of highly educated and sophisticated. Gradually the discoveries of science are being generally accepted among African Pentecostals. There is a higher appreciation of the benefits of science which is seen as part of God's gift to humankind.

Yet such acceptance and appreciation is seen also to re-affirm the traditional African Christian and African Pentecostal confession of God as creator, and to underscore God's greatness rather than depreciate faith in him. To the degree that science is capable of being understood as confirming God's existence and creative power, to that same extent the general African Pentecostal attitude, as one has observed it develop over the years, is increasingly that creation and science should not form such a radical opposition. Today, African Pentecostal hermeneutics suggest the two must be seen together as affirming the existence of God and the wonder of his hands and his impenetrable wisdom. The world and everything in it reflect God's majesty as revealed to us in Jesus Christ.

11

Meaning-Making and Religious Experience

A Cognitive Appraisal Model of Pentecostal Experiences of the Holy Spirit

Edward E. Decker, Jr.

Amos Yong has recently challenged Pentecostals to become involved in an ongoing conversation regarding a broader psychological understanding of the Pentecostal experience. In fact, he stated that it was "essential" to do so, and that failure to engage in the ongoing conversation "could undermine the vitality and future of Pentecostal scholarship."[1] In order to prompt the conversation he reiterated three areas of previous research that have focused on various phenomena of the Pentecostal experience. These data stipulate that experiences central to Pentecostal believers facilitate entry into dissociative states, various trance states, and altered states of consciousness. These states, in turn, seem to be conducive to, if not causative of, various phenomena characteristic of

1. See Amos Yong, "Academic Glossolalia? Pentecostal Scholarship, Multi-disciplinarity, and the Science-Religion Conversation," *Journal of Pentecostal Theology* 14 (2005) 61–80, quotes from 65 and 63 respectively.

Pentecostalism. Yong implies that the integration of Pentecostal theology and the behavioral and social sciences holds promise for the ongoing conversation.[2]

If the behavioral and social sciences, psychology in particular, have demonstrated anything, they have demonstrated that people and groups differ in their sensitivity and vulnerability to certain type of events, as well as in their interpretations and reactions to those events.[3] As might be imagined, this is true of Pentecostal experiences of "the Holy Spirit."[4] These differences may be due to differing theologies,[5] personality differences,[6] or group norms.[7] However, individual (and group) differences may also be related to individual cognitive processes that mediate between one's stated experience of "the Spirit" and one's response to the same.

Christian scripture is replete with references to the interaction of the Holy Spirit with humanity. These references reveal three perspectives

2. To Yong's credit, he has also contributed to the conversation by suggesting a typology of "Spirit" which calls for further illumination of the *hagios pneuma*; see Yong, "Discerning the Spirit(s) in the Natural World: Toward a Typology of 'Spirit' in the Religion and Science Conversation," *Theology & Science* 3 (2005) 315–29; cf. Yong and Paul Ebert, "Christianity, Pentecostalism: Issues in Science and Religion," in J. Wentzel van Huysteen, ed., *Encyclopedia of Science and Religion* (New York: Macmillan, 2003) 1:132–35.

3. Gordon Stanley, William K. Bartlett, and Terri Moyle, "Some Characteristics of Charismatic Experience: Glossolalia in Australia," *Journal for the Scientific Study of Religion* 17 (1978) 269–77; Mark J. Cartledge, *Charismatic Glossolalia: An Empirical Study* (Burlington, VT: Ashgate, 2002); and Leslie J. Francis and Mandy Robbins, "Personality and Glossolalia: A Study among Male Evangelical Clergy," *Pastoral Psychology* 51 (2003) 391–96.

4. When quotation marks are placed around the term "the Spirit," "Holy Spirit," and "the Holy Spirit" it is to demonstrate that this is an idiosyncratic term often used by Pentecostals to identify individual religious encounters that are thought to parallel the experiences so named in biblical text. No attempt is made in this chapter to ascertain the extent to which the Spirit may or may not interact with humanity.

5. Henry I. Lederle, *Ecumenical Theology* (Pretoria: University of South Africa, 1990); Frank D. Macchia, "Pentecostal Theology," in Stanley M. Burgess and Eduardo M. Van Der Mass, eds., *The New International Dictionary of Pentecostal and Charismatic Movements* (Grand Rapids, MI: Zondervan, 2002) 1120–41.

6. Adams Lovekin and H. Newton Maloney, "Religious Glossolalia: A Longitudinal Study of Personality Changes," *Journal for the Scientific Study of Religion* 16 (1977) 383–93.

7. Felicitas Goodman, *Speaking in Tongues: A Cross-cultural Study of Glossolalia* (Chicago: University of Chicago Press, 1972).

of this divine-human interaction. The Spirit is depicted as an indwelling Spirit who cultivates an inner life in persons in order to call them to salvation and to produce fruit of the Spirit. The Spirit is presented as a guide to truth in that the Spirit prompts memory and promotes thoughts regarding the words and deeds of Jesus. The Spirit is also depicted as an empowering Spirit who provokes persons to action, endows insight not previously possessed, and guides in the execution of the intended actions. These same scriptures also depict individual responses to the experience of the Spirit, including glossolalia, inspired speech, and unusual knowledge.

This essay suggests that each person who encounters what he or she identifies as the empowering (or prompting) of the Spirit, knowingly and (most likely) unknowingly, engages in a cognitive appraisal process. This process begins with an internal or external experience. The appraisal occurs automatically, and engages the person in a series of nonconscious decisions as to whether or not the experience is personally meaningful. It also enables the person to make attributions concerning the source of the experience. The appraisal process can be affected by a variety of circumstantial, situational, and personal factors. Ultimately, this process leads to determinations regarding the meaning of the experience and the appropriate response.

What follows below is an explication of this proposed cognitive appraisal process. The discussion begins with an explanation of cognitive appraisal as a meaning making endeavor. The interaction of religious events and the cognitive appraisal process is then identified, and a four step cognitive appraisal process is proposed as a way to understand the response of Pentecostals to what they refer to as an experience of the Holy Spirit.

Cognitive Appraisal as Meaning-Making

The concept that humans engaged in a cognitive appraisal process to understand the events they encounter grew out of research related to military combat. It was evident that different people responded in different ways within the environmental demands and pressures of war. Under comparable conditions, for example, one person responded with anger, another with depression, and still another with valor.[8] Richard

8. See Richard S. Lazarus and Susan Folkman, *Stress, Appraisal, and Coping* (New

Lazarus and Susan Folkman note, "in order to understand variations among individuals under comparable conditions [it became necessary] to take into account the cognitive processes that intervene [mediate] between the encounter and the reaction or response, and the factors that affect the nature of the mediation."[9]

Lazarus and Folkman's cognitive appraisal model has also shown that the factors that influence cognitive mediation include the characteristics of the person on the one hand (e.g., neuroticism, religiosity), and the nature of the environmental event on the other (e.g., beneficial or threatening). Other relevant factors involved in the appraisal process include such things as the presumed cause of the experienced event and the context within which the experience occurs. The appraisal is also influenced by a determination of what is salient for one's well-being in a given event. The subjective meaning of an experience is the result of the appraisal of the various elements of an experience within the context of various personal and environmental factors. The net result of the appraisal process is a determination of an appropriate response to the experience.

Cognitive Appraisal Process and Religious Events

Other researchers like Crystal Park and Lawrence Cohen stipulate that religious events stimulate a similar appraisal process.[10] As is true of the appraisal process in general, the search for religious causation of events is informed by the immediate environmental context in which the experience occurs.[11] In support of these earlier findings, I have suggested

---

York: Springer, 1984) 1–21, for a complete review of the development of the cognitive appraisal process. This chapter includes a number of excellent references.

9. Lazarus and Folkman, *Stress, Appraisal, and Coping*, 23. Although appraisal theory and the appraisal process was conceived in relation to stress and coping it clearly has broader application to any experience people encounter.

10. Crystal L. Park and Lawrence Cohen, "Religious Beliefs and Practices in the Coping Process," in Bruce N. Carpenter, ed., *Personal Coping: Theory, Research, and Application* (Westport, CT: Praeger, 1992) 185–98; cf. also Craig S. Smith and Richard L. Gorsuch, "Sanctioning and Causal Attributions to God: A Function of Theological Position and Actors' Characteristics," *Research in the Social Scientific Study of Religion* 1 (1989) 133–52.

11. Nina P. Azari and Dieter Birnbacher, "The Role of Cognition and Feeling in Religious Experience," *Zygon* 39 (2004) 901–17; Bernard Spilka and Daniel N. McIntosh, "Attribution Theory and Religious Experience," in Ralph W. Hood, ed., *Handbook of*

that persons who are convinced of God's reality and presence ascribe causation to God as a central component of the appraisal process.[12]

Other religiously-related personal factors, such as one's religious orientation, affect the meaning-making process and consequently influences how one interprets events or occurrences.[13] In the same manner, one's God-concept is important in the interpretation of events and occurrences.[14]

A Four-Stage Cognitive Appraisal Model

People utilize a cognitive appraisal process as a way of understanding (making meaning of) the various experiences they encounter. One way to more accurately understand individual (and group) differences related to Pentecostal experiences is to identify the cognitive processes that seem to mediate between one's stated experience of "the Spirit" and one's response to the same. The four-stage cognitive appraisal process identified below draws especially on the previously referenced work of Lazarus and Folkman and Park and Cohen (albeit to be supplemented by other research) and is presented as a model to facilitate such understanding.

The appraisal process, often depicted in a linear fashion, is usually considered to be circular in nature. It may be understood as a decision-making process that occurs in a manner that is consistent with a person's personality and belief structure. The outcome of such a decision-making process is personal meaning, which may in turn lead to further participation in, or rejection of, a particular experience or anticipated response. Table 1 describes the various elements of the appraisal process, each of which is described below.

Religious Experience (Birmingham, AL: Religious Education Press, 1995) 421–25.

12. Edward E. Decker, Jr., "Attributions to God: Implications for Religious Meaning Belief Systems" (lecture given at Oral Roberts University, Tulsa, OK, 2006).

13. Joseph H. Fichter, *Religion and Pain: The Spiritual Dimension of Health Care* (New York: Crossroad, 1981); K. Jill Kielcolt and Hart M. Nelson, "The Structuring of Political Attitudes among Liberal and Conservative Protestants," *Journal for the Scientific Study of Religion* 27 (1988) 48–59; and Crystal L. Park, Lawrence Cohen, and Lisa Herb, "Intrinsic Religiousness and Religious Coping as Life Stress Moderators for Catholics versus Protestants," *Journal of Personality and Social Psychology* 59 (1990) 562–74.

14. Craig A. Schaefer and Richard L. Gorsuch, "Situational and Personal Variations in Religious Coping," *Journal for the Scientific Study of Religion* 32 (1993) 136–47.

Appraisal

An appraisal is a cognitive task a person engages in when encountering an event, occurrence, or interpersonal transaction. The appraisal of the sensory processes experienced in the event, occurrence, or interpersonal transaction is stimulated by the need to make an evaluation of the occurrence as it is experienced by the person. The appraisal is also necessary to manage the emotions accompanying the event, occurrence, or interpersonal transaction, as well as to determine the meaning, or significance, of the same.

The appraisal of the person-environment occurrence includes an evaluation of the personal significance of the event as well as an evaluation of the options in response to the event or occurrence, including the personal resources to cope with the event. This appraisal process is also thought to be influenced by one's personal beliefs and commitments. While originally viewed as a conscious activity appraisal is now thought to also include an immediate and undeliberate, non-conscious, component.[15]

Table 1. Meaning Making and Religious Experience

Experience	Appraisal	Relevant factors	Outcomes
Internal or external	Primary appraisal	Contextual characteristics	Meaning
	Secondary appraisal	Situational constraints	Feeling of knowing
	Attribution	Personal characteristics	Response
	Reappraisal	Prior experiences	Reappraisal

Primary Appraisal

The primary appraisal of an event or occurrence has to do with the evaluation of the personal significance of the occurrence for the person. In this regard, initial appraisals of religious events are deemed as relevant or irrelevant for a person given his or her beliefs and values and the contextual characteristics of the event or occurrence. Events or

---

15. Richard S. Lazarus, *Stress and Emotion: A New Synthesis* (New York: Springer, 1999); Pawel Lewicki, Maria Czyzewska, and Thomas Hill, "Nonconscious Information: Process and Personality," in Diane C. Berry, ed., *How Implicit is Implicit Learning?* (New York: Oxford University Press, 1997) 48–72.

occurrences within an explicitly religious context are more likely to be deemed as relevant for the person. If the event or occurrence is deemed as irrelevant it is ignored. If, however, the event or occurrence is assessed to be relevant, the first step in assigning meaning to the event has taken place.

Secondary Appraisal

A secondary appraisal entails the evaluation of one's ability to respond to the event or occurrence. It is a complex evaluative process that takes into account various response options and the likelihood that any one of them may be effectively applied. Lazarus refers to this as "part of an active search for information and meaning."[16] One's religious beliefs influence the secondary appraisal process by allowing for a wider range of potential activities for use in coping with the event, should it become necessary to do so.

Attributions

The third element in the appraisal process is an attribution, or a series of attributions, made by the person encountering certain experiences. Attributions, which may be conscious or nonconscious, are attempts to link an event with its causes. Indeed, "understanding the influences that lead to the making of religious attributions is the key role for the psychology of religion."[17]

Not surprisingly, religious attributions are informed by the immediate environmental context in which the experience occurs. Attributions are also influenced by the implicit knowledge and norms of the attributor. As an extension of these findings, I suggest that the stronger one's belief to in the supernatural, the stronger the attribution to God.

Reappraisal

Current literature indicates that a reappraisal often follows the initial appraisal of an event, occurrence, or interpersonal transaction. The reappraisal is intended to confirm, for the person, the initial conclusions of the initial appraisal or alter it based on new information.

16. Lazarus, *Stress and Emotion*, 76.

17. Bernard Spilka, Ralph Hood, and Richard Gorsuch, *The Psychology of Religion: An Empirical Approach* (Englewood Cliffs, NJ: Prentice-Hall, 1985) 21.

Relevant Factors

Cognitive appraisal processes are informed by contextual, situational, personal, and experiential factors.

Contextual Characteristics

As has previously been stated, a person's understanding of an event or occurrence is shaped by the contextual characteristics of the event. This is especially evident for religious people when the event or occurrence is within a religious framework. These contextual characteristics, identified by Lazarus as environmental variables, have been defined as a) demands (implicit or explicit pressures from the environment to act in certain ways and to manifest socially correct attitudes and behaviors), b) constraints (clear expectations as to what people should not do), and c) opportunities (the fortunate timing of an event or occurrence and the wisdom to recognize the opportunity by taking the right action at the right time).[18]

Situational Characteristics

Whereas the contextual characteristics of an occurrence or event have to do with the framework within which an event or occurrence is experienced, the situational characteristics of the event have to do with the specific situation itself. Three situational factors that lead to various understandings of an occurrence or event are a) its novelty, b) its predictability, and c) its ambiguity. In what appears to be the classic scenario of research demonstrating the obvious, Miller found that individuals were better able to respond to a situation if it was one with which they were familiar.[19]

Personal Characteristics

There are a large number of religiously-related personal factors that affect the meaning-making process. To begin, one's religious orientation influences how one interprets events or occurrences. Personality

18. Lazarus, *Stress and Emotion*, 61–70.

19. Suzanne M. Miller, "Individual Differences," in Bruce N. Carpenter, ed., *Personal Coping: Theory, Research, and Application* (Westport, CT: Praeger, 1992) 77–91.

variables are also thought to influence appraisals.[20] Some of the most commonly discussed of these personality characteristics include hope, optimism, hardiness, and self-efficacy. Neuroticism, optimism, and openness to experience have also been identified as influencing appraisals.[21] The Five-Factor theory as well as the Myers Briggs Type Indicator may prove to be informative regarding the appraisal process in regard to persons with a religious orientation.[22] These instruments identify personality patterns that are descriptive of personal proclivities regarding one's interaction with other people, one's sensitivity to internal or external stimuli, and one's preferred method of managing information.

Prior Experiences

Prior experience is another relevant factor thought to influence one's appraisal of religiously-oriented occurrences or events. People with prior appraisals of religiously-oriented occurrences or events are thought to be able to adapt to changing situations and contexts. Prior experience provides some guidance in the selection of responses to the initial appraisal, depending on what seems useful at the time.

Additionally, persons with prior experiences of self-reported successes in appraisals of and subsequent responses to religiously-oriented events or occurrences, form self-efficacy judgments. These judgments seem to influence future responses. While there may be no singularly correct way to respond to an appraisal of any particular religiously-oriented event or occurrence, given the relevance of the situation for a given person in a given situation, the words of Lazarus seem apropos: "[A successful response] depends on an appraisal process that seeks the most serviceable meaning available in the situation, one that supports

20. Crystal L. Park and Susan Folkman, "Meaning in the Context of Stress and Coping," *Review of General Psychology* 1 (1997) 115–44; Genevieve Bouchard, Annie Guillemette, and Nicole Landry-Leger, "Situational and Dispositional Coping: An Examination of their Relation to Personality, Cognitive Appraisals, and Psychological Distress," *European Journal of Personality* 19 (2004) 221–38.

21. Robert R. McCrae and Paul T. Costa, "Validation of the Five-factor Model of Personality across Instruments and Observers," *Journal of Personality and Social Psychology* 52:1 (1987) 81–90; Robert R. McCrae and Oliver P. John, "An Introduction to the Five-factor Model and Its Applications," *Journal of Personality* 60 (1992) 175–215.

22. Isabel Briggs Myers, Linda K. Kirby, and Katharine D. Myers, *Introduction to Type: A Guide to Understanding Your Results on the Myers-Briggs Type Indicator* (Palo Alto, CA: Consulting Psychologists, 1998).

realistic actions while also viewing that situation in the most favorable way possible."[23]

Outcomes

The final step in the appraisal process is an outcome. More than being the initiation of a specific behavior or series of behaviors, an appraisal results in a) the meaning of the experience for the person making the judgment, b) a feeling of knowing that is related to the extent to which one feels confident about his or her appraisal, c) intended responses, to what one believes to be true, and d) a reappraisal of the entire appraisal process.

Meaning

In regard to the appraisal process, the generation of meaning seems to be related to the primary and secondary appraisals previously discussed. Embedded in the attributional aspect of the appraisal process, which closely follows the primary and secondary appraisal, meaning arises from questions such as "what does all this mean?," "what does this mean for me?," and "what am I to do with what I now think I know?" Because attributions made in religious contexts by persons who are oriented toward religious outcomes tend to be religious in nature, the questions cited immediately above in a Pentecostal context could be stated as "what meaning does God have for me?" and "what does God want me to do with what I know?" The outcome of the meaning-making endeavor would be different in another, say liturgical, religious context.

To a certain extent, the meaning of an appraisal is related to memories of previous events. Memory systems record, retain, and retrieve experiences, facts, knowledge, and skills that form an essential framework for thoughts, emotions, and behavior, elements of consciousness that provide meaning.[24] Memories of events are stored in regard to their meaning,[25] and successful memory formation depends on the organi-

23. Lazarus, *Stress and Emotion*, 124.

24. David Y. Hwang and Alexandra J. Golby, "The Brain Basis for Episodic Memory: Insights from Functional MRI, Intracranial EEG, and Patients with Epilepsy," *Epilepsy and Behavior* 8 (2006) 115–26.

25 Robert A. Bjork, "Memory and Meta-memory Considerations in the Training of Human Beings," in Janet Metcalf and Arthur P. Shimamura, eds., *Metacognition: Knowing about Knowing* (Cambridge, MA: MIT Press, 1994) 185–205.

zation of the information at the time of encoding.[26] For example, the activity component of an event provides better access than the location, time, and participants involved.[27]

But more than the recalling of explicit memory, it is the cognitive schema, the unconscious ways in which people perceive and organize information, and the pre-existing, non-conscious, inferential (encoding) algorithms that influence the meaning of an event. The rules involved in this encoding process are not available to the perceiver's conscious awareness and they operate with such speed that they are practically unnoticeable to the perceiver, who experiences only the outcome, a subjective impression. These encoding algorithms translate objective stimuli, for example, auditory or visual stimuli from the extroceptive and introceptive systems of the brain, into subjectively meaningful impressions and interpretation.

Feeling of Knowing

The first aspect of the outcome is a personal sense of meaning about the event. If the appraisal process produces a sense a) that the event is relevant for the person, b) that she or he has the resources to respond, c) that there is a cause of the experience (i.e., the "Holy Spirit," as opposed to pizza, or the need for personal affirmation), and d) that the contextual and situational characteristics of the event correspond to prior experiences, then with all likelihood the event will have meaning for that person. This triggers the second aspect of the outcome of the appraisal process: a feeling of knowing.

A feeling of knowing is an individual judgment, again often made according to non-conscious algorithms that attribute the source of one's experience as well as the veracity and salience of the information received. Often the results of "feeling of knowing judgments" include a sense of confidence and a state of believability,[28] and lead to decisions to

26. Atsuko Takishima, Ole Jensen, Robert Oostenveld, Eric Maris, Mara van de Coevering, and Guillen Fernandez, "Successful Declarative Memory Formation is Associated with Ongoing Activity during Encoding in a Distributed Neocortical Network related to Working Memory: A Magnetoencephalography Study," *Neuroscience* 139 (2006) 291–97.

27. Katinka Dijkstra and Mine Misirlisoy, "Event Components in Autobiographical Memories," *Memory* 14 (2006) 846–52.

28. Janet Metcalfe, "Preface," in Janet Metcalfe and Arthur P. Shimamura, eds., *Metacognition: Knowing about Knowing* (Cambridge, MA: MIT Press, 1994) xi–xiii.

continue with a particular task.[29] If the information about which one is making a judgment is new or novel, the feeling of knowing is reduced; there is a decrease in confidence as to believability of the appraisal and one's ability to respond. However, if the information is familiar to the person, his or her feeling of knowing is enhanced.

Response

The third element of the outcome of an appraisal regarding an event or occurrence is a response. As is true of other elements of the appraisal process, one's response is related to the aforementioned relevant characteristics (see Table 1). The response is most often consistent with the religious context of the person.

Reappraisal

Making meaning of a religiously-oriented event or occurrence is an ongoing process, with complex feedback loops and constant updating.[30] Thus, as the various elements of the appraisal progress over time, one's sense of meaning about a religiously-oriented event or occurrence may change, as might one's responses. One's response changes the situation, and the appraisal begins again.

Case Example of a Cognitive Appraisal of a Pentecostal Experience

This essay suggests that people engage in a cognitive appraisal process to understand the events they encounter. The appraisal process suggested in Table 1 demonstrates how meaning making occurs for individuals. These encounters are usually stimulated by internal or external experiences. The appraisal of these perceptions ultimately results in a response to the experience. It has also been suggested the one's religious orientation influences his or her response.

For example, Frank Macchia's narrative regarding a religious experience he had shortly after arriving at college, and his subsequent expe-

29. Thomas O. Nelson and Louis Narens, "Metamemory: A Theoretical Framework and New Findings," *The Psychology of Learning and Motivation* 26 (1996) 125–73.

30. Bruce N. Carpenter, "Issues and Advances in Coping Research," in Bruce N. Carpenter, ed., *Personal Coping: Theory, Research, and Application* (Westport, CT: Praeger, 1992) 1–29.

rience of glossolalia, serve to demonstrate the appraisal process.[31] His experiences, the attribution to God of these experiences, and the manner in which contextual, situational, and personal factors contributed to the outcome of his experiences will be demonstrated. The meanings he attaches to glossolalia in his depiction of Pentecostal theology and the outcomes of Spirit baptism he suggests in *Baptized in the Spirit* may be seen as the result of the appraisal process.

Macchia's narrative begins with his recollection of memories as a child and then as an adolescent in the home of a Pentecostal preacher. He tells of his involvement in the life of the church, although it is recalled as being at the behest of his mother, and documents his time away from faith and his desire to escape from the environment of his Pentecostal home. These dynamics initiated an emotional encounter with his father and his subsequent "surrender to God."

Macchia's arrival on a Bible school campus filled him with anxiety that was dissipated as he read his Bible and was "drawn into" stories concerning the risen Christ and Pentecost. The starkness of his dormitory room and the loneliness he felt seem to be significant. It is also noteworthy that in his narrative he recalls memories of his previous encounters with these Bible stories: "I was familiar with several of the stories." The result of this encounter with scripture fostered a desire to be "like them."

His story continues as some new friends invited him to the chapel to pray. "No sooner had I entered the room that I fell to my knees and began to pray. I began to cry and to search for words that I could not find. I felt a fountain well up within me. It grew stronger and stronger until it burst forth with great strength. I began to pray in tongues . . . [and] I felt God's powerful presence embrace me."

Analysis

Consistent with the model presented in Table 1, Macchia cites a number of internal and external experiences, all of which were subject to an appraisal process. However, for the purposes of this chapter the emotions

---

31. See Frank D. Macchia, *Baptized in the Spirit: A Global Pentecostal Theology* (Grand Rapids, MI: Zondervan, 2006) esp. 12–13. All Macchia quotations in the rest of this essay are from these pages unless otherwise noted. Thanks to Dr. Macchia for permission to use his testimony as a case study.

he was experiencing as he entered the chapel immediately after having encountered "the reality of God" in the stories of the Bible seems to be most salient.

APPRAISAL

Macchia's testimony is illuminated by the cognitive appraisal model presented here.

Primary Appraisal

Although it can only be inferred, it appears as though his immediate, and most likely non-conscious, appraisal was that what he was experiencing (i.e., the overwhelming emotions) had salience for him, perhaps as a result of his life in the church as the son of a Pentecostal preacher. In fact, the tenor of the language he uses now to express his experience indicates that those particular moments had great religious significance for him. In this way, his experience is entirely consistent with what the cognitive appraisal model would lead us to expect: that the initial appraisal of a religious event is related to its relevance for a person, given one's beliefs and values.

Secondary Appraisal

A secondary appraisal entails a person's analysis of his or her ability to respond to the salience of the experience as determined in the prior appraisal. This appraisal involves a search for information and meaning, which are most often found within the factors relevant to the experience. In this regard, it seems evident that Macchia made an instantaneous judgment that he could, and would, respond. The rapidity of the appraisal and meaning-making process may be seen in Macchia's next statement after describing the emotionality he felt following his encounter with the stories of the Bible: "I determined *in that moment* . . . ." (emphasis added).

Attribution

In keeping with the research indicating that persons who are convinced of God's reality and presence utilize attributions to God as a central component of their interpretation of events,[32] Macchia seems to have attributed his emotional response to the biblical stories he had just read. He also attributed to divine origin the invitation of his new acquaintances to go to the chapel for prayer.

Relevant Factors

The schema of a particular religious tradition, the presence of others who are also having (the same or similar) religious experiences, or some other environmental cue, all serve to create a mental set through which the religious person interprets any given religious experience.[33] Macchia's experience seems to be entirely consistent with these findings.

Contextual Characteristics

Given his life-long involvement in Pentecostal churches, and his memories of the experiences he observed and personally encountered, the chapel seems to have been an especially relevant factor for Macchia's appraisal of the experience he encountered. The setting of the chapel tapped into a mental set of safety, salience, and significance. Macchia seems to take note of the contextual importance for he is able to recount one of these contextual characteristics many years later: the presence of a cross "on the wall facing the door."

In a similar fashion, Macchia's experience was aided by the fact that his friends were having the same experiences. This awareness further added to the salience and significance of the contextual characteristics involved in Macchia's experience.

Situational Constraints

Macchia was asked by friends to pray, an activity and experience with which he was thoroughly familiar. As stated previously, the predictability of an event or occurrence serves to diminish the threat of the event. Consequently, he entered into that activity, immediately and apparently

---

32. Patricia W. Cheng, and Laura R. Novick, "A Probabilistic Contrast Model of Causation," *Journal of Personality and Social Psychology* 58 (1990) 545–67.

33. Raymond F. Paloutzian, Thomas G. Fikes, and Dirk Hautserat, "A Social Cognition Interpretation of Neurotheological Events," in Joseph Rhawn, ed., *Neurotheology: Brain Science, Spirituality, Religious Experience* (San Jose, CA: University Press, 2002) 215–22.

with total abandon. Macchia's reading the "familiar" stories of the Bible is another situational factor.

Personal Characteristics

Because mine is a post hoc theoretical analysis of Macchia's experience, suggesting aspects of his personality that may lend itself to the appraisal process and his subsequent response would be the ultimate in hubris. It seems safe to say, however, that his appraisal was influenced by his personal characteristics. Perhaps something of these may be seen in his urgency to call his parents following his experiences in the chapel.

Prior Experiences

Having grown up in the home of a Pentecostal pastor no doubt provided a backlog of prior experiences from which Macchia could draw for the appraisal process. His appraisal seems to be consistent with research suggesting that people with prior experiences of appraisals regarding religious experiences are thought to adapt to changing situations and contexts.[34] It seems that in all likelihood then, this reservoir of previous experiences prepared him for his experience in the chapel, and for his as yet to be determined outcomes.

OUTCOMES

This is the culmination of the initial appraisal process. Personal meaning of an event or occurrence is determined here, as is the sense of confidence one supplies to the meaning he or she discovers. A particular response, or set of responses, follows, as does a reappraisal process.

Meaning

Meaning is developed from the specifics of the primary and secondary appraisal, in conjunction with memories of previous experiences. The meaning of Macchia's experience was determined within the context of his Pentecostal faith and the religious setting in which he experienced it. In his mind, he was having a genuine divine-human encounter.

---

34. Lazarus, *Stress and Emotion*, 77.

Feelings of Knowing

Because the experiences he encountered in his dorm room and in the chapel were similar to other experiences he had, Macchia could enter into his experience. The confidence he seems to have felt seems to have persisted as he continues to be actively Pentecostal to this day. The veracity with which he imbued his preliminary experience also allows him, no doubt the result of many subsequent appraisals, to expand the Pentecostal experience to include persons from other Pentecostal orientations although their particular experiences of meaning-making may be different from his own.

Response

Macchia's response to the cognitive appraisal process is clearly stated: "I began to speak in tongues." This was in response to another appraisal associated with his being overwhelmed with emotion as he entered the chapel. Each of the activities reiterated by Macchia regarding his experience that day are the result of an appraisal process.

Reappraisal

As previously stated, meaning-making is an ongoing process. Macchia's work seems to demonstrate that he has nonconsciously, and without a doubt, consciously entered time and again into the reappraisal process. Each appraisal brings a differing response, and the appraisal process begins again.

In this regard, it seems that Macchia continues to discover new meanings for glossolalia. This is evident in his work as a Pentecostal theologian and in the emerging focus of his global Pentecostal theology. In the former, it seems as though subsequent appraisals have enabled Macchia to suggest some new meanings for the experience of glossolalia.[35] The latter clearly represents his continued search for the meaning of glossolalia in an ecumenical and world context. Indeed, the

---

35. See, e.g., the following essays by Macchia: "Tongues as a Sign: Towards a Sacramental Understanding of Pentecostal Experience," *PNEUMA: The Journal of the Society for Pentecostal Studies* 15:1 (1993) 61–76; "Groans too Deep for Words: Towards a Theology of Tongues as Initial Evidence," *Asian Journal of Pentecostal Studies* 1:2 (1998) 149–73; and "The Tongues of Pentecost: A Pentecostal Perspective on the Promise and Challenge of Pentecostal/Roman Catholic Dialogue," *Journal of Ecumenical Studies* 35:1 (1998) 1–18.

last chapter in his recent book is entitled "expanding the boundaries of Spirit baptism."

Summary

One way to explain the various responses of Pentecostals to a stated experience of "the Spirit" is to utilize a cognitive appraisal methodology. Such a methodology stipulates that one's response to any given experience is the result of an appraisal process composed of conscious and non-conscious processes. These cognitions mediate between the encounter and the person's reaction or response.

What makes an understanding of the cognitive appraisal process so salient for the experiences of Pentecostals is that religious events stimulate an appraisal process similar to that identified above. In this regard, the appraisal of a religious event operates within the religious framework of the person while taking into account the context of the occurrence or event. For example, appraisals of religious events are deemed as relevant or irrelevant for a person given one's beliefs and values, and religious orientation. Persons who are convinced of God's reality and presence ascribe causation to God as a central component of the appraisal process.

A four-stage cognitive appraisal process, drawing on the work of Lazarus and Folkman and Park and Cohen, has been presented as a model to facilitate an understanding of Pentecostal responses to religious experiences. These experiences begin an initial appraisal that is influenced by factors relevant to the person and the situation in which the experience is encountered. The outcome of such a decision-making process is personal meaning which in turn serves to guide the development of a response—one consistent with the contextual and situational influences on the appraisal process.

Future Research

The cognitive appraisal process as applied to Pentecostal experiences remains theoretical. What is needed is a rigorous plan of research into the various components of the suggested cognitive appraisal process. That people make appraisals, and that these appraisals are influenced by religious factors, is without question. However, what is not known is whether or not aspects of the "Pentecostal experience" will affect appraisals in the same way as other religious experiences. For example, what would the primary and secondary appraisals be for persons without a Pentecostal or charismatic background who manifest, at least phenomenologically, characteristics accompanying Pentecostal experiences of being filled with the Spirit? Would these appraisals be similar to those whose "experience of the Spirit" is more like Macchia's?

It has also been established that contextual and situational factors influence the appraisal process. However, to date no research has been developed that assesses the extent to which religious contexts and situations affects one's appraisal of the "experience of the Spirit." Would such an experience be affected by loud music and praying (often the norm for Pentecostal believers)? Would the presence of a powerful person, a well-known evangelist or pastor, influence one's "experience of the Spirit"?

Do differing personality attributes affect the appraisal process? It is expected that persons with high scores on the Extroversion and Openness to Experience scales of the Five Factor Theory of Personality as developed by McRae and Costa would have a different response to "the Spirit" than would those high on the Neuroticism scale.[36] To what extent do prior experiences in a Pentecostal environment, or with "an experience of the Spirit" influence appraisals? What factors influence one's feeling of knowing (confidence) regarding his or her appraisal of an "experience of the Spirit?"

Certainly, there is much to do in this regard concerning the conversation between religion, specifically Pentecostalism, and psychology. What an exciting possibility!

36. See McCrae and Costa, "Validation of the Five-factor Model of Personality across Instruments and Observers."

12

Teaching Origins to Pentecostal Students

Michael Tenneson and Steve Badger

Introduction

Professors in the life sciences at Pentecostal colleges and universities typically struggle with two enormous challenges. The first is how to present various theistic perspectives on origins in a way that reinforces students' faith in the Creator and the trustworthiness of the Bible while inculcating confidence in the merits of the scientific enterprise. The second is how to assess the breadth and depth of the knowledge and opinions of their students regarding origins.

Teaching creation-evolution is, at the very least, controversial and can even be job threatening, as evidenced by the recent conflicts between intelligent design proponent Bill Dembski and Baylor University,[1] science journal editor Richard Sternberg and the Smithsonian

---

1. Fred Heeren, "The Deed Is Done," *American Spectator* 33:10 (December 2000) 28.

Institution,[2] and marine biologist Nathaniel Abraham and Woods Hole Oceanographic Institution.[3]

Both of the authors teach science classes at a Pentecostal liberal arts university, and one of us (Steve Badger) also teaches Bible and theology courses. Through the years we've experimented with a variety of classroom approaches that are designed to be less likely to polarize our students while developing their critical thinking skills. We've learned the importance of discussing how epistemological theory, presuppositions, descriptions of scientific methods, and patterns of integrating knowledge affect a person's conclusions.

As part of our strategy for improving instruction, we developed a survey to measure the opinions and distribution of opinions vis-à-vis origins. This undertaking was facilitated by a pilot study conducted by one of us.[4]

We hope that instructors will use the survey to examine their students' opinions about origins before covering this topic. Instructors can also evaluate the effectiveness of their instruction by administering the survey before and after teaching on origins. We think that origins can be taught with a minimum of conflict by following our recommendations. We also posit that teachers can improve the quality of instruction by examining students' views before and after teaching about origins.

Teaching Goals

Educators need to assess their teaching methods. What constitutes success? We consider our approach to teaching origins successful when our students:

1. Find their Pentecostal faith strengthened, not weakened.
2. Move from a dogmatic "one right view" to accepting Christians with a different theistic view as genuine believers.

2. Michael Powell, "Editor Explains Reasons for 'Intelligent Design' Article," *The Washington Post* (19 August 2005).

3 Beth Daley, "Biologist Fired for Beliefs, Suit Says: Woods Hole States Creationist Stance at Odds with Work," *Boston Globe* (7 December 2007) available online: www.boston.com/news/local/articles/2007/12/07/biologist_ fired_for_beliefs_suit_says/.

4. Michael Tenneson, "The Development and Validation of Scientific Attitudes and Attitudes Toward Evolution and Creation Instrument for Christian College Biology Students" (PhD diss., University of Missouri, 2001).

3. Understand the philosophical underpinnings of the natural sciences (e.g., uniformitarianism) and of theology (e.g., the nature of God).

4. Recognize the difficulties in correctly interpreting Scripture and the difficulties in correctly interpreting nature.

5. Recognize the limitations of biblical hermeneutics and the limitations of scientific methods.

6. Describe clearly and succinctly the strengths and weaknesses of the common Western positions on creation and evolution.

7. Recognize how a person's presuppositions can control his or her conclusions.

8. Choose an appropriate integrative approach (complementarism or concordism) rather than non-integrative models (e.g., "nonoverlapping magisteria").

9. Demonstrate an awareness of the current issues being debated (e.g., punctuated equilibria, intelligent design).

10. Know and use technical terms correctly (e.g., microevolution, macroevolution, natural selection).

11. Know and use effective approaches to discussing origins with those with whom they disagree.

12. Respond to survey items consistently with the approach they claim to embrace (young earth creationism, old earth creationism, evolutionary creationism).

The results of our origins survey and conversations with students and alumni have helped us to assess the achievement of our teaching goals. Student responses on tests also provide insights, and we hope to develop a brief self-reporting survey for students to further enable us to determine how well we are achieving these goals.

Pedagogical Approaches

We want to teach origins in a way that encourages students in their Pentecostal faith and strengthens and broadens their understanding of the scientific endeavor—including its strengths and limitations. The elements essential to accomplishing these goals are discussed here in the order that we've found most effective in our teaching.

Presuppositions and Worldview

Science textbooks rarely identify the presuppositions used by scientists. As we begin teaching a unit on origins, we list several of these presuppositions. Here is a short list of presuppositions that we have used:[5]

- The physical realm exists independent of the mind.
- The physical world is orderly and knowable.
- Physical constants of the universe have not changed over time (uniformitarianism).
- The senses and the mind are reliable.
- Inductive reasoning is reliable.
- The laws of logic (e.g., law of non-contradiction) are true.
- Human observations of physical phenomena are trustworthy (the correspondence theory).
- Measurements yield accurate and useful information.

Our presuppositions largely control our conclusions. For instance, if a person does not believe God exists, she will not be likely to embrace any theory of creation. Or if a person thinks the scientific method is the only reliable method of gaining knowledge of the physical world, he will be more likely to hold an evolutionary theory. An awareness of presuppositions improves the quality of dialogue vis-à-vis origins.

Epistemology

Not all of our students have had an introductory course in philosophy. Thus, while most of them are familiar with scientific methods, they often are not familiar with the variety of other ways people gain knowledge. We discuss several of these, including testimony of an authority, the senses, reason, self-revelation, intuition, and serving an apprenticeship.[6] This knowledge of epistemology enables students to think more critically about science and faith.

5. J. P. Moreland, *Christianity and the Nature of Science* (Grand Rapids, MI: Baker, 1989) 108–33.

6. Dallas M. Roark, *Introduction to Philosophy* (Emporia, KS: Dalmor, 1982) 12–23.

METHODS OF SCIENCE

When we describe the methods of the natural sciences, we emphasize their weaknesses and limitations along with their strengths—even as we affirm our confidence in scientific methods to answer certain types of questions and solve certain types of problems. Students rarely have difficulty seeing that these methods of science are not applicable to answering questions of ethics or aesthetics. However, many students are unaware that scholars debate what is and is not *science*.

METHODS OF BIBLE INTERPRETATION

Many of our students are familiar with criteria for sound biblical interpretation, but they don't always apply those criteria when interpreting the creation accounts in Genesis. We emphasize that although we place great confidence in the trustworthiness of the Scriptures, we must distinguish between "the Scriptures" and a person's interpretation of the Scriptures.

Showing students the difficulties scholars have in interpreting the first part of Genesis helps students appreciate the complexity. The first challenge is identifying the genre of Genesis 1–2. Should we read and interpret it as historical (chronological) narrative? If we do, this raises the problem of light being created on day one while the celestial bodies that provide light being created on day four. And while the Hebrew of Genesis 1 is not poetry, it does appear to be poetical. Scholars also debate the range of meaning of the Hebrew word *yôm* (day). In Genesis 1, must it mean a 24-hour day or may it have a figurative meaning as well?[7]

COMMON WESTERN PERSPECTIVES ON ORIGINS

Students often think there are only two positions on origins: young earth creation and atheistic evolution. We teach that contemporary attempts to answer the questions of origins can be arranged into five general viewpoints: young earth creation (YEC), old earth creation (OEC), evolutionary creation (EC), deistic evolution (DE), and atheistic evolution (AE).[8]

7. Bruce K. Waltke, "The Literary Genre of Genesis, Chapter One," *Crux* 27 (December 1991) 2.

8. Richard T. Wright, *Biology Through the Eyes of Faith* (San Francisco: Harper-Collins, 2003).

We strive to avoid exalting or denigrating any one of the three theistic views, however we remind students that the DE and AE positions are inconsistent with Christianity. People who belong to any of the first three camps (YEC, OEC, and EC) believe in the God of the Bible and agree that the Bible is God's Word (although they disagree about how the creation accounts in the Bible should be understood).

Further, no group is monolithic—proponents in a camp usually disagree about the details. So we teach our students a general description of each of the five camps and use the popular names of each group despite objections by some as to what they want to be called. Here is how we describe each group to our students.

Young Earth Creationists (YEC) like to call their position "Scientific Creation." YECs typically interpret the biblical creation accounts as scientifically accurate historical narrative. They claim that both the Bible and scientific evidences support these conclusions: (1) God suddenly made the physical realm and life, (2) out of nothing, (3) in six consecutive 24-hour periods, (4) about 6,000–15,000 years ago. All theories of macroevolution are rejected, as is a universe that is billions of years old. John Whitcomb and Henry Morris and Jonathan Sarfati are modern proponents.[9]

Old Earth Creationists (OEC) accept the scientific evidences for a universe that is billions of years old, but they argue that God created everything—including life—by a series of creative acts that were separated by long periods of time. This position is also known as "Progressive Creation." Although adherents often disagree on when each of these creative acts occurred, they do believe that God directly created life pretty much as it exists today. They reject macroevolutionary theory. Creation accounts in the Bible are interpreted as historical narrative but not necessarily as a scientific explanation of how God created the earth. This view has been popularized by Bernard Ramm and Hugh Ross.[10]

Evolutionary Creationists (EC) accept the scientific evidence for a universe that is billions of years old and embrace contemporary bio-

9. John Whitcomb and Henry Morris, *The Genesis Flood: The Biblical Record and Its Scientific Implications* (Grand Rapids, MI: Baker, 1979); and Jonathan Sarfati, *Refuting Compromise: A Biblical and Scientific Refutation of 'Progressive Creationism' (Billions of Years) As Popularized by Astronomer Hugh Ross* (Green Forest, AR.: Master, 2004).

10. Bernard Ramm, *The Christian View of Science and Scripture* (Grand Rapids, MI: Eerdmans, 1954); and Hugh Ross, *The Fingerprint of God* (Orange, CA: Promise, 1991).

logical theories of evolution, but they stress that God guided the evolution of existing life forms from the original life forms that He created. Creation accounts in the Bible are not thought to be historical narrative or scientifically accurate. ECs generally attempt to harmonize theories of macroevolution with the biblical account of origins. This position is also known as "theistic evolution." Contemporary representatives of this position are Howard van Till, Kenneth Miller, and Francis Collins.[11]

The fourth group, the *Deistic Evolutionists* (DE), claims that God is no longer involved in the physical realm. They also usually maintain that the physical realm is a superior and more trustworthy revelation of God than the Bible, which is usually rejected as neither inspired nor authoritative. DEs argue that if God created the physical realm, He left it to evolve on its own. This was Charles Darwin's viewpoint.[12]

Since *Atheistic Evolutionists* (AE) deny the existence of God, they propose that life arose from non-life via natural causes. They also posit that one kind of life changed into other kinds of life by natural processes. AEs do not consider the Bible to be God's Word. People who are not necessarily confirmed atheists but who attempt to answer the questions of origins without invoking God (methodological naturalists) could also be included in this camp. Some people call this "Ateleological (purposeless) Evolution." A well-known spokesperson for this view is Richard Dawkins.[13]

While some people (e.g., Buddhists and Hindus) may not fall into one of these five groups, this is a general description of the vast majority of Westerners today. Since a Christian cannot be an atheist or a deist, we encourage our students to adopt one the three theistic positions (YEC, OEC, and EC).

11. Howard J. Van Till, "The Fully Gifted Creation," in J. P. Moreland and John Mark Reynolds, eds., *Three Views on Creation and Evolution* (Grand Rapids, MI: Zondervan, 1999) 161–247; Kenneth Miller, *Finding Darwin's God: A Scientist's Search for Common Ground between God and Evolution* (New York: HarperCollins, 1999); and Francis Collins, *The Language of God: A Scientist Presents Evidence for Belief* (New York: Free, 2006).

12. Cornelius Hunter, *Darwin's God: Evolution and the Problem of Evil* (Grand Rapids, MI: Brazos, 2001).

13. Richard Dawkins, *The God Delusion* (Boston: Houghton Mifflin, 2006).

EVIDENCES FOR MACROEVOLUTION

As we show students the typical arguments and evidences that lead some people to embrace contemporary macroevolutionary theory, we do not present these as certain knowledge, but as the reasons that some people find convincing. Here are some of the reasons we present:

1. *The age of the earth.* The majority of scientists think that empirical evidences point to a physical realm that is billions of years old.
2. *Natural and artificial selection.* The findings of many empirical studies fit the theory of natural selection.
3. *Biogeography.* The study of the geographic distribution of life forms (both living and fossils) is consistent with macroevolutionary theory.
4. *The fossil record.* Many people (including some theists) find the catastrophic flood explanation insufficient to explain the distribution and abundance of discovered fossils.
5. *Vestigial structures.* Vestigial structures are anatomical features that have no known or greatly reduced function compared to apparent ancestors. These are thought to be ancestral remnants.
6. *Biochemistry.* The structures of a variety of biochemicals correlate with the ancestral relationships inferred from the fossil record.
7. *Logical and reasonable.* Generally, macroevolution fits two common truth tests: the coherence theory of truth and the correspondence theory of truth.[14]

INTEGRATIVE APPROACHES

Scholars have proposed patterns of integrating scientific and religious knowledge.[15] We show students the different ways Christians integrate their understanding of science with their faith, and the credence they place on general revelation (nature) versus special revelation (the Bible). Five general patterns of integration follow.

---

14. For a summary of these theories of truth, see J. P. Moreland and William Lane Craig, *Philosophical Foundations for a Christian Worldview* (Downers Grove, IL: Inter-Varsity, 2003) 135–44.

15. Richard Bube, *Putting It All Together: Seven Patterns for Relating Science and the Christian Faith* (Lanham, MD: University Press of America, 1995) 56–187, and Moreland, *Christianity and the Nature of Science*, 46–58.

No Common Ground: Conflict is impossible by definition because natural science and biblical theology have no common ground. This pattern is called the two worlds view, compartmentalism, or nonoverlapping magisteria (NOMA).[16]

Both Are Right: Science and religion both provide valid insights into the nature of reality but from different perspectives. This is often called complementarism.

Both Are Wrong: The apparent conflict between a scientific and a biblical account of origins is due to human imperfection in both. Scientists and theologians should work to achieve an integrated understanding of reality. This is often called concordism.

Scientists Know Best: When science and religion conflict, both cannot be right. In any conflict, science is always right. We call this conflictism 1.

Theologians Know Best: When science and religion conflict, both cannot be right. In any conflict, theology is always right. We call this conflictism 2.

We encourage our students to reject NOMA and both conflict patterns for the following reasons. If God exists, there is no warrant for excluding him a priori from the origins model. We believe that neither the natural sciences nor biblical theology provides a complete picture of reality. For these reasons we encourage our Pentecostal students to favor some integrative approach (e.g., concordism or complementarism).

Current Issues

After going over the five integrative models, we usually end the unit on origins with a review of contemporary issues. These include intelligent design (ID), age of the earth, macroevolution, punctuated equilibria, and the finely tuned universe. For each of these topics, operational definitions are discussed along with proponent and detractor statements.

Classroom Atmosphere

Because this topic is controversial and some people see their views on origins as foundational to Christianity itself, we strive to minimize

16. Stephen Gould, "Nonoverlapping Magisteria," *Natural History* 106 (March 1997) 16.

emotionalism. First, we attempt to establish ourselves in our students' eyes as orthodox Pentecostals who honor the Scriptures and recognize God as the Creator even as we teach them how to use the methods of the natural sciences.

Further, we attempt to provide students with a classroom that is a safe place to discuss and disagree on issues. This approach includes a lecture tone that is often informal and conversational while avoiding sarcasm and ad hominem comments—and discouraging student from the same.

We avoid disclosing our positions to students before they have a chance to form their own. Then if they discover their view is not ours, we don't try to convince them to abandon their position and embrace ours.

Finally, our use of self-effacing humor can also disarm otherwise antagonistic students. Student evaluations of our teaching and conversations with students support our conclusions that this classroom atmosphere is helpful.

Use of Graphs and Illustrations

We have designed a few figures to help students visualize and comprehend important concepts. For example, one illustrates the relationships among belief, truth, and knowledge, another represents the differences between historical science and empirical science, and a third illustrates the effect of presuppositions on conclusions about origins. A group of five illustrations describes patterns of integrating science knowledge with faith knowledge. All of these illustrations are used in our classroom presentations and are included in a book that is required in some of our courses.[17]

Suggestions for Productive Dialogue

Can people with different opinions discuss theories of origins productively? Or must we have only heated arguments? Both parties must be committed to a non-confrontational, non-adversarial approach to dialogue productively. We offer the following suggestions to students who

17. Stephen Badger and Mike Tenneson, *Christian Perspectives on Origins* (Springfield, MO: Evangel University, 2007).

want to discuss origins with a friend who holds an opinion different from theirs.

Things Students Should Know

1. Know your purpose and goals in discussing origins.
2. Recognize your pattern of integrating faith and science.
3. Understand your position before you try to understand your friend's.
4. Natural science can neither prove nor disprove God's existence.
5. Recognize your presuppositions.
6. Many Pentecostal Christians who embrace the Bible as God's Holy Word disagree on the genre of the creation account in Genesis.
7. Accepting an old earth theory of origins does not mean that you accept a theory of macroevolution.
8. Some Pentecostals accept the scientific evidence for a universe that is billions of years old.
9. Many Pentecostals think there is biblical evidence for a universe that is only thousands of years old.
10. The natural sciences are not the only way to gain reliable knowledge and cannot find the answer to every question or the solution to every problem.

Things Students Should Do and Not Do

1. Do learn the biblical and scientific evidences for the age of the universe and earth.
2. Do help your friend identify his/her presuppositions.
3. Do honestly consider your friend's arguments.
4. Do define terms to be sure that you both mean the same thing by a particular word.
5. Do not misrepresent your friend's position by bringing up outdated, discarded arguments.
6. Do not make your position the litmus test for scientific orthodoxy or for religious orthodoxy.
7. Do not assume you know your friend's motive for embracing his/her position.
8. Do choose an appropriate pattern of integrating faith and science (e.g., do not relegate science and religion to two separate domains).

9. Do listen to your friend the same way you want him/her to listen to you.
10. Do not attack the other person; instead, discuss the merits of the evidence.
11. Do educate yourself by reading articles and books by those who hold opinions different from yours.

The Online Origins Survey

In an attempt to understand our students and to evaluate and improve our instructional methods, we created a survey to measure attitudes and beliefs about origins. Retrospectively, developing the survey and studying students' responses have had a dramatic effect on both our thinking and teaching. Those who teach origins should consider creating their own survey or using ours.

The origins survey consisted of 62 statements and was taken online. A Likert[18] scale response set (strongly agree, agree, uncertain, disagree, strongly disagree, decline to answer) was used within the framework of the five commonly held positions on origins: young earth creation, old earth creation, evolutionary creation (i.e., theistic evolution), deistic evolution, and atheistic evolution.

Two types of validity were considered in the development of this survey: content and construct. Content validity is the degree to which survey statements represent the ideas intended to be investigated.[19] The evidence for content validity depended on the verdicts of five subject experts and was determined before administration of the instrument. The subject experts all possessed terminal degrees in science or theology and had much background in the study of origins. These reviewers evaluated items for inclusion in the survey. Items were included when at least 80% of the judges were comfortable that they accurately fit the views of people with that particular camp affiliation.

Construct validity measures the degree to which survey responses seemed to fit the theoretical model, that is, the degree to which a respondent's self-identified position on origins determined how a person

18. Rensis Likert, "A Technique for the Measurement of Attitudes," *Archives of Psychology* 140 (1932) 152.

19. Robert K. Gable and Marian B. Wolf, *Instrument Development in the Affective Domain: Measuring Attitudes and Values in Corporate and School Settings*, 2nd ed. (Boston, MA: Kluwer, 1993).

responded to the survey statements.[20] Construct validity was evaluated by administering the instrument to the sample population (students, faculty, staff, and administrators at Assemblies of God institutions of higher education in the United States) and subsequently performing exploratory factor analyses using the Statistical Package for the Social Sciences (SPSS) computer program. This analysis indicated that subjects responded to survey statements using five mental constructs (or factors).

The factors for the students were: 1) evolutionary creation, 2) old earth creation, 3) young earth creation, 4) historic and scientific accuracy of Genesis, and 5) fiat creation. For the faculty, the factors were: 1) old earth creation, 2) evolutionary creation, 3) science over theology, 4) young earth creation, and 5) anti-deism. Analysis identified the same three factors (YEC, OEC, and EC) for both students and faculty, as we predicted before the survey was administered.

The unanticipated factors "historic and scientific accuracy of Genesis" and "fiat creationism" for students and "science over theology" and "anti-deism" for faculty may indicate some ambiguity or confusion on the part of the respondents.

We conclude that the survey exhibits strong content and construct validity, as supported by evaluations of the five content validity judges and by the principal components (factor) analysis. This analysis indicated that three of five empirical factors closely corresponded to our three theoretical categories (YEC, OEC, and EC).

We also examined item and instrument reliabilities. Reliability examines the precision or level of internal consistency or stability of the measuring device over time. Both validity and reliability were examined since a reliable measure may be consistent but not valid. The SPSS software was used to calculate the Cronbach alpha reliability coefficients.[21] Overall survey and individual factor reliabilities were all very near or greater than 0.70. These reliability data, taken together, indicate the instrument is reliable.

In summary, this survey is both valid and reliable. That is, it measures what it purports to measure with high consistency.

20. Anton E. Lawson and John Weser, "The Rejection of Nonscientific Beliefs about Life: Effects of Instruction and Reasoning Skills," *Journal of Research in Science Teaching* 27 (1990) 331.

21. Lee J. Cronbach, "Coefficient Alpha and the Internal Structure of Tests," *Psychometrika* 16:3 (1951) 297.

SURVEY RESPONSES

In 2004, faculty, students, staff, and administrators from Assemblies of God colleges and universities in the United States (numbering 1,032) completed the survey. Since then, it has been used in a number of different settings. It was utilized in a controlled experiment (effects of conditioning on views on origins) in a psychology class at a Pentecostal university. It was also used as a pre/post teaching measure of attitude/belief change in a natural science class at a Pentecostal Bible college, an introductory theology class at a Pentecostal liberal arts university, a zoology class at a Pentecostal liberal arts university, and a Genesis and science course at a Pentecostal seminary. Members of three Pentecostal churches have also taken the survey.

DEMOGRAPHIC DATA

Respondents to the survey given in 2004 were 40% male and 60% female. Nearly two-thirds of the respondents (63%) were students, 19% educators, 11% staff, and 3% were administrators. A majority (74%) indicated that they were affiliated with the Assemblies of God. The three largest majors represented were education (18%), biblical studies (14%), and pastoral ministries (13%). A smaller number of science majors (12.3%) took the survey.

From the 2004 survey, it is apparent that Assemblies God students and educators hold diverse views on origins (Table 1). The plurality position of both students and faculty is young earth creation, followed by old earth creation and evolutionary creation, respectively. Approximately one-fifth of the respondents did not commit to a position. We were surprised by the large number of OEC and EC respondents in our sample.

If respondents agreed with four (80%) or five (100%) of the top five items (based on factor loadings) within each position, we felt survey responses were consistent with stated positions (see Table 2). A large percentage (95%) of self-described YEC students responded consistently to the model predictions for YEC. Faculty did not do as well (85%). Faculty who aligned with the OEC position were more consistent (75%) than students (66%), and EC faculty were very consistent (96%) relative to students (70%). The OEC camp, overall, had the lowest congruence between self-described camp affiliation and response pattern.

These inconsistencies may reflect a need for better instruction on the central tenets of each viewpoint or attempts of the respondents to combine YEC and non-YEC statements. Teachers could use this survey to reveal any inconsistencies between a person's perceived and actual camp affiliations.

Evaluation of Instruction

Comparisons between camp affiliation changes (YEC, OEC, and EC) and individual survey item response differences before and after instruction provided us with valuable insights into the consistency and understanding of the positions taken by students. SPSS allowed us to make these analyses with ease.

During the spring semester (2006), one of us (Badger) administered the survey as a pre- and post-instruction measure of origins attitudes and beliefs in a general education biology class at a Pentecostal Bible college. Although the sample was too small for statistical analysis of camp changes (twenty-eight pretest and nineteen post-test respondents), about half of the YEC and OEC students abandoned their positions, and the EC position disappeared. The "undecided" and "blank" responses more than doubled (from 28% to 68%). This shift may indicate an increased awareness of unanswered questions in this discussion (see Table 3).

The survey was also used by a theology professor in his introductory theology classes at a Pentecostal liberal arts university as a pre- and post-instruction measure (see Table 4). A chi-square (χ^2) association analysis indicates the distribution of students among the self-described camps is significantly different before and after the instructional unit on origins ($\chi^2 = 86.60$, df = 36, p ≤ 0.01). Seven items also showed significant change in responses. These responses indicate that students changed both camp affiliations and attitudes/beliefs about individual origins propositions (see Table 5).

A psychology professor used the survey in the fall of 2007 in a controlled experiment on the effects of conditioning on views on origins in a psychology class (35 participants) at a Pentecostal university. The variable tested was scripture reading. It did not have a significant effect on survey responses between the test and control groups.

In the spring of 2008, twelve zoology students at a Pentecostal liberal arts university took the survey before and after a unit of instruction on origins by one of the authors (Tenneson). The sample was too small for statistical analysis of camp affiliation change, but paired sample t-tests found four significant item response changes (see Table 6).

Most recently, the survey was used as a pre/post teaching measure of attitude/belief change in a Genesis and Science course at a Pentecostal seminary. The opinions of the students changed significantly on five of the survey statements (see Table 7).

Individual teachers will have different reasons for this kind of instructional evaluation. Although some may want to influence their students' camp affiliations, we think a more appropriate use is to evaluate the effectiveness of various instructional approaches. The survey can be used to evaluate the development of critical thinking skills such as being willing to change one's viewpoint in light of new evidence and holding positions that are internally consistent. Similarly, valuable insights into students' preexisting opinions may be gained before a unit of instruction.

LIMITATIONS

Our work has a few limitations. For example, our evidence for successful instruction is largely anecdotal. We have not used controlled experiments to compare instruction with and without the various suggestions cited in this article.

Further, due to the lack of data, we made no examinations of the DE and AE camps. We hope to include them in the future. Although we think the length of the survey discouraged multiple submissions, no other mechanism prevented this. The 2004 survey sample was limited to people in Assemblies of God higher education. We would like to expand the sample to include other groups such as faculty and students at Coalition of Christian Colleges and Universities and at secular colleges and universities.

Conclusions

We encourage students to evaluate assumptions and evidences for several scientific propositions: uniformitarianism, the age of the universe, and evolution. We also encourage students to evaluate several theological propositions: the Bible is God's Word, God is the Creator, and God is immanent in his creation.

Our approach to teaching this controversial subject has not resulted in angry responses (yet!) from constituents or parents. We think that this is because we frame the discussion around letting the proponents and detractors present their arguments and evidences. We then let the students adopt the theistic view that is most congruent with their epistemological preference, view on applicability of science and hermeneutics, and integrative paradigm. They own their knowledge and have a wealth of information on the range of various viewpoints on each topic. We emphasize which origins viewpoints are outside a theistic worldview (deism and atheism) and which patterns Christians should avoid (dualistic models like NOMA and the two conflict views).

We tell our students that each of us must arrive at a position on origins that fits his or her model of interpreting the Scriptures and science. We also must be able to articulate and defend our position.

Students and educators at Assemblies of God colleges and universities hold diverse views on origins and could strengthen the internal consistency of their camp affiliations (YEC, OEC, and EC) through a deeper examination of the reasons for embracing a viewpoint. Some respondents were not well-informed about their camp and the reasons for choosing their position. Almost a fourth of the respondents were undecided about which position they embrace. Is this as it should be? Maybe, maybe not. Holding opinions loosely on this topic may be healthy. The origins survey can provide teachers with valuable insights into their student's views on origins and the effectiveness of their approaches to teaching origins.

Students and faculty vary somewhat in their origins perspectives. A larger percentage of faculty favor the ancient creation camps (OEC and EC) while students favor YEC. EC faculty and YEC students demonstrated the most consistent understanding of their camp tenets.

The teaching approaches that we've found most effective follow. The effects of epistemology, presuppositions, and worldviews on beliefs about origins (including science and biblical interpretation) must be examined. Let the advocates for each theistic camp (YEC, OEC, and EC) speak to that view's strengths, and let the detractors summarize the weaknesses. Teach that intelligent, informed, genuine Pentecostals can embrace different theistic positions on origins that still honor God as the creator. A position on origins should be based on an honest attempt to integrate the biblical creation accounts and the theories of the natural sciences.

The areas of agreement among YEC, OEC, and EC are greater and more important than the areas of disagreement. Pentecostals should stop fighting over origins and join together to address other, more important, spiritual and social issues.

Our research has found no uniquely Pentecostal perspective on creation-evolution. Instead, Pentecostals are found in each of the three theistic camps (YEC, OEC, and EC). In this respect, we probably are similar to the larger Evangelical community, although non-Pentecostal Evangelicals may distribute differently among these three groups.[22]

Appendix: Tables

Table 1. Self-Reported Position of 763 Student and 224 Faculty Respondents (2004)

Self-Reported Position	% Students	% Faculty
Young Earth Creationists	51.1	34.8
Old Earth Creationists	17.6	30.8
Evolutionary Creationists	8.5	12.1
Undecided and Blank	22.5	21.4
Atheistic/Deistic Evolutionists	0.2	0.8

22. We gratefully acknowledge the assistance of these friends: Robert Spence, Commissioner, Assemblies of God Commission on Christian Higher Education, and Dayton Kingsriter, Director, Assemblies of God Commission on Christian Higher Education. These friends at Evangel University were also helpful: Glenn Bernet (Vice President for Academic Affairs) Robert Berg (Director, Lifeworks) Mike McCorcle (Chair, Department of Science and Technology) Diane Awbrey (Associate Professor of English) and Erica Harris (Assistant Professor of Biology). Finally, we appreciate these colleagues for using our survey and sharing their data: William Griffin (Associate Professor of Old Testament and Hebrew) and Geoff Sutton (Professor of Psychology). Portions of this essay were presented at the Oxford Round Table, Oxford University, Oxford, England, in August, 2007 and at the Society for Pentecostal Studies, Durham, NC, in March, 2008.

Table 2. Comparison of Stated Positions and Responses to Top Five Items (2004)

Camp	Students	Faculty
YEC	95%	85%
OEC	66%	75%
EC	70%	96%

Table 3. Significant Changes in Responses to Origins Survey Statements of Bible College Students in a Biology Class Before and After an Instructional Unit on Origins

(1 = Strongly Disagree, 2 = Disagree, 3 = Uncertain, 4 = Agree, 5 = Strongly Agree)

Survey Item	Mean Score before Instruction	Mean Score after Instruction
1. Every detail of the Genesis creation narrative is historically accurate	4.5	3.75
4. Adam and Eve were not two actual people.	1.13	1.88
14. The creation account in Genesis has much historical significance, but the divine and human authors wrote it primarily to communicate theological truths—not to reveal precisely how God created everything.	2.56	3.63
26. The universe is at least several billion years old.	2.13	2.69
46. The creation account in Genesis has little if any historical accuracy.	1.25	2.13
47. Accepting evolutionary theory leads to the destruction of biblical moral and ethical values.	3.31	2.19
60. Macroevolution and the Genesis account of creation are mutually exclusive—both cannot be true	3.69	2.69

*dependent samples t-tests (p ≤ 0.05), n = 16

Table 4. Significant* Changes in Self-Reported Origins Positions Before and After an Instructional Unit on Origins in an Introductory Theology Class at a Liberal Arts College

Camp	% Before (n = 57)	% After (n = 57)
Young Earth Creationists	45.6	50.9
Old Earth Creationists	10.5	12.3
Evolutionary Creationists	21.1	14.0
Undecided, Blank, Other	22.8	22.8

* χ^2 test for association, $p \leq 0.01$

Table 5. Significant* Changes in Responses to Origins Survey Statements of Christian Liberal Arts Students in an Introduction to Theology Class Before and After an Instructional Unit on Origins

(1 = Strongly Disagree, 2 = Disagree, 3 = Uncertain, 4 = Agree,
5 = Strongly Agree)

Survey Item	Mean Score before Instruction	Mean Score after Instruction
3. Life originally came into existence spontaneously from non-life, without any divine activity.	1.09	1.24
28. Macroevolution did not happen by chance; God guided it.	2.69	2.24
34. God is still using macroevolution to produce new life forms (kinds).	2.59	2.14
53. Genuine Christians accept only the Young Earth Creation model and reject all other models of origins.	2.41	1.97
58. Spiritually mature Christians accept only the Young Earth Creation model and reject all other models of origins.	2.31	1.95
60. Macroevolution and the Genesis account of creation are mutually exclusive: that is, both cannot be true.	2.62	3.09
62. Unity among Christians is more important than the creation-evolution controversy.	2.64	4.10

*dependent samples t-tests ($p \leq 0.05$), n = 57

Table 6. Significant* Changes in Responses to Origins Survey Statements of Christian Liberal Arts Students in a Zoology Class Before and After an Instructional Unit on Origins

(1 = Strongly Disagree, 2 = Disagree, 3 = Uncertain, 4 = Agree, 5 = Strongly Agree)

Survey Item	Mean Score before Instruction	Mean Score after Instruction
2. God created everything that exists.	4.33	1.33
4. Adam and Eve were not two actual people.	1.25	1.67
56. The origins debate is useful for bringing non-Christians to faith in Christ	3.67	2.83
60. Macroevolution and the Genesis account of creation are mutually exclusive—both cannot be true.	2.50	3.50

*dependent samples t-tests ($p \leq 0.05$), n = 12

Table 7. Significant* Changes in Responses to Origins Survey Statements of Pentecostal Seminary Students Before and After a Course on Genesis 1–11 and Science

(1 = Strongly Disagree, 2 = Disagree, 3 = Uncertain, 4 = Agree, 5 = Strongly Agree)

Survey Item	Mean Score Before Instruction	Mean Score After Instruction
6. Questions about origins are better answered by natural scientists than by Bible scholars.	2.50	1.30
23. God specially created Adam and Eve millions of years after He created plants.	2.60	3.40

Survey Item	Mean Score Before Instruction	Mean Score After Instruction
29. No solid scientific evidence exists that challenges a literal interpretation of the Genesis account of creation.	2.40	1.80
33. Noah's flood (in Genesis) explains the geological layers.	3.60	2.70
62. Unity among Christians is more important than the creation-evolution controversy.	4.00	4.70

*dependent samples t-tests ($p \leq 0.05$), n = 10

Contributors

Peter Althouse (PhD, University of St. Michael's College, Toronto) is Assistant Professor of Theology, Southeastern University, Lakeland, Florida

J. Kwabena Asamoah-Gyadu (PhD, University of Birmingham) is Vice-President, Trinity Theological Seminary, Accra, Ghana

Steve Badger (PhD, University of Southern Mississippi) is Professor of Chemistry, Evangel University, Springfield, Missouri

R. Jerome Boone (DMin, Columbia Theological Seminary, Atlanta area) is Professor of Old Testament and Christian Formation, Lee University, Cleveland, Tennessee

Shane Clifton (PhD, Australian Catholic University) is Academic Dean and Lecturer in Theology, Southern Cross College of the Assemblies of God, Sydney, Australia

Edward E. Decker, Jr. (PhD, Kent State University) is Professor of Christian Counseling, Oral Roberts University, Tulsa, Oklahoma

Scott A. Ellington (PhD, University of Sheffield) is Associate Professor of Christian Ministry, Emmanuel College, Franklin Springs, Georgia

Gerald W. King is a PhD candidate at the University of Birmingham, Birmingham, United Kingdom

David S. Norris (PhD, Temple University) is Professor of Biblical Theology, Urshan Graduate School of Theology, St. Louis, Missouri

Matthew Tallman is a PhD Candidate at the Regent University School of Divinity, Virginia Beach, Virginia

Michael Tenneson (PhD, University of Missouri-Columbia) is Professor of Biology, Evangel University, Springfield, Missouri

Bernie A. Van De Walle (PhD, Drew University) is Associate Professor of Theology, Ambrose University College, Calgary, Alberta

Robby Waddell (PhD, University of Sheffield) is Associate Professor of New Testament, Southeastern University, Lakeland, Florida

Amos Yong (PhD, Boston University) is Professor of Theology and Director of the PhD Program in Renewal Studies, Regent University School of Divinity, Virginia Beach, Virginia

Author Index

Subject Index

CPSIA information can be obtained at www.ICGtesting.com
Printed in the USA
BVOW06*2347010916

460882BV00009B/7/P